The
Theatrical Public
in the time of
Garrick

HARRY WILLIAM PEDICORD

THE
THEATRICAL PUBLIC
IN THE TIME OF
Garrick

SOUTHERN ILLINOIS UNIVERSITY PRESS

Carbondale and Edwardsville

FEFFER & SIMONS, INC.

London and Amsterdam

To ADAH *and* ALISON

PREFACE

WHEN David Garrick and Samuel Johnson came up to London in March, 1737, the metropolis was supporting no fewer than four and often five major legitimate theatres and a number of minor playhouses. In addition to the Theatres Royal in Drury Lane and Covent Garden, the major playhouses included Lincoln's Inn Fields (new theatre), Goodman's Fields in Ayliffe-street, and the Little Theatre in the Haymarket. To stage-struck young men from the provinces it must have seemed an era of unlimited opportunity and prosperity. But had they been invited behind scenes in the professional world of the theatres they would have found that all was in turmoil.

Most of the gossip and speculation centered about Henry Fielding, manager of the Little Theatre in the Haymarket. His satiric attacks against the Government had become notorious, and it was momentarily expected that an irate ministry would retaliate. The extent of such disciplinary action was of vital concern to every member of the theatrical profession, transcending in importance the uncertain fate of Manager Fielding. Actually the existence of most major and all minor playhouses was in jeopardy. And three months after Garrick's arrival in London the blow fell. On June 21, 1737, the actors' worst fears were confirmed with the passage in Parliament of a Licensing Act establishing the stage under the absolute control of the Lord Chamberlain, restricting legitimate drama to the two Patent theatres in Drury Lane and Covent Garden, and investing the Lord Chamberlain not only with power to license theatres but also with inclusive powers of censorship over all future dramatic productions.

For a time after the passage of the Licensing Act man-

agers of outlawed playhouses used every possible strategy
to evade the law and keep their theatres open. Lincoln's Inn
Fields, the Little Theatre in the Haymarket, and Goodman's
Fields all announced themselves as "the late theatres" and
resorted to productions considered outside the strict reading
of the law. Garrick himself made his London debut as
Richard III (October 19, 1741) in a performance at Goodman's Fields which was given "gratis by persons for their
diversions"; the play was inserted between two parts of a
concert of music for which admission had been charged. By
such devices the managers kept their houses going for a brief
time, staging performances more and more sporadically each
season. But it was already a lost cause, and by the time
Garrick purchased his half of the Drury Lane patent these
theatres had been effectively silenced and all legitimate
activity was confined to Drury Lane and Covent Garden
theatres.

The monopoly thus enjoyed by the patentees of the
Theatres Royal remained unbroken throughout the years
of Garrick's management, except for the unusual grant
bestowed by the Crown upon Samuel Foote in 1766, whereby
he was permitted to erect and operate a new Little Theatre
on the site of the old one in the Haymarket. Here Foote
was allowed to produce dramatic entertainments, but only
in those months in which both Patent houses were closed
for the season.

When we speak, therefore, of "the theatrical public" we
are centering attention solely upon the patrons of Drury
Lane and Covent Garden theatres, except in those instances
in which it will be necessary to contrast this public with audiences of the earlier years before the Patent monopoly was
established. When reference is made to so-called "minor
theatres" during the period, it must be remembered that
these were playhouses in which only productions of a non-
dramatic nature were countenanced — musical entertainments, pantomimic spectacles, vaudeville, and animal acts

— for the minor theatres as defined in the years before the Licensing Act did not achieve new life until the last decades of the eighteenth century. (For a list of the London theatres of this time see Allardyce Nicoll, *A History of Late Eighteenth Century Drama 1750–1800*, Cambridge, 1927.)

All previous studies of London theatre audiences in the eighteenth century have been limited to brief sketches providing the necessary background for discussion of the broader subjects of acting, stagecraft, and the literature of the theatre. In the main such sketches have interpreted the available evidence correctly as to the social categories, the behavior, and the taste of the theatrical public. They have, however, left unanswered such important questions as the size of the audiences, the economic aspects of eighteenth century playgoing, the quality of the spectators and that of the repertoire as measured in terms of popularity at the box office. While this study will not change the prevailing conception as to audiences of this period, it does attempt to answer these questions and to underscore by further evidence such impressions as we now possess.

Most accounts stem from the spirited chapters on theatre audiences included by Dr. Doran in his *Their Majesties' Servants: Annals of the English Stage* (2 vols., London, 1860). Later writers have accepted his contrasting of early and late eighteenth century audiences in matters of behavior and taste. They have added to his sketches pertinent materials drawn from the plays, from the prologues and epilogues, and other contemporary memorabilia. The most exhaustive and usable accounts to date have been those of Allardyce Nicoll in the two volumes of his history devoted to this period, and a critical study by James L. Lynch which appeared after this book had gone to press: *Box, Pit, and Gallery; Stage and Society in Johnson's London* (University of California Press, 1953). Others who have considered the theatrical public in some detail are G. C. D. Odell (*Shakespeare from Betterton to Irving*, 2 vols., New York,

1920) and Alwin Thaler (*From Shakespeare to Sheridan: a Book about the Theatre of Yesterday and Today,* Cambridge, Mass., 1922). John A. Kelly's *German Visitors to English Theaters in the Eighteenth Century* (Princeton, 1936) provides a valuable commentary on the behavior and taste of English audiences as seen through the eyes of foreign travelers.

For their courtesy in permitting me to quote from copyrighted works my acknowledgments are due to the Cambridge University Press for use of the text of *The Chances,* from *The Works of Francis Beaumont and John Fletcher,* edited by Arnold Glover and A. R. Waller, for excerpts from *Dr. Campbell's Diary of a Visit to England in 1775,* edited by James L. Clifford, and for quotations from E. G. Dowdell's *A Hundred Years of Quarter Sessions* and Allardyce Nicoll's two volumes devoted to the eighteenth century in *A History of the English Drama 1660–1900;* to Harvard University Press for quotations from Elizabeth Gilboy's *Wages in Eighteenth Century England* and R. G. Noyes's *Ben Jonson on the English Stage 1660–1776;* to the Houghton Mifflin Company for excerpts from *Some Unpublished Correspondence of David Garrick,* edited by George P. Baker; to Alfred A. Knopf, Inc., for extensive excerpts from M. Dorothy George's *London Life in the Eighteenth Century;* to Dougald MacMillan and to the Oxford University Press for permission to tabulate the repertoire and to quote from *Drury Lane Calendar 1747–1776;* to the North American Newspaper Alliance for an excerpt from a column of dramatic criticism by Mr. Lawrence Perry; to the Princeton University Press for extensive quotation from John Kelly's *German Visitors to English Theaters in the Eighteenth Century;* to the editors of *Studies in Philology* for excerpts from articles by George Winchester Stone, Jr.; and to Yale University Press for quotations from Fielding's *Covent Garden Journal,* edited by G. E. Jansen.

Without the cooperation and kindness of librarians in

many cities in the United States and England this work would not have been possible. It is with pleasure that I acknowledge my indebtedness particularly to the librarians of the University of Pennsylvania, the Historical Society of Pennsylvania, and the New York Public Library; to Mr. Edward Robertson, Librarian of the John Rylands Library of the University of Manchester, England, for his kind permission to use Rylands English Ms. No. 1111 for statistical purposes; to the Folger Shakespeare Library, Washington, D. C., its Director, Dr. Louis B. Wright, and especially to its Curator of Books and Manuscripts, Dr. Giles E. Dawson, for permission to quote extensively from the diaries of William Hopkins and Richard Cross, prompters at Drury Lane Theatre during Garrick's management, from the account books of Drury Lane and Covent Garden Theatres, and from a Notebook of Clippings, 1770-1777.

I am grateful to Professor Emmett L. Avery for his invaluable criticism of statistical methods employed in Chapter I, and I am also obliged to Professors W. Rex Crawford, Alfred B. Harbage, and Matthias Shaaber, for their reading of the manuscript and for much helpful criticism and advice. Dr. Harbage's own work *Shakespeare's Audience* (New York, 1941) has provided many hints as to investigation procedure. I wish to acknowledge also the courtesy of Mr. Maynard Morris of New York City in allowing me to verify certain facts from Garrick manuscripts in his possession, and the material assistance of the Reverend Harry F. Gardner, Vice-President of Waynesburg College. But I am under greatest obligation to Professor Arthur H. Scouten, friend and teacher, whose extensive knowledge of the period and genial understanding of my problem have followed my work and assisted in every way.

HARRY WILLIAM PEDICORD

Pittsburgh
January, 1954

Contents

Errata

Page   1, line 4 : *For* Hall *read* Hull
Page 48, line 27 : *For* Rodgers *read* Rogers
Page 60, line 17 : *For* Norn's *read* Norris
Page 192, line 17 : *For* Bosford *read* Besford
Page 216, line 32 : *For* Moseen *read* Mozeen
Page 247, line 21 : *For* Bosford *read* Besford
Page 255, line 28 : *For* Hull, Thomas, 212–13, 218–19, 222– *read*
                          Hull, Thomas, 1, 212–13, 218–19, 222–
Page 258, line 50 : *For* Moseen *read* Mozeen
Page 259, line 13 : *For* Norn *read* Norris
Page 261, line 26 : *For* Rodgers *read* Rogers

1. THE ELBOWED CROWD

Let cits point out green paddocks to their spouses,
To me, no prospect like your crowded houses.
    Prologue to THE RUNAWAY (*Drury Lane, February 15, 1776*)

ON MARCH 18, 1775 Thomas Hall's alteration of Thomson's *Edward and Eleonora* was acted at Covent Garden Theatre as a benefit for Mrs. Barry. Two days later the critic of *The Morning Chronicle* commented on that benefit audience as follows: "The audience, which was more brilliant and numerous than any ever yet seen in this theatre, confessed their sensibility, and wept applause." [1] Most contemporary evidence as to the number of persons attending eighteenth century London playhouses is couched in just such generalities. A popular bill draws "a crowded house" or "a thin house." Actors are applauded or damned by "a large and brilliant crowd" or by one that is "not above the charges of the house." No report tells us what we wish to know: what was an "average audience" on an "average night" in Garrick's time? Nor should we expect it to be otherwise, perhaps, in the nature of so complex a problem. What we wish to know must be based upon particular theatre buildings, and indeed upon the particular state of those buildings at the moment of writing. We need first of all a knowledge of the total capacity of each theatre. At Drury Lane, for example, we must know whether reference is made to the Wren structure inherited by Garrick and Lacy, to one of the successive enlargements made in the early years of their management, or to the auditorium designed by the brothers Adam.

We might expect something more explicit from the theatre

managers. But they were extremely reluctant to discuss their
business affairs in public and issued only the most cautious
statements. Garrick will commit himself only to general
estimates even in his private correspondence, admitting that
"Hamlet was ye most crowded house we ever had and
Archer [*The Beaux' Stratagem*] was a most splendid one,
tho not quite so profitable. . . ." [2] Even the daybooks of
playhouse functionaries prove disappointing. Richard Cross,
prompter at Drury Lane, underscores an important September evening by saying that "The House was crowded in ten
minutes," [3] while another occasion draws "the greatest
crowd I ever saw since the Delevals play'd." [4] In fact, the
only tangible evidence is found in estimates given in
box office parlance, as "a £200 house," or "enlarged by
£40 a night." But here again we face an indefiniteness
which is exasperating. We must know the number of seatings in each portion of the theatre — pit, boxes, galleries;
we need to know how the spectators distributed themselves
in such seatings; we need to compare the capacity of the
theatre with these box-office totals to learn the proportion of
this "crowded house" represented in the customary "orders,"
complimentary tickets issued by the management.[5] It is
indeed unfortunate that one Jedediah Buxton on his visit
to Drury Lane limited his "astonishing calculations" to the
number of steps taken by the dancers and the number of
words Garrick spoke that evening! [6]

Among the early historians of the eighteenth century
theatre only Fitzgerald and H. Barton Baker deal with the
problem of attendance, and then only indirectly. Both were
content to state the capacities of the two Patent theatres in
terms of the box office.[7] Later authorities repeat these estimates without question until they reach solid ground in the
architectural specifications [8] for the Drury Lane Theatre
of 1794. Odell dismisses the matter by saying, "We are not
called upon to record many changes in the actual shape of

the theatres during Garrick's time. At the beginning of the
Lacy-Garrick management, the theatre in Drury Lane was
enlarged to the extent of holding more by forty pounds a
night." [9] Allardyce Nicoll summarizes the earlier information in terms of the box office and adds the known capacities
of Drury Lane in 1794 and after.[10] Miss E. P. Stein antici-
pates our own method when she writes, "The size of Drury
Lane before Garrick enlarged the auditorium (1762), can
be estimated from the receipts of a well-attended but non-
gala performance." But she leaves the problem there, adding
only that "the amount usually ranged from one hundred and
twenty-five to one hundred and thirty pounds." [11] No
attempt has been made to interpret such materials as are at
hand in terms of numerical capacities, average attendance,
or the proportion of playgoers to the population of metropolitan London. We shall attempt to make such an interpre-
tation and to arrive at certain reasonable if not positive
conclusions about the numerical strength and influence of
Garrick's audiences.

The history of the Patent theatres in so far as their
spectator-capacities are concerned is briefly as follows. The
older house, Drury Lane, was designed by Sir Christopher
Wren and erected in 1674.[12] When its rival was built in
Covent Garden (1732), this Wren structure was considered
old, a patchwork of successive alterations,[13] and rumored by
its enemies to be unsafe.[14] This was the Drury Lane Theatre
inherited by Garrick and Lacy as they planned their first
season, 1747–48, a house three fourths the size of its com-
petitor.[15] Little wonder that the new managers resolved to
refurbish it, increasing their box office potential "by £40 a
night" before the September opening.[16] Two further enlargements were made during Garrick's management, one in 1762
providing for £354 gross income,[17] and the other designed
and executed by Robert and James Adam for the final season
in 1775.[18] Five years after Sheridan assumed management

the house was remodeled so as to hold an estimated 2,000 persons,[19] only to be torn down completely in 1792–93 and replaced by the cavernous edifice of 1794.[20] Meanwhile, we may assume that Covent Garden Theatre continued to operate at the capacity originally established by Rich in 1732, a box office gross of £200.[21] In any event there is no record of any enlargement until fifty years later, when it underwent two alterations within a decade — one in 1782 and the Holland structure of 1792, a partial rebuilding.[22]

Thus we find at the end of the century one completely new theatre and another which differed substantially from its predecessors. It is at this point that we encounter the architectural specifications referred to by historians, enabling us to count accurately the total number of places in the theatres and to establish the number of seats in each division of the auditoriums.

Drury Lane Theatre, 1794 [23]		*Covent Garden Theatre, 1792* [24]	
Upper Gallery	308 persons	Upper Gallery	361 persons
First Gallery and slips	675 persons	First Gallery and slips	820 persons
Boxes	1,828 persons	Boxes	1,200 persons
Pit	800 persons	Pit	632 persons
Total capacity	3,611 persons	Total capacity	3,013 persons

These figures in themselves are of no great assistance. They cannot take us beyond the barrier erected by the chain of alterations in both houses from the beginning to the end of the century. At this point, however, another set of figures is available. It is curious that historians have not called attention heretofore to the figures given by the contemporary architect George Saunders for the Covent Garden Theatre of 1782. In *A Treatise on Theatres* [25] Saunders argued for a theatre auditorium shaped like a horseshoe. He compared his own designs with the oblong auditorium in Covent Garden.

. . . An advantage this form possesses over every other, respecting the number of spectators it will contain, I shall prove by comparing it with Covent Garden theatre. In this designed theatre every spectator would be well accomodated (*sic*), and the different ranges of boxes and galleries maintained of a spacious height. A person seated in the most remote part of the scene, would be 15 feet nearer the scene than a person so situated in Covent Garden theatre. And yet,

In Covent Garden theatre,		In the designed theatre,
The upper gallery will contain 384 persons		525
First gallery and slips	700	927
Boxes	729	600
Pit	357	368

By Saunders's count, made at least two years prior to the second alteration, Covent Garden Theatre in 1782 would contain a total of 2,170 seated persons distributed as above. Such a memorandum is invaluable because the manner in which people were seated about the house forms the most baffling part of the problem of interpreting box office receipts. We shall have opportunity to check Saunders's figures later.

According to Fitzgerald and Baker the original Covent Garden Theatre was calculated to hold approximately £200.[26] If this be true, then the Saunders figures for 1782 may be used to establish a proportion as follows: 2,170 (capacity) is to £325 (estimated gross at standard prices) as X is to £200.[27] The resulting estimate of the number of persons this theatre would hold in 1732 is 1,335. Drury Lane, on the other hand, was reckoned as only three fourths the size of its rival in 1733.[28] A subtraction from the original estimate for Covent Garden gives a total of 1,001 spectators at Drury Lane [29] and a box office gross of £150.[30]

When David Garrick assumed his management in 1747 he immediately enlarged his theatre to hold "more by £40 a night," or upwards of £190 and a capacity of 1,268 persons.[31] Such a figure agrees with prevailing contemporary opinion as to the comparative capacities of the two Patent theatres. The Earl of Carlisle, writing in 1800, echoes this opinion when he says,

Persons now living can remember the dramatic contest between
Barry and Garrick; the former acting at Covent Garden, and
the latter at Drury Lane. The Covent Garden theatre has been
much enlarged since that period; but before that increase of
size, held to be too extensive, and giving a great advantage to
Garrick, then treading a much smaller stage.[32]

We learn, however, from the *Memoirs of the Colman Family*
that Drury Lane was remodeled in 1762 from a previous
gross of "220 guineas" or £231 to "337 guineas" or
£354.[33] If so, these figures will give us a far greater number
of spectators: 1,542 persons in 1747 and 2,362 persons in
1762. If, however, as Joseph Knight states,[34] the gross in
1762 was only £335, then the total capacity became 2,206.
This is a closer approximation of Baker's estimated 2,000
persons before the alteration of 1780.[35] We may assume at
least this much: that Drury Lane held about 1,001 persons
at capacity (and exclusive of any seating on the stage)[36]
in 1732, and that Garrick had enlarged it to hold at the
outside 2,362 persons by 1762. Meanwhile, the rival house
seems to have maintained its capacity at 1,335 persons
(exclusive of stage seatings) until it was increased to 2,170
in 1782.[37]

   Unfortunately, only a very few accounts of the two Patent
Theatres list the number of persons included in gross receipts
for a particular day or the manner in which these people
were distributed throughout the house.[38] Least of all are such
figures often available for an ordinary evening. Many entries
giving detailed receipts are for the annual round of benefit
performances. But while benefit statistics may be suspect in
calculating daily attendance averages,[39] they will be useful in
demonstrating the capacity of the theatres. The spectre of
unpaid house charges was sufficient to goad the poorest
salesman among recipients of benefits into trying to reach
capacity attendance on his night. Certainly a Garrick, Barry,
or Powell, drawing excellent houses all season, might expect

capacity attendance at their benefits.[40] It is possible, then, from a study of the account books of both theatres, to obtain a fair sampling of this material in the critical years before and after each alteration or enlargement. Such information will serve to test our estimates above and at the same time throw some light upon attendance habits.

Four benefit performances listed in the *Covent Garden Account Book* for the season 1740-41 [41] are the earliest entries I have been able to find in which the distribution of ticket purchasers is shown.

Wed. Nov. 19 Recruiting Officer and School Boy

        Tickets deliv'd out by a Gentlewoman under misfortune to be taken this night.

        Rece[d] 74 . 5 . 0 money

           46 . 14 . 0 Seals

        An acc[t] of the Tickets that came in this night

        Box 48 12 : 0 : 0

        Pitt 160 24 : 0 : 0 Delivered

        Gall 107 10 : 14 : 0

                    46 : 14 : 0 ½ is 23 : 7 : 0

  Dec. 12 Provok'd Husband and the Dragon

        Rece[d] 43 . 7 . 6 money

           34 . 12 . 0 Seals

        The acc[t] of the Tickets that came in y[s] night

	Box	Pitt	Gall	Value	½ Value
for Mrs. Dupre	7	95	85	24 : 10 : 0	12 : 5 : 0
for Mrs. Price	9	18	33	8 : 5 : 0	4 : 2 : 6
for Mrs. Gould	1	0	16	1 : 17 : 0	0 : 18 : 6
	17	113	134	34 : 12 : 0	17 : 6 : 0

Wed. April 1st Oroonoko and Merlin

        Rece[d] 40 : 14 : 6 money

          71 : 3 : 0 Seals

        An acc[t] of The Tickets that Came in this Night

	Box	Pitt	Gall	full Value	½ Value
For Mr. Dan French	20	150	85	36 : 0 : 0	18 : 0 : 0
Mr. Farquhar's Daughters	15	118	137	35 : 3 : 0	17 : 11 : 6
	35	268	222	71 : 3 : 0	35 : 11 : 6

Wed. April 8 Double Dealer & Yᵉ King & Miller
                Receᵈ   20 : 11 : 0 money
                       149 : 2 : 0 Seals
            An acctᵗ of The Tickets that came in this Night

For	Box	Pitt	Gall	full Value	½ Value
Mr. E. Roberts	125	407	177	110 : 0 : 0	55 : 0 : 0
Mrs. Chambers	93	91	22	39 : 2 : 0	19 : 11 : 0
	218	498	199	149 : 2 : 0	74 : 11 : 0

From these accounts we may make one deduction. There
must have been at least the following capacities at Covent
Garden in each category: boxes 218 (April 8), pit 498
(April 8), first gallery 222 (April 1) — a total of 938 possible spectators in all. But this does not account for the
persons included in the "money" receipts. Knowing, however, the amount of tickets or "Seals" included in the gross
receipts, it should be possible to approximate their number.
If we could assume that these people distributed themselves
in the same proportion as those presenting tickets, a simple
equation would suffice. But we know that one section of the
house, the upper gallery, has been omitted from the ticket
account altogether.⁴² Due allowance for this factor will have
to be made by a subtraction from the "money" receipts
before any equation is possible.

We may argue that at Covent Garden the upper gallery
certainly would be filled on a gala or benefit night; indeed,
it would on most evenings, for the entrance fee was but a
shilling. It is also probable in this particular theatre that few
alterations affecting capacity were carried out until 1782.
Almost certainly there were none in this upper region. We
have seen that the 1792 alteration reduced the upper gallery
seats from 384 to 361. Lacking contrary evidence we will
probably not err greatly in selecting the larger figure given
by George Saunders as not only proper for 1782, but as the
probable total for this section from the erection of the theatre
in 1732. "The gods" ultimately had to make way for those
patrons able to pay a higher price for their entertainment.

Until the erection of entirely new theatres their seats would be the ones sacrificed in any partial alteration.

If we consider 384s. as the probable gross for the upper gallery when full, and accordingly deduct £19 4s. from the "money" receipts, we may distribute the balance of "money" proportionately among the other three categories and arrive at as honest an estimate as possible without further direct evidence. The receipts for November 19 will then give us 315 ticket patrons, 384 upper gallery patrons, and 377 persons to be distributed in pit, boxes, and first gallery, or a grand total of 1,076 in attendance. Similarly, 829 persons attended on December 12, 1,072 on April 1, and 1,311 on April 8 — all within the computed capacity of 1,335 persons and yielding gross receipts well within the estimated £200 house of 1732. Six years later, in the season of 1746–47, only three performances at Covent Garden grossed more than the £200 limit.[43] They were: February 12, the opening night of Benjamin Hoadly's *The Suspicious Husband*,[44] £205; April 4, *The Distress'd Mother* and the new farce *Miss in Her Teens* (opened January 17) for the benefit of Mrs. Cibber, £267; and a third benefit on May 11, *The Way of the World*, £207.

A further opportunity to check the Saunders figures for Covent Garden is afforded by detailed receipts for 37 performances recorded in the *Covent Garden Cash Book 1759–60*.[45] Twenty-nine of these performances were benefits and the remaining eight doubtless were, although not so designated by the accountant. The number of tickets sold has been recorded in the usual manner, omitting the upper gallery. Now granting that these records will not cover the entire house on any given evening, nevertheless a total of the largest number of tickets issued in each category ought to give us some idea of the greatest number of spectators it was theoretically possible to accommodate in these seats during the 1759–60 season. On December 21, 1759, a total of 519 box tickets were taken for the benefit of the General Lying-in Hospital, Grosvenor Square; on May 2, 1760, 830 pit tickets were taken; and on May 19, 1760, 824 persons bought seats in the first gallery. To be sure, benefit tickets were not always used when purchased; nor can we ever be certain of a manager's whim on benefit evenings, whether his pit and boxes were "laid together," even when he had so advertised,[46] or other special arrangements made. We do know by simple arithmetic, however, that for this series nothing over standard prices was charged (boxes 5s., pit 3 s., first gallery 2s.). There was then a total of 2,173 possible spectators in boxes, pit, and first gallery on this hypothetical evening (a £336 house), or only three more seats than Saunders has allowed for the total capacity of the theatre in 1782. Nor have we accounted for the upper gallery and its 384-shilling customers. This will bring the total to 2,557 persons. Of this number, if we allow for about 200 stage seatings,[47] 187 persons are represented as actually overtaxing the capacity. No claim can be made for the validity of such a total in 1759–60, of course, but the comparison with Saunders's figures is most encouraging. If we could prove it, we would be able to push back by some twenty years the date to which his estimates apply. It is enough, perhaps, to note that our gross of £200 and capacity of 1,335 are not seriously challenged either by the 1746–47 or the 1759–60 receipts. In the 181 playing nights of the latter season, only 8 non-benefit performances grossed more than £200, and half of this number are well within the range of approximation understood in the £200 limit.[48]

Receipts listing the number of persons by category in the gross at Drury Lane are few, and I have been unable to discover any in the earlier years with which to test our estimates. We have conjectured a theatre enlarged by its new management in 1747 to a gross of about £190 and a capacity

of approximately 1,268 persons. We know certainly that this
house was enlarged again in 1762 to at least £335 and 2,206
persons, perhaps to £354 and a capacity of about 2,362. The
following are accounts of four Theatrical Fund benefits
which took place between the enlargement of 1762 and the
alterations made in 1775.[49] While they do not contain sufficient information upon which to base a mathematical approximation, they show that the changes made in 1762 provided ample seating which was not really overtaxed by the
time Garrick was discussing his final alterations with the
Adam brothers in 1775.

191st Night   Susp. Husband & Daphne [50]
                   For Theatrical Fund
                                      Cash £ 87 . 16 . 0

          Cash in the Galleries   88 . 0 . 0
          From Mr Johnston   211 . 18 . 0
                                  ───────────
                                  299 . 18 . 0
              paid sundries   16 . 5 . 6
                                  ───────────
                                  £ 283 . 12 . 6
          Box Tickets   680   £ 170───────
          Cash   87 . 16
                                  ─────────
                                  £ 257 . 16

June 2nd   *For the Theatrical Fund* [1772]
           K. Richard 3d & Devil to Pay
    182d Night . . . . Cash   97 . 2 . 6
                                            Acct   — 18 . 6
                                                   ──────────
          Mr. Johnston for   98 . 1 . —
          848 Tickets sold . . . .   215 . 3 . 3
                                                   ──────────
              Total Reced   313 . 4 . 3
                  Do paid   17 . 12 . —
                                                   ──────────
          Bala paid
          Wm Hatsell   295 . 12 . 3

          For the Theatrical Fund [1774]

May 17th K. Lear & Neck or Nothing
179th Night .... Cash   89 . 12 . —
                         After Money — — —
                                      89 . 12 . —
          Mʳ Johnston for
          826 Tickets sold   210 . 11 . 6
              Total rec'd   300 . 3 . 6

          Theatrical Fund [1775]

May 25th Wonder & Rival Candidates
186ᵗʰ Night .... Cash Record 87 . 11 . 6
                         A. M.   — . 5 . —
          Mʳ Johnston for   87 . 16 . 6
          860 Tᵗˢ sold   221 . 14 . —
              Total Rec'd   309 . 10 . 6

To the above let us add the following account of a capacity
house at Drury Lane during the same period. It appeared in
the *Theatrical Monitor,* No. 18, April 16, 1768, in support
of a criticism of the managers' conduct. While it may be
wholly unreliable, its 1,900 paying customers and unesti-
mated number of "free servants" offer a further check on
our estimates.

A Teller's Account of a crowded House at *Drury Lane* Theatre.

Side, front and green boxes,	600	people	at 4/	120 . 0 . 0
Pit	500	"	at 2/6	62 . 10 . 6
First gallery	700	"	at 1/6	52 . 10 . 0
Second gallery; besides	100	"	at 1/0	5 . 0 . 0
free servants				
Night's Receipts				240 . 0 . 0
Nightly expenses (as at benefits)				66 . 0 . 0

It is significant that none of these figures exceeds the gross
limit of 1762. In fact, daily receipts throughout this period
seldom go beyond a £300 gross.[51]

Contemporary accounts of the Adam alterations in 1775

lead one to believe that size was less a consideration than
architectural magnificence and luxurious appointments. According to one account the only remarkable interior alteration affecting capacity consisted of "new side boxes, both
upper and under, which are far more spacious and commodi-
ous than the former. . . ." [52] The impression given is of
contraction rather than of expansion of the seating capacity,
although it is unlikely that the Adam interior appointments
would reduce a £354 theatre to anything near the £230 gross
which Fitzgerald gives as his estimate of Sheridan's remodel-
ing in 1780. [53] The clearest conception of the seating proportions, if not the total capacity, of the 1775 theatre can be
obtained from accounts of the oratorio season which began
February 19, 1779. [54] Out of 11 evenings given over to this
form of musical entertainment the 10th proved the greatest
at the box office, not only in attendance but in the number
of persons in each of the four seating categories. On the 10th
night, 1,241 persons are accounted for as follows:

10th Night

			£		s		d
Boxes	170	....	89	"	5	"	0
Pitt	286	....	71	"	10	"	0
1st Gall:	526		92	"	1	"	0
2nd Gall:	259		25	"	18	"	0
			£ 278	"	14	"	0
Am 9th Nt	....			"	7	"	6
			£ 279	"	1	"	6

A summary of findings concerning the approximate capacities of the two Patent theatres during the years of Garrick's
management and beyond may be stated in terms of the traditional rivalry between the houses. Garrick and Lacy inherit
an old theatre seating about 1,001 persons. They begin their
management by challenging the 1,335 seats at Covent Garden with 267 additional ones at Drury Lane. When they
refurbish their theatre and accommodate the public with new

approaches to the house and its boxes in 1750 and 1752, it
is with little desire of increasing the capacity; they have
noted their advantage over Covent Garden in the current
"battle of the Romeos." But the success of pantomime and
increased patronage of musical pieces of all kinds creates a
demand for more places and a stage cleared of all spectators.
The two managers at Drury Lane covet this increased patronage and decide that the time has come for drastic alteration. Drury Lane must completely overshadow its com-
petitor in the number of spectators it will hold. So the theatre
of 1,762 provides for a nightly attendance of 1,027 more
playgoers than the neighboring house. However, the managers are not entirely justified in their anticipation: they
have increased capacity and cleared their stage, but patronage does not so much decline as fail to increase to match the
additional places. Garrick's personal popularity as an actor
reaches its lowest ebb and he leaves London for a European
tour.[55] The advent of young Powell and a new pantomime
momentarily save the day until Garrick's return. Then a
revival of interest in the manager's acting brings at least an
appearance of normality. When Drury Lane is again refur-
bished in 1775, it is for the last time. Garrick is interested
in beautifying his house inside and out, in making it attractive and enticing to the public love for show and comfort,
and in making the theatre still more valuable as property in
the forthcoming sale of his share in the Patent. But he is not
as interested in enlarging its capacity. The theatre he leaves
at his retirement will probably seat an audience numbering
somewhat under the maximum of 2,362 persons established
for the 1762 alteration.

If both Patent theatres had operated every evening at
peak capacity, we have to assume that the maximum number
of their patrons in metropolitan London was as follows:
2,336 persons nightly, 1732–47; 2,603 persons, 1747–62;
and 3,697 persons from 1762 to the end of our period. These

figures are obtained by adding the estimated figures of both
theatres for the three periods of alterations. They afford a
maximum weekly potential of 14,016 persons, 1732–47;
15,618 persons, 1747–62; and from 1762 on, 22,182 persons. But let us now consider what actually occurred in the
matter of daily and weekly attendance.

From the Drury Lane accounts I have selected daily
receipts in the critical years before and after each alteration.
These have been totaled for each season and divided by the
number of performances that season in order to secure the
average daily gross.[56] I have equated these averages with the
maximum gross and maximum capacity conjectured for
each alteration to establish the probable number of daily
playgoers. Results are grouped according to the periods in
Drury Lane's architectural history.[57]

Season	Total of Performances		Total Receipts	Average Daily Receipts	Average Daily Attendance	Estimated Capacity
1741–42	191		£18,276	£ 96	642	1,001
1747–48	173		£25,390	£147	984	1,268
1749–50	[175]	173	£23,266	£134	897	1,268
1758–59	[186]	139	£21,010	£151	1,011	1,268
1763–64	[186]	159	£26,809	£169	1,131	2,362
1772–73	[188]	135	£25,446	£188	1,255	2,362
1774–75	188		£33,615	£179	1,198	2,362

Unfortunately receipts for Covent Garden are not available
to match the above figures season by season. At three points,
however, I have been able to find records which are but a
season apart.[58]

Season	Total of Performances	Total Receipts	Average Daily Receipts	Average Daily Attendance	Estimated Capacity
1740–41	170	£19,501	£115	768	1,335
1746–47	166	£22,195	£134	894	1,335
1759–60	181	£26,211	£145	968	1,335

Elsewhere will be found charts of theatrical attendance based

upon these particular seasons.[59] Mondays, Thursdays, and
Saturdays seem to have been the most favored days for
attendance, even when we allow for the custom of alternate
performances at the two houses for several weeks at the
beginning of the season. Holidays show no particular ad-
vance over regular daily patronage. The months of November, January, and February find the largest crowds in the
theatres, except those during the annual "benefit season"
which began in mid-March and continued through April
and May.[60]

The figures listed above give us a daily average of 1,410
persons and a weekly average of 8,460 persons for the combined attendance at the Patent houses in the period 1740–42,
and 1,878 daily and 11,268 weekly in the period 1746–48.
In fifteen years these averages had become 1,979 persons a
day and 11,874 persons a week (1758–60).

It is with considerable satisfaction that we can produce at
this point the one known instance of specific contemporary
testimony corroborating our estimate of London's playgoing
population. And the fact that our witness happens to be
Samuel Foote adds weight to what otherwise might be dismissed as guesswork. For the manager of the Little Theatre
in the Haymarket was as shrewd and calculating an authority in theatrical finance as Garrick himself, and he underscores our conservative estimate of 11,874 weekly theatre
patrons emphatically, stating that "Upon the least favourable Calculation, the Number of those called Play-Followers,
cannot be rated at less than twelve thousand in this Metropolis. . . ."[61] If by independent and far from perfect means
we have approximated the true potential audience in London's population at this time, we shall be content to have
our estimate termed "the least favourable Calculation."

When Foote speaks of the London metropolis, he uses the
contemporary term describing the cities and liberties of
London and Westminster together with the Borough of

Southwark and its adjacent parts.[62] The population of this area served by the two Patent theatres is estimated to have been 676,250 by 1750, rising to 900,000 by the end of the century.[63] If we relate our audience estimates to the total population from 1750 on, we discover that 1.7 percent of the people, or only 17 persons in every 1,000, attended these theatres during the period of Garrick's management. How far his contemporaries who were not theatrical people could misjudge this audience potential is shown by Mrs. Brooke in her attack on Garrick for rejecting one of her tragedies:

Would it not have been wiser, as well as more manly, to have said in the clearest and most ambiguous terms, "Sir, we have no occasion for new pieces while there are only two English theatres in a city so extensive and opulent as London; a city which, in the time of Elizabeth, when the frequenters of the theatre were not a tenth part of the present, supported seventeen.[64]

On the other hand, even though the percentage of theatre-goers in the total population appears so small, this cannot mean that only one particular group attended. To be sure, one reads a contemporary diary such as that of Isaac Reed [65] and receives the impression that a company assembled of an evening at Drury Lane was much the same as one at Covent Garden. We know that people alternated between the two theatres from day to day throughout the season. This was particularly true of a good proportion of pit and boxes, but not necessarily of the two galleries. Here would be found the more casual patrons, those who could not afford to indulge themselves with such frequency. But we must also take into account a curious statement made by that even more curious and short-lived manager, Theophilus Cibber. Discussing the audience from the box office point of view Cibber says, "As every seven years is allow'd to be a new Stage of Life, consequently the Majority of our theatrical Auditors, may be said to be renew'd at the End of every such Period." [66]

If I interpret Cibber correctly, this statement is significant for the whole question of theatre patronage. Certainly it explains the secret of the success of the repertory system as practiced in the eighteenth century. While only 17 people in 1,000 attended the theatre in any one season, the actual number of "Play-Followers" was renewed with each generation and guaranteed that patronage was much more diffused within the population limits. Many or few, however, Foote's expression "Play-Followers" does speak for the definite majority of eighteenth century playgoing people.

"THE world is a theatre; mankind are the comedians; chance composes the piece, and fortune distributes the parts; theologists and politicians govern the machines; and philosophers are the spectators. The rich take their places in the pit and upper boxes, the powerful in the front and sides, and the galleries are for the poor. The women distribute fruit and refreshments, and the unfortunate snuff the candles. Folly composes the overture, and time draws the curtain. . . ." The anonymous author *Honestus* calls this effusion *The Universal Farce displayed*.[1] While we are not concerned with his private quarrel with destiny, the use *Honestus* makes of the public playhouse as a universal symbol shows how completely the mold had set in a hundred-odd years of cataloguing audiences in prologue and epilogue. The "four estates" constituting theatre patronage were described with monotonous regularity as to pit, boxes, middle gallery, upper gallery. If Richard Estcourt was saying in the Epilogue to Mrs. Centlivre's *The Basset Table*,

> This goodly Fabrick to a gazing Tarr,
> Seems Fore and Aft, a Three Deckt-Man of War:
> Abaft, the Hold's the Pit, from thence look up;
> Aloft! that's Swabber's Nest, that's the Main-Top.
> Side Boxes mann'd with Beau, and modish Rake,
> Are like the Fore-castle and Quarter-Deck.[2]

Thomas King was provided with the following Prologue written for the opening of the same theatre in 1776:

Another simile, we mean to broach —
A new one too! — the stage is a stage coach. —
A stage coach! — why? — I'll tell you if you ask it.
Here (*boxes*) some take Places, and some mount basket. (*Gall.*)
Our cattle too, that draw the stage along,

Are of all sorts and sizes — weak and strong,
Brown, grey, black, bay, brisk, tame, blind,
        lame, fat, lean, old and young!
If as we're jogging on, we sometimes stop,
Some scold within, and some asleep will drop.
While sailors and their doxies sing and roar a'top![3]

The typical distribution of the eighteenth century theatre
audience exactly paralleled the box office tariffs, as they in
turn implied the rigid social distinctions of that day: the
beau monde in front and side boxes; wealthy tradesmen in
the pit and first gallery; and "the Mob" in the upper gallery.
Theophilus Cibber in characteristic humor denominates them
as the "Noble, Gentle, or Simple, who fill the Boxes, Pit,
and Galleries, . . . as K——g, L—rds and COMMONS . . .
make that great Body the Nation." [4]

Even if such a simplification is accepted, we still do not
know very much about these people. Mrs. M. D. George
reminds us of the fact that

Eighteenth-century London inevitably suggests the brilliant
society which made up the world of politics and fashion. This
small world of statesmen and politicians and placemen, of wits
and rakes and fops, was so self-sufficient, so conscious that it
was the only world that counted, that it imposes its point of
view on us. The social life of the eighteenth lives for us chiefly
in the letters and memoirs of these people, their houses, their
portraits, their furniture. . . . We know little of the artisans
and labourers, the shopkeepers and clerks and street-sellers,
who made up the mass of the population. . . . We are apt to
see them through the eyes of that other world as the Mob, the
Fourth Estate as Fielding called it.[5]

This is just what we do not wish to do. Our task is to
scrutinize such cataloguing in terms of Foote's 12,000 "Play-
Followers" in metropolitan London. Who were these 17
persons in every 1,000 of population? Especially, who were
the people who frequented the lower-priced seats of the middle and upper galleries?

In 1709 Daniel Defoe divided the English population into seven categories, placing his median in the fourth class:

1. The great, who live profusely.
2. The rich, who live very plentifully.
3. The middle sort who live well.
4. The working trades who labour hard, but feel no want.
5. The country people, farms, etc., who fare indifferently.
6. The poor, that fare hard.
7. The miserable, that really pinch and suffer want.[6]

This classification persisted throughout the century. Another writer thus described the Londoners of 1807:

1. The great.
2. The opulent tradesman and merchant.
3. Persons of small income.
4. The journeymen.
5. Citizens of the lowest class.[7]

While there is no statistical answer for London itself, such descriptions will be sharpened for our purpose by a glance at the empire estimates of Patrick Colquhoun made soon after 1800.[8] Basing his figures upon an estimated population of fourteen millions, Colquhoun divided the people into six classes. His figures have been reduced to percentages in the following analysis:

Category	Percent
Aristocracy	3.0
Traders and employers	5.3
Public employees and professional classes	3.6
Innkeepers and publicans	3.1
Working classes, paupers and vagrants	64.0
Freeholders and farmers	21.0

In the grouping of working trades with paupers and vagrants, we meet with what Mrs. George calls the hopeless confusion as to the make-up of the lower classes of English society, a confusion bitterly denounced by Francis Place as the jumbling together of "the 'lower orders,' the most skilled and the most prudent workman, with the most ignorant and imprudent labourers and paupers, though the difference is great indeed, and indeed in many cases will scarce admit of comparison." [9]

Daily wages for both journeymen and their laborers were more or less stable throughout the period of our investigation. In London, where wages were highest, a typical journeyman's wage in the building trades was 3s. a day in 1720, an amount which prevailed until sometime after 1780.[10] The journeyman-mason received 12s. to 14s. a week, the journeyman-saddler 12s. to 15s., the journeyman-printer 14s. to a guinea.[11] Those employed as day labor received an average of 1s. 8d. a day, rising in certain trades to 2s. from 1700 to 1787.[12] Among the many extant budgets collected by the economists, the two following will show something of London life in this period. The first is that of a single journeyman-tailor in 1752.[13] It is set down here in brief.

Item	£	s.	d.
One day's expences	0	0	11
Sunday's expence	0	1	0
The other five days' expence.............	0	4	7
Lodging for a week	0	1	0
Washing for a week	0	0	8
Shaving for a week	0	0	4
	0	8	6

The second budget is that of a journeyman-saddler, his wife and three children, in 1779.[14]

Item	£	s.	d.
The man being obliged to work from home early every morning, breakfast for his wife, and children every day for six days at 1s. per day..................	0	6	0
Breakfast and dinner for the man and supper for the whole family at 1s. per day..	0	6	0

Lodgings, coals, candles, soap and other
   necessities cannot amount to less than.. 0   5   0
Sunday's breakfast, dinner, and supper for
   the whole family 0   2   0
                                          0 19   0

Now if the journeyman-saddler draws a wage of 15s. a week and his living necessities amount to 19s. a week, it is obvious that he will have to supplement his income in some manner. At any rate, we should not expect him to be an habitué of even the cheapest gallery seat at Covent Garden or Drury Lane. If we were to find him there, we would suppose it a rare holiday occasion. And yet we do find him there, impatient at the doors long before the time for the performance! This phenomenon was a constant surprise to the travelers who visited London. Their accounts remark upon the passion of London workmen for the playhouse and other places of amusement.[15]

Mrs. Gilboy reminds us that money wages in the eighteenth century do not offer in themselves a basis for estimating the condition of the London laborer.[16] There are the perquisites of his particular trade, payment in kind, and the earnings of the other members of his family.[17] She believes, on the basis of statistical data as to the relation of the price of wheat and wages, that a distinct increase in the standard of living occurred between 1710 and 1736 which remained unchallenged, despite rising costs in the middle of the century until the great rise in prices of the nineties.

It is precisely during the period of increasing wages and decreasing prices, [she writes,] that we find most contemporary complaint of an orgy of gin-drinking, of gaming, of attendance at interludes and frolls. . . . The wide participation in these activities by the poorest members of the London community can be partly explained by the wage and price figures. Since the family bread cost less, at a time when wages were rising, there was obviously more surplus to spend.

But what is even more important, Mrs. Gilboy concludes by
saying, "The popular fever for excitement went further,
however, and not only surplus income, but that which should
have gone for necessities, was squandered at the tavern or
the play." [18] A contemporary physician, Dr. George Fordyce,
agrees with this viewpoint in discussing the health of his
patients. He says that these workmen earn large sums,

which they spend in drinking, exposing themselves at the same
time to the inclemency of the weather; always idle when they
have any money left, so that their life is spent between labor
and attention above their powers, and perfect idleness and
drunkenness. Their women also, passing from affluence to distress almost every week, are forced, though soberly inclined,
to lead very disorderly lives.[19]

Here is the heart of our problem. The matter of wages
and budgets is not enough. The fact that members of the
working classes continually deprived themselves and their
families of necessities in order to purchase amusements
makes any exactitude impossible. An examination of the
various amusements available to these people, however, may
lead us to certain conclusions as to their custom.

In 1768 Thomas, Bishop of Bristol, addressed an open
letter to the inhabitants of the three united parishes of St.
Mary-le-bow, St. Pancras, and Allhallows Honey-Lane,
complaining that the people had suffered the subscription
for daily prayers to dwindle almost to the vanishing point.

All that I desire of you [he wrote,] is, that of the better sort,
every one would subscribe ten shillings a-year, that is half a
crown a quarter, and of those in lower circumstances every
one would subscribe five or four shillings a year, that is, at
least a shilling a quarter. . . . You cannot surely think so small
and inconsiderable a sum any loss or burden to you. You may
easily make it otherwise, by riding out a Sunday or two less
in a year, or by giving an evening or two less in a year to
Vauxhall or Ranelagh, to the Tavern or the Play. This you

will do, if you are not "lovers of pleasure more than lovers of God." [20]

We may speculate on the results of this familiar clerical appeal, but one thing is certain. The good Bishop understood his parishioners — those "of the better sort" and those "in lower circumstances" — and he has catalogued their chief modes of entertainment.

"Riding out a Sunday" and visits to the parks and public gardens would appear to be a primary source of pleasure for all classes. They might be expected to appeal especially to the workingman. Malcolm tells us that Mary-le-bon Gardens were opened some time before 1737 and were frequented by all classes gratis. But ". . . the company resorting to them becoming more respectable, Mr. Gough, the keeper, determined to demand a shilling as entrance-money, for which the party paying was to receive an equivalent in viands." [21] Two explanations are possible: first, we might conclude that "the company resorting to them becoming more respectable" means that the Gardens had fallen from favor with the working classes; second, that Mr. Gough, either from business acumen or under pressure from "the better sort," fixed his shilling entrance-money deliberately to exclude not only paupers and vagrants, but also the London workman. The latter undoubtedly is the true explanation. Mr. Gough merely anticipated the practice at Ranelagh and Vauxhall. The former charged half a crown admission, including tea, coffee or punch; the latter held to a lower admission fee but priced its refreshments exhorbitantly. We may presume, then, that London journeymen frequented such places on rare occasions only, if at all. Even the citizen described by Bonnell Thornton,[22] who took his wife and two daughters to Vauxhall, grumbled over his chicken "no bigger than a partridge," which cost half a crown, and vowed that the ham they ate cost a shilling an ounce. Leaving the place he was heard to mutter, "It would not have cost me above fourpence-half-

penny to have spent my evening at Sot's Hole; and what
with coach-hire, and all together, here's almost a pound gone,
and nothing to show for it." Henry Fielding settles the
matter when he explains that "though Ranelagh and Vauxhall, by reason of their price, are not entirely appropriated to
the people of fashion, yet they are seldom frequented by any
below the middle rank." [23]

Public eating places to which the London workman could
resort on occasion were limited. The cheapest served a filling meal for threepence-halfpenny and were patronized by
"a company of hackney coachmen, chairmen, draymen, and
a few footmen out of place or on board wages." [24] Here the
workman would no doubt dine; for the price was right and
the food plain and possibly wholesome. The "Ordinary"
was more expensive, about tenpence for "two dishes and a
pastry, including a penny to the waiter; and the company
generally consisted of literary characters, a few Templars,
and some citizens who had left off trade." [25] Chophouses,
according to Thornton, were patronized by "the jemmy
attorney's clerk, the prim curate, the walking physician, and
the captain upon half-pay." [26]

If we may believe Francis Place, the main entertainment
for London workmen centered about the tavern. There they
obtained their pot of beer for 3d. and could add to it on a
lucky day other pots, or perhaps a quartern of gin, winnings
from games of chance or dexterity. Says Place:

Until lately, all the amusements of the working people of the
metropolis were immediately concerned with drinking—chair-
clubs, chanting-clubs, lottery-clubs, and every variety of club,
intended for amusement were always held at public-houses.
In these clubs every possible excitement to produce excess was
contrived . . . skittles, dutch-pins, bumble-puppy, drafts, dom-
inos, etc., were all provided by the publicans . . . these were
the *only* amusements within reach of the working people.[27]

Allowing an average weekly wage of about 12s., let us

tabulate the price of eighteenth century amusements and
their modern equivalents and compare them with what an
Elizabethan workman paid for his "pleasures." [28]

Place or Mode of Entertainment	Cost to 18th Century Workman (Pence)	Cost to Modern Workman at 18th Century Rates (Dollars)	Actual Cost of Modern Equivalent (Dollars)	Cost to Modern Workman at Elizabethan Rates (Dollars)
Patent Theatres:				
Upper Gallery	12	4.56	1.95 (Average	.62
First Gallery	24	9.12	2.60 legitimate	.93
The Pit	36	13.68	3.25 theatre)	1.86
Minor Theatres:				
Gallery	6	2.28	(Average	.31
The Pit	12	4.56	.79 movie	.62
The Boxes	30	11.40	admission)	.93
Ranelagh	60	28.80	(Small night-	
Vauxhall	36	13.68	3.00 club minimum	
"Sot's Hole"	3 (?)	1.14 (?)	cover charge)	
Pot of Beer	3	1.14	.35	1.24
Cheapest dinner	3½	1.33	.75	.93
Transportation	3	1.14	.10	.93
Reading matter	3	1.14	.05 (Newspaper)	.31
A small book	36	13.68	.50 (Magazine)	3.72

Considering the cost of amusements in relation to the
London workman's budget, the testimony of Place seems
reasonable. Our tabulation shows that the eighteenth century
Londoner was much less able to attend the theatre than his
modern counterpart in American industry. He was also less
able than the Elizabethan workman. And yet there is ample
proof of his appetite for theatrical entertainment. Theophilus
Cibber in his *Two Dissertations on the Theatres* (1756)
quotes at length from a Parliamentary speech of 1733 in
defense of the playhouse.[29] In the course of debate the speaker

answers the old charge that theatres entice apprentices from
their masters' business :

As to 'Prentices, and Persons of the like Class, 'tis evident they
will spend their leisure Evenings somewhere abroad; if they
go to a Play, it will cost 'em but one Shilling for the whole; if
they go to a Tavern, or even an Alehouse, it must needs cost
them more, besides the Danger of coming Home drunk, and
setting Fire to their Masters Houses.

Granting the workman's appetite for the theatre, two
questions arise : How often was he a member of the audience
at one of the Patent houses? How often did he attend theatrical amusements in general? Neither question can be
answered with any degree of exactitude, but we may hazard
an approximation for the first. If Covent Garden held 384
persons in its shilling gallery in 1782,[30] and if we assume
that Drury Lane's upper gallery held about the same number, we can estimate that 4,608 persons in the one-shilling
class attended the Patent theatres every week, or 0.6 percent
of London's total population.[31] The answer to the second
question is anybody's guess. Despite his economic status, it
appears that the London workman attended some theatrical
performance often enough to cause deep concern to moralists
and those in authority who professed to be alarmed at what
was always termed the "debauching" of the lower classes
by the playhouse.[32] Certain factors of this problem should be
recognized however — the box office rates in the few
"minor theatres" in operation after the Licensing Act of
1737,[33] and the custom of "half-price" admission to Drury
Lane and Covent Garden.

The Government legally limited its citizens to these two
Patent houses, but certain "minor" theatres continued to
circumvent the law by producing spectacular shows, musical
entertainments, and pantomimes. *The Daily Advertiser* for
July 10, 1744, estimated the crowd attending a performance
of *The Sorceress; or, Harlequin Savoyard* at the New Wells,
Clerkenwell, as "Upwards of 500 people present, including

100 sailors." On August 28, 1744, the same newspaper estimates that 600 persons were present at Sadler's Wells to witness a performance of *Happy Despair*. Such houses were few in number, but their importance in the life of working people cannot be ignored. Here the workman might occupy the same seat as at Drury Lane, but at 6d. instead of the usual shilling for a full evening's entertainment. If so minded he might indeed pay his shilling, but to sit in the pit and become a part of "society" for an evening! At the minor theatre he would be regaled by a splendid aquatic show, an animal or variety show, a musical entertainment, or a pantomime.[34] That such theatres must have won the support of a large following of "the meaner sort" is shown not only by the fact that they were able to keep open in the face of the Patent monopoly, but also in the challenge which they brought to their great rivals in the field of the spectacular.

Attempts at Covent Garden and Drury Lane to abolish the custom of "half-price" led to serious and prolonged rioting and the usual destruction of playhouse furnishings. At last the managements were forced to yield to popular sentiment.[35] According to custom, those who were either too busily engaged to come at the beginning of the evening's bill, or who preferred to witness only the second and lighter portion, or who could not afford the full price of admission — all these were admitted after the close of the third act of the principal item on the bill. It was no mob fancy which began the Half-Price Riots of 1763. Back of the vanity and impertinence of Grub-streeters such as Francis and Fitzpatrick, who conceived and led the rioting, was the sound economic necessity of the more humble in London's playgoing population. Nor was it mere whimsy on the part of the managers to place the lighter portions of their entertainment *after* seven o'clock in the evening. Percy Fitzgerald describes this policy in terms of the audience:

There can be no doubt that this half-price was an equitable

practice in the large theatres and under the patent limitations, for as the choice of entertainment was thus restrained, and there were but two or three houses, it was deemed fair that the audience should be allowed to select what portion of the entertainment it should attend. The performance, too, began very early, and was so arranged as to be, as it were, in two divisions, each of which might suit a different class of spectators. The farce in those days was not the sketchy imperfect thing it is now [1882], but a feature of the night, and worth the reduced rather than half price that was paid for it.[36]

Fitzgerald no doubt alludes to the eighteenth century equivalent of our modern "tired businessman" with his marked preference for relaxation at so-called "girlie shows," or to contemporary men-about-town such as Isaac Reed, whose diaries reveal an overwhelming liking for the second half of theatrical performances. We may assume that the London workman also made up a considerable portion of the "latter Account" at half-price time. A German visitor said of English theatres in 1791, "A unique feature . . . was the afterpiece, in which the greatest variety of entertainment was offered, and for which the seats, hitherto comparatively empty, were invariably filled to capacity; for after the first acts of the main play, the price of admission was reduced by half." [37]

We have noted that whether his weekly earnings would permit or not, our London workman did attend the theatre, and that he went, if at all, with some regularity. In his amusements his choice naturally rested between the tavern and the playhouse; the former in all probability cost him far more of an evening, while the playhouse fee was inclusive for the night's diversion. Those who would choose the theatre in preference to a tavern had their choice between a full performance at a house like Sadler's Wells or a half-evening in a Patent theatre. We conclude that the workman's patronage, perhaps divided between the two, veered strongly toward the cheaper entertainment.

In 1696 Gregory King estimated that 13 percent of the London population belonged to the servant class.[38] Making allowance for an increase in population during the century, and of this class in particular, we can estimate the servants of 1750 conservatively as numbering about 88,000. Unfortunately their theatre ways cannot be charted, because they aped their betters, because some were on board wages, and because their duties often demanded their presence in a particular theatre and determined what part of the auditorium they were to occupy. James Townley's *High Life Below Stairs* (Drury Lane, 1759), although broad in its comedy is nevertheless a faithful picture of retainer habits. Sir Harry's Servant meets the Servant of the Duke while taking the air in the Park:

Duke: Well, baronet, and where have you been?

Sir Harry: At Newmarket, my lord: we have had devilish fine sport.

Duke: And a good appearance, I hear; plague take it, I should have been there; but our old duchess died, and we were obliged to keep house, for the decency of the thing.[39]

Davy, in Garrick's *Bon Ton* (Drury Lane, 1775), reminds Sir John of a promise:

Sir John: Why, what did I promise you?

Davy: That I should take sixpen'oth at one of the theatres tonight, and a shilling place at the other to-morrow.

Sir John: Well, well, so I did. Is it a moral piece, Davy?

Davy: Oh! yes, and written by a clergyman; it is called the "Rival Cannanites; or the Tragedy of Braggadocia."

Sir John: Be a good lad, and I won't be worse than my word; there's money for you. (*Gives him money*)[40]

While Garrick's Davy spent his evenings in the upper gallery, we can be certain that the Duke and Sir Harry would be seen only in the best seats they could afford or usurp.

We have next to consider the group Malcolm has termed "persons of small income." As he distinguishes these from

the "opulent tradesman and merchant," we may suppose that
it corresponds with Defoe's class called "the middle sort."
In any event the class will include the small businessman,
the shopman, the experienced clerk, and those "persons of
small income, who are compelled . . . to occupy furnished
and unfurnished first and second floors." [41] While an average
shopman of the period earned a yearly wage of about £20,
such wages were customarily in addition to his board and
lodgings; more industrious men could earn £30 to £40 in
the more responsible positions.[42] An experienced clerk in a
wealthy tradesman's office could earn about £50 a year.[43]
In this class also would be the wealthy widow, Moritz's
landlady, who told him she always fixed on one day each
year in which, without fail, she hired a coach and drove to
Ranelagh.[44] Most of these people, however, were not far
removed from the income of a good London journeyman.
They might very well be able to afford a seat in the first
gallery at Drury Lane on occasion; but if they attended at
all frequently, they must have taken cheerfully the shilling
places at the top of the house.

Among the people of "the middle sort" we should expect
to find also the professional man and the public servant.
Since their incomes vary considerably, they will be found
in either gallery or in the pit. The lowly usher, or assistant
schoolmaster, with his £10 to £20 a year plus board,[45] will
have to choose carefully between the two galleries, while
Mr. Rice, "the instructor of English," sits in a front box.[46]
The lawyer-author Arthur Murphy enjoys the freedom of
the house while his benefits from a single play amount to
a clear profit of £789 16s. 6d. in three nights.[47] Murphy's
place will be in the pit. A like choice must be made by the
impoverished "blackcoat" whose drab living amounts to but
£50 a year,[48] in splendid contrast indeed to those of the
Reverend Doctors Young and Brown seated near the pit
doorway.[49] Beside such ranking clergymen will be found

men whom it did not suit either to be at the expence of dress, or who had not the time to equip themselves. . . . This of course comprehended a large description of persons, such as belonged to the inns of court, men of liberal pursuits and professions; and who, by an uniform attendance at the playhouse, became no incompetent judges of the drama.[50]

A disastrous instance of mob hysteria at the pit door of the Haymarket Theatre in 1794 allows us to add to an already varied list of persons to be found in this section of the house. There was a command performance of a triple bill, and the following persons died, according to the coroner of St. Martin's Parish, an "accidental death by suffocation, and being trampled upon at the pit-door." [51]

Mrs. Fisher, sister-in-law to Mr. Brandram of Tooley-street.
Miss Brandram, niece of Mr. Brandram.
Mr. Brandram, his nephew.
Benjamin Pingo, Esq., York Herald, of the heralds' college.
J. C. Brooke, Esq., Somerset Herald, of ditto.
Mrs. and master Willis, wife and son of Mr. Willis, attorney, of Gray's Inn.
Mr. Garbutt, late master of the Three Sisters, of Whitby.
Mrs. Gwatkin, wife of Mr. Gwatkin, dancing master, Bartlett's Buildings.
Mrs. Spencer, St. James's Market.
Miss Williams, Pall-mall. . . .
Mr. Robinson, of Coleman-street, farrier.
Miss Bushnel. . . .
Mrs. Edgar and son of Pall-mall.
In all 15 persons.

It is in the pit and boxes that we shall encounter the wealthy traders and employers.

A play-house, what a place! I must forswear it.
A little mischief only makes one bear it.
Such crowds of city folks! — so rude and pressing!
And their horse-laughs, so hideously distressing!

> Whene'er we hiss'd, they frown'd and fell a swearing,
> Like their own Guildhall Giants, fierce and staring! [52]

These are the fellows of whom Charles Knight wrote that they were "accumulating wealth and losing respectability," citizens at the beginning of the century and "a hybrid of fashion before its close." [53] No longer were the boxes the sole privilege of the aristocracy, which indeed was being slowly engulfed by the rise of these upper-middle-class merchants. If the Fine Lady, Mrs. Riot, can shout at Aesop in the Shades,

Your taste here, I suppose, rises no higher than your Shakespeare and your Johnsons: oh you *Goats and Vandils!* in the name of barbarity take 'em to yourselves, we are tir'd of 'em upon earth: — one goes indeed to a Playhouse sometimes, because one does not know how else one can kill one's time — every body goes, because — all the world's there — [54]

the tradesman's daughter confides to her Diary that she

Got up at eleven, rather fatigued with last night's entertainment; breakfasted about twelve, when Mr. *Crochet,* the music master, came to give me a lesson on the harpsichord; desired him to call to-morrow, being indisposed; . . . drest myself by three to dine with my papa and mama; at half past four retired to my room to rest myself a little; at a quarter before five began to dress for the play; made a shift to get into the front boxes by half past six; from thence set off for Mrs. *Draper's* rout; lost about five guineas at quadrille; and I believe it might be three at whist; came home at three in the morning, not a little chagrined at my loss. [55]

Foreign visitors would ordinarily sit in the boxes or in the pit. We read of J. J. Rousseau sitting in the Garricks' box, of Judge Samuel Curwens' visits to both Covent Garden and Drury Lane, and even to the Patagonian Theatre in Exeter Exchange. [56] Travelers such as von Archenholz, who professed to have witnessed Garrick's *The Jubilee* twenty-eight times, Count Kielmansegge, Friedrich von

Gunderode, and the Baron Grimm — all these wrote extended accounts of their experiences as London playgoers.[57] Sometimes their reactions were unfavorable, especially as to the deportment of their fellow auditors; more often they were enthusiastic and complimented the production skill of English companies. Finally, the foreign ambassadors appear to have attended quite frequently. We know the ambassador of Morocco attended a performance of *Henry VIII* and the pantomime *The Genii* at Drury Lane; the Tripoline ambassador favored the same historical drama but with the pantomime of *Harlequin Ranger,* and particularly desired the pairing of *The Careless Husband* with *The Englishman in Paris* on the occasion of Miss Dawson's benefit.[58] The visit and marriage of the King of Denmark in the summer and fall of 1768 was punctuated by no less than six appearances at the Drury Lane theatre alone.[59]

One class remains to be surveyed: those persons whom Grosley insisted should be distinguished "not only from persons of condition, most of whom walk a-foot merely because it is their fancy, but even from the lowest class of shopkeepers" [60] — the porters, sailors, chairmen, the street workers, and so on. Of the sailors as a class their love for entertainment was proverbial. Their presence atop the shilling gallery is the theme of many a prologue and epilogue. And we have already noted their presence in considerable numbers at "minor theatres." The parliamentary speech quoted earlier contains a singular picture of their influence: [61] ". . . the Theatre in Goodman's Fields is chiefly supported by Captains of Ships, and seafaring Men, who thereby carry abroad a Taste of Politeness and Generosity, and give the World a better Idea of *English* Manners; they are roused from their Barbarity, and taught to think like human Creatures." And then the crowning argument: ". . . a considerable Sum of their Money is left here to circulate, which might otherwise, perhaps, be carried abroad." Enough has

been said! If no others in this class could afford the theatre,
His Majesty's sailors must have had money to spend. As
for the porters, at possible earnings of at least £25 a year,[62]
they too must have been able to conjure up sixpence or a
shilling for gala occasions. With the exception of the sailors,
however, it is unlikely that any majority of this lowest class
in eighteenth century London ever sat in even the upper
gallery of a Patent house. The Patent monopoly retarded all
progress toward a return to a more democratic audience.
It remained for the twentieth century to bring it about most
completely for the legitimate drama in the early work of
London's Old Vic Company and the recent establishment of
a National Theatre.

While we have shown that all but the very lowest class of
Londoners could actually afford now and then the price of
some theatrical entertainment, the traditional hours of performance at the Patent theatres must have had a decided
effect upon the box office and the make-up of audiences.
During Garrick's management performances usually began
at six o'clock.[63] Theatre doors were open early in the after-
noon, usually somewhere between three o'clock (the earliest
hour for dining) and five o'clock.[64] The rule was "first come,
first served" for the best seats in each section of the house.
The custom afforded sufficient time for theatre lovers to
secure favorite seats and for the Quality to send footmen to
hold the better places. An audience demonstration in October, 1768, in protest against opening theatre doors earlier
than five o'clock forced the Drury Lane management to
establish such a policy. Hopkins the prompter writes that
Tom King appeared before the audience to say that

he was desired by the Managers to tell them the Doors for the
future should not be opened till Five, ' — A great Clap, — He
added that (the) Managers was always willing to oblige the
Publick in every thing that was in their Power; but they
thought that on very full Nights it would be attended with

some Inconveniences.' — They would not hear of any Alteration, he then told them, "the Doors should always for the future be opened at five, unless the Publick applyed to have it altered." [65]

It is apparent that such a practice did not work in favor of the London business world or that of the laboring classes. The following summary of working hours in certain trades has been compiled from information derived from Mrs. George. [66]

London tailors, 6 a.m. - 8 p.m. (1721) ; 6 a.m. - 7 p.m. (1768)
Bookbinders, 6 a.m. - 9 p.m. (1747) ; 6 a.m. - 8 p.m. (1785)
Handicrafts, 6 a.m. - 8 p.m. (1747) ; 6 a.m. - 9 p.m.; 5 a.m. - 9 p.m.
Building trades, 6 a.m. - 6 p.m. (during daylight hours)
Ropemakers, 8 p.m. - 8 a.m.
Shopkeepers, 7 a.m. - 8 p.m. (1747) ; 8 a.m. - 10 p.m. (1786)
Tambour workers (women), no limit.
Charwomen and laundry workers, no limit.

From such a sampling of working hours it is reasonable to believe that opening time and time of performance at the Patent theatres were established with little respect for this class of people. Unless the journeyman were among the "idle and profligate" (as many undoubtedly were), or unless he went to the theatre on a holiday, [67] the hour of performance must have excluded him. Malcolm, in describing the journeyman's life, says he will not discuss the thousands who

have been steady well-behaved youths, in the practice of passing their evenings and holidays in rational pursuits with parents and friends, and who enter upon their profession determined to render themselves respectable, and their connexions happy . . . there is too much still-life for description in the man who rises at six in the morning, and works without cessation till six in the evening. His intervals of amusement may be directed to the same objects, Tea-gardens, public Exhibitions, and the Theatres ; but his conduct is so properly governed, that Temperance and Pleasure dance in his features. [68]

As for his less reputable brothers, Malcolm says that they worked perhaps three days in the week.

. . . Sunday they appropriate to the same species of relaxation to which they accustomed themselves in apprenticeship: Monday is sainted with them. And who will work on *Saint Monday?* Not the idle Journeyman and Labourer of London. Unfortunately the votaries of this Saint celebrate his name with libations of Beer and Gin, the fumes of which render them unfit for work on Tuesday. On Wednesday they begin the week; not by a close attention to their business, as their employers find to the extent of vexation and disappointment. . . . At the close of the week necessity compels this description of madman to work; for, Saturday arriving, he must procure the means of redeeming his own and his wife's clothes from that *most respectable member of society* the Pawnbroker. And this is the labouring life of at least thirty thousand persons at present in London.[69]

Such hours, then, would not be conducive to playgoing except at intervals. When the better class of laborer did attend it was probably at seven o'clock, or thereabouts, the half-price time. His employer no doubt was under the same constraint in his working hours, for John Brownsmith the prompter, in the Preface to his curious handbook *The Dramatic Timepiece* (1767), mentions as one of its selling points that,

. . . It will likewise be infinitely serviceable to *all those* whom Business may prevent attending a Play till after the Third Act, which is commonly called "The latter Account of it;" for by only allowing seven Minutes between each Act, for the intervening Music, they will always be certain of the Time *any Act* will be *over.*

A random glance at box office figures showing the relation between "After-Money" and the full admission price will show the importance of this concession to working hours. *The Covent Garden Cash Book 1759–60*[70] lists receipts such as the following: November 30, £51 10s., After-

Money, £206 19s. 6d.; December 12, £113 19s., A-M.,
£49 16s. 6 d.; December 18, £123 Os. Od., A-M., £55 10s.
6 d.; December 21, £142 6s. Od., A-M., £56 Os. Od., etc.
Indeed, the importance of the working hours was recognized early by the minor theatres in their struggle for patronage. The Theatrical Booth in Southwark, for example,
advertised a performance of *The Recruiting Officer* and
The Lying Valet "to begin positively at six and to conclude
about 9 o'clock." [71] If the great houses were bogged down
by custom and the convenience of the Quality,[72] these lesser
managers knew where to strike a telling blow. At Goodman's
Fields Theatre in 1733 one was asked to ". . . consider the
better Class of People that frequent it, — which are Merchants, Tradesmen, their Wives, or Daughters: Can it any
Way interfere with their Business, it never beginning till
the Hour that all Business is over, and has constantly done
by Ten at farthest, which is no unseasonable hour." [73]

The closing hour, especially in the great theatres, is a
perplexing problem, and we are grateful for this hint from
Goodman's Fields. Ten o'clock must have been the suitable
closing hour at all theatres, although it is certain that on
gala and benefit nights the ideal was not always achieved.
Two plays timed by Brownsmith were played on the same
evening and totaled 3 hrs. 4 min.[74] Arthur Murphy's comedy
All in the Wrong in five acts lasted 1 hr. 44 min. The other
half of the bill was Samuel Foote's three-act piece *The
Minor,* which had a running time of 1 hr. 20 min. "By
adding half an hour to the Time of the whole Play," says
Brownsmith, "you may be certain of the Time it will be
over." [75] This will mean one hour to be added to the time
of the two plays to allow for entr-acte music and other
entertainments. If the performance began at 6:00 p.m. sharp,
the Murphy comedy would end at 8:14 p.m. and the entire
evening's bill would conclude at 10:04 p.m. Except on
benefit nights, I am of the opinion that ten o'clock was the

customary closing time at most eighteenth century theatres.

Of those who could afford to attend the theatres and had leisure to indulge themselves, there was undoubtedly a great number who did not go at all. Perhaps they had no relish for this form of entertainment. Perhaps they had personal religious or moral scruples. The extension of the controversy begun by Jeremy Collier in 1698 through the efforts of people such as John Tillotson, Arthur Bedford, or William Law, reflects not only a general dissatisfaction with the social tone of the century which persisted in groups such as the Society for the Reformation of Manners, but it also reflects what must have been the attendant confusion in the public mind as to the propriety of going to the theatre. The Church in the eighteenth century took little official notice of the theatres, although its aloofness is understandable in the light of its historic prejudices. Many clergymen attended performances, some of them cherishing lifelong ambitions as authors. With the majority, however, such ambitions must have been severely controlled. They always had to reckon with ecclesiastical authority. Indeed the Reverend John Hoadly's reluctance to acknowledge the authorship of several pieces, "to bring himself upon the public stage," is an amusing example of official disapproval.[76] His father was a bishop! Perhaps some of the more disappointed joined their voices with their zealot brothers who used pulpit and press to denounce the theatres in terms of institutionalized blasphemy and depravity.

The presence of the clergy in the pit of a Patent theatre is apt to deceive us into thinking that the Collier controversy was dead by the time that David Garrick became manager. Nothing is farther from the truth. From 1698 to 1800 over fifty diatribes against playhouses were published, more than twenty appearing *after* 1747.[77] Not that any of them had many new indictments. The issues were the old ones — playhouses provided opportunities for "whoredom and adultery" and enticed the working population into idleness and the general discredit of trade, while the plays burlesqued religion, abounding in blasphemous epithets, and as a survival of paganism corrupted all morality by neglecting to exact punishment of their characters for some very attractive vices. In answer over twelve publications appeared between 1748 and 1800.[78] They argued a defense of the stage which, while often admitting the charge of licentiousness, upheld the theatre as an instrument of reform. Some suggested that matters might be settled by increasing censorship. For the most part, however, the answers flung back the charge of immorality against the contemporary pulpits, insisting that the clergy had mistaken the effect for the cause. " 'Tis not the Playhouse makes them lewd, but (if it is so) they the Playhouse; and unless you can deprive People of their Appetites, you do nothing: A Man that is viciously inclined will be so at Church, as well as a Playhouse." [79] While Methodists, Quakers, and others bore the brunt of savage satire from the stage,[80] and must have pondered doubtfully the allurements of playgoing, it is reasonable to suppose that many others were in a similar state of incertitude. The Wesleyan revivals and the moral reformation led by Wilburforce were certain to be felt at the box office.

Secular authority seems not to have wavered to any great extent either in its censure. The standard form of indictment was set forth early by the Grand Jury of Middlesex impaneled July 7, 1703:

We the Grand Jury of the County of Middlesex do present, that the Plays which are frequently acted in the play-houses in Drury-Lane and Lincoln's-Inn-Fields in this County are full of prophane, irreverent, lewd, indecent, and immoral expressions, and tend to the great displeasure of Almighty God and to the corruption of the auditory, both in their principles and their practices. We also present, that the common acting of plays in the said play-houses very much tend to the debauching and ruining the youth resorting thereto, and to the breach of the peace, and are the occasions of many riots, routs, and disorderly assemblies, whereby many murders and other misdemeanors have been frequently done, and particularly the barbarous murder of Sir Andrew Slanning, which was very lately committed as he came out of one of the said playhouses; and further that the common acting of plays at the said play-houses is a public nuisance.[81]

By the end of the century, officials were making the same charges concerning Palmer's Royalty Theatre in Well Close Square. It was a threat to morality, industry, and commerce. The magistrate for the Tower Division called it ". . . the rendezvous of bawds and prostitutes, who as soon as it is opened make it their constant resort." [82] We smile at the lack of originality in these charges, but Mrs. George reminds us that ". . . the puritanic attitude towards sports and amusements from the middle ages to the early nineteenth century cannot be understood without a knowledge of the very real social evils which seemed to be inevitably connected with them." [83]

One class of spectators which rapidly increased in this century is difficult to classify as to the location of its seats. To Garrick's Farmer returned from London the location seems to have been the first gallery.

> Above 'twas like Bedlam, all roaring and rattling!
> Below, the fine folk were all curts'ying and prattling:
> Strange jumble together — Turks, Christians, and Jews!
> At the Temple of Folly, all crowd to the pews.[84]

While feeling was running high all over England at the passage of the Naturalization Bill in 1753, it is only to be expected that we should find a demonstration taking place at the theatre. Richard Cross writes of the Drury Lane performance on September 8th, "Ye Naturalizing Bill having made some Noise against the Jews, some people call'd out for ye Merchant of Venice, & a Letter was thrown upon ye Stage desiring that play instead of the Opera, but we took no notice of it, some little hissing but it dy'd away." [85] At about the same time Samuel Foote was getting a laugh in his prologue at Drury Lane with the following lines:

> The many various objects that amuse
> These busy curious times, by way of news,
> Are plays, elections, murders, lott'ries, Jews; [86]

In 1775, on the night of the first performance of Garrick's afterpiece *May Day,* the Drury Lane prompter wrote in his Diary, "This Musical Farce of one Act was wrote (by Mr. Garrick) on Purpose to introduce Miss Abrams, a Jew Girl, upon the Stage. . . . Both the Piece and the Young Lady were received with great Applause." Two days later *The Public Advertiser* commented, "The Number of Jews at the Theatre is incredible." [87]

The composition of Garrick's audience was heterogeneous. Men and women from all walks of life frequented his theatre as they were inclined or financially able. That we are correct, however, in describing this theatre as "essentially a theatre of the upper-middle class" [88] has been demonstrated both on the social and the economic level. The Patent monopoly insured this circumstance throughout the eighteenth century by way of the box office. While the number of middle-class spectators grew, crowding the more aristocratic patrons and changing the tone of the presentations, it yet remains that only 17 people in every 1,000 attended Covent Garden and Drury Lane. And we rightly assume that, except for the servants in the upper galleries, the truly "meaner sort" were excluded from these theatres. If this class and a percentage of their more fortunate fellow citizens looked to such minor houses as survived and approved their lower tariffs, it is merely another indication of the self-destructive nature of the policies pursued by the Patentees.

III. In the Name of Freedom

The eighteenth century had a rigid conception of the make-up and distribution of its theatre audiences, but later historians have held to their own fixed impression of the behavior of these playgoers. It is an all too convenient formula. It begins the century in rowdyism, riot, and brutality, traces a gradual softening of this barbarity through the influence of middle-class social pretensions, and arrives at the end of the period in what Allardyce Nicoll has termed an "equitable calm." This is indeed the broad outline of change which occurred. But too much has been made of the contrast between early and late eighteenth century audience behavior. Nicoll admits that "no decided cleavage can be traced between the audiences of the early and those of the late eighteenth century"; but, he continues, "slowly the main features of the typical body of spectators were changing during those years. In spite of recurring riots, in spite of rowdyism during and after the performance of plays, the playgoers of 1770 were quieter and less uproarious than their predecessors of 1730." [1] He then proceeds to chart a series of theatre disturbances which have no parallel in the earlier period!

Now a change in audience taste does not imply an automatic change in manners or behavior. In order to reach the years when public taste is reflected "in the highly decorous comic operas of the age, in the more than decorous sentimental comedies and even in the moral melodramas," [2] there is a tendency to overstress the bad behavior of early audiences and to credit later playgoers with a higher degree of decorum than the facts warrant.

The uproar before the play begins is indescribable. . . . Not

only orange-peels but sometimes even glasses of water or other
liquids are thrown from the gallery into pit and boxes, so that
frequently spectators are wounded and their clothing is soiled.
In short, such outrages are committed in the name of freedom
that one forgets one is in a playhouse which claims in its adver-
tisements the title of a Royal Theatre. In Germany such disorder would never be tolerated even at a marionette theater in
a village inn. At Drury Lane I wished to look around at the
gallery in order to examine its structure, but a heap of orange-
peels, striking me with considerable force in the face, robbed
me of all curiosity. The best plan is to keep your face turned
towards the stage and thus quietly submit to the hail of oranges
on your back. On one occasion my hat was so saturated (I really
do not know with what watery ingredients) that I was compelled to have it cleaned next day at the hatters.[3]

This is the behavior, not of audiences in the early years of
the century, but of playgoers in 1791 as seen through the
eyes of a foreign visitor.

So much for the galleryites. What of the other parts of
the house? Perhaps we shall find more decorum there. Dr.
Campbell attended Drury Lane Theatre as a member of the
large audience of March 4, 1775, at a performance of Robert
Jephson's *Braganza* and Henry Bate's *The Rival Candidates*
which did not end until eleven o'clock because of the uproar
in the audience.[4] The Doctor describes the tumult occasioned
by a sudden desire for prologue and epilogue, both ordinarily discontinued after the ninth night.

When the overture for the farce began to be played the Epilogue
was called for — the musick ceased for it could not be heard —
a long interval ensued — the players came on — they stood
their ground for a long time — but were hissed at length off —
Mr. Vernon attempted to speak, but he would not be heard —
still the cry was off, off, the epilogue, etc. — after a long pause
the bell rang for the musick — this set the house in an uproar
— the women however who were singers came on in hopes of
charming these savage beasts — but they were a second time
pelted off — *etc.*

The usual roaring and a hail of oranges came from the galleries. But what was most impressive to Dr. Campbell was the conduct of some in the pit beside me — some were more moderate and asked others why they made such a noise — one before asked another behind, how he dared make such a noise and told him — after some altercation — that he deserved to be turned out of the pit — This produced no other effect but to make my friend behind me more vociferous.[5]

If the boisterousness of early audiences is admitted, their reputation for brutality is questionable. If we grant a change in taste on the part of later audiences, we must also examine their claim to better behavior.

Perhaps the real reason for over emphasizing the brutality of early playgoers has been the sheer weight of publicity given to the various attempts of the Justices to suppress playhouses, fairs, and similar gatherings, and to the attacks of those who considered it their duty to regiment the morals of the common people. From 1700 to 1737 in particular the public airing of these protests by the authorities did much to malign the average playgoer. In all this the brunt of the attack was felt by the minor theatres.

We have already considered the stereotyped form of the indictments.[6] All playhouses are surrounded by "a halo of brothels," all are frequented by pickpockets and cutthroats, and thither consort all the profligates, whores, and riotous drunkards of London. All this leads to the debauching of the citizens. With the passing of the Licensing Act of 1737 the authorities seem to have relaxed their vigilance or to have been moderately successful in their purpose. From 1737 until almost the end of the century we hear less and less from civil authorities, except for individual instances. In 1751, for example, action was brought against a Justice, Sir Samuel Gower, landlord of the notorious New Wells Theatre in Goodman's Fields. In defiance of his brother magistrates Gower had licensed brothels and disorderly houses in the

region about his playhouse. As proprietor he gave "all countenance and encouragement . . . commending and otherwise
encouraging the actors." [7]

Public notice of such conditions surrounded early playgoing with a sinister atmosphere, but it should not be
charged to the bulk of the audiences of the minor theatres.
It is significant also that the Patent houses are never mentioned in the general indictments. E. G. Dowdell admits that
these amusements "against which the more respectable magistrates set their faces were too often disreputable and
degrading." [8] But he continues, "unfortunately the campaign
for their suppression was waged mainly in the belief that
ordinary people should have no public entertainments and a
purely negative attitude of this kind was hardly more defen-
sible than successful." We are inclined to approve of the
sentiments of *Heraclitus Ridens* in his reactions to the
pronouncements of the Grand Jury of Middlesex in 1703:

Earnest. But the Grand Jury tell you, in their presentment,
that the toleration of these houses corrupts the City youth,
makes them dissolute and immoral, and entices them to take
lewd courses.

Jest. I am sorry to hear the Citizens' instructions bear so
little weight with them, and am apt to think they are not so
exemplary in their lives and conversations as they have been
supposed to be. Would their masters keep a strict hand over
them, there would be no reasons for complaints; and I dare be
persuaded, there is more debauchery *occasioned by pretending
to eat Custards* towards Hampstead, Islington, and Sir George
Whitmore's in a week, than is possible to be brought about by
a Playhouse in a twelvemonth.[9]

The sinister atmosphere attributed to playhouses consisted
largely of the activities carried on in the immediate environs
rather than within the theatres themselves. *The Universal
Spectator* put its finger upon the realities of the problem as
it existed in 1735:

What will ensue from *new* play-houses being erected may be
seen by that at Goodman's-fields: the street where it is built
used formerly to be inhabited by silk-throwsters, ribband-weav-
ers, and others whose trades employed the industrious poor;
immediately on setting up this Playhouse, the rents of the
houses were raised, as the landlords could then let them to
more *profitable* tenants; and now there is a bunch of grapes
hanging almost at every door; besides an adjacent Bagnio or
two; an undoubted proof that innocence and morality are not
the certain consequences of a Playhouse.[10]

With surroundings such as these the Patent houses were
familiar too. But within the theatres themselves the criminal
element appears to have been limited to pickpockets and
prostitutes. As for the graver crimes, except for "the barbarous murder of Sir Andrew Slanning" very early in the
century, we have no record of any violence. Slanning's death,
be it noted, occurred "as he came out of one of the said
playhouses," and not within the theatre proper.[11]

In the press for places the cry of "pickpocket!" was usual
throughout the century. When Mr. and Mrs. Furrow come
up to London and take their son Frank to Drury Lane they
are reminded of the perils of the City.

Constable. Have a care of your pockets, gentlefolks!

Fur(row). 'Ecod, that's right — have a care of thy metal
watch, Frank! Mind your pockets, dame Furrow! A plaguy
pickpocket place, this same playhouse, I promise you.[12]

Samuel Rodgers remembered the one time he had seen Garrick act. He tells of the great crowding, of waiting long in
a dark passage on his way to the pit.[13] When the doors are
opened "a dangerous trial of skill ensues; every person
endeavours to enter first; the space is clogged; and pushing,
screams, and execrations follow."[14] An entry in Richard
Cross's Diary for December 26, 1757, shows that the upper
gallery passages were even more perilous: "This Night by
the Crowd upon the upper Gallery Stairs two Women and a

Man were kill'd." [15] A final Hogarthian touch is provided by Malcolm's account of this region: "we witness constant disputes often terminating in blows, and observe heated bodies stripped of the outward garments, furious faces, with others grinning horribly." [16] All this must have been fruitful hunting ground for petty thievery.

But that the pickpocket was more prevalent in theatres than elsewhere is highly improbable in an age in which street robbers infested the whole metropolis. In 1744 conditions were such that the Justices, while maintaining that their own campaign was progressing with all speed, petitioned the Duke of Newcastle for additional support. They feared that such thievery would persist "and, from robbing foot passengers in the streets, soon reach to the coaches and dwelling-houses of His Majesty's subjects." [17] They urged the need for more legislation for strengthening the watch, increasing the lighting of streets, and the putting down of disorderly assemblies. Like the Slanning murder, these indictments were far too common everywhere to lodge the blame with playhouse patrons. We must remember too, the method of punishment for culprits caught in the theatre was not one to encourage this crime within so confined an area. Theft of a handkerchief was enough to transport a thief for seven years.[18] Still more would he fear the retribution implied in the general audience cry to "Throw him over!" (that is, from gallery into pit).

The presence of a great number of prostitutes was taken for granted by the audience. Their seatings in theatres were supposed to be well-defined. The Earl of Carlisle writes of the "women of the town" who "quietly took their stations in the upper boxes, called green boxes." [19] He adds that these women "were never permitted in the boxes below stairs, with the single exception of the beautiful Kitty Fisher, whose appearance occasioned great dismay among all the frequenters, male and female, of the hitherto unpolluted front boxes." But such segregation was not always so scrupulously observed. Bonnell Thornton reviews the problem in an amusing essay on audiences:

I must take notice of that division of the upper boxes properly distinguished by the name of the flesh market. There is frequently as much art used to make the flesh exhibited here look wholesome, and, as Tim says in the farce, "all over red and white, like the inside of a shoulder of mutton," as there is by the butchers to make their veal look white; and it is as often rank carrion and flyblown. If these ladies would appear in any other quarter of the house, I would only beg of them, and those who come to market, to drive their bargains with as little noise as possible; but I have lately observed with some concern, that these women deign to appear in the lower boxes, to the destruction of all order, and great confusion of all modest ladies. It is to be hoped, that some of their friends will advise them not to pretend to appear there, any more than at court; for it is as absurd to endeavour the removal of their market into the front and side boxes, as it would be in the butchers of St. James's market to attempt fixing the shambles in St. James's Square.[20]

Under date of November 7, 1753, Richard Cross makes a brief but illuminating entry — "a whore taken out for Noise in Green Boxes." [21] All of which infers that prostitutes were a conspicuous element in the audience and that management was none too successful in keeping the "noise" of solicitation at a minimum. And yet it is unlikely that such conduct was in a class with doings at masquerades and other social gatherings in London. A *Ridotto al fresco* at Vauxhall in 1732 attracted about 400 persons, in the proportion of ten men to one woman, and 100 soldiers were required to preserve order until the company broke up between three and four in the morning.[22]

Audience acceptance of these criminal aspects of playgoing is clearly shown in verse exercises written by two boys of

thirteen, after they had attended their first play at Drury
Lane.[23] The youngsters wrote under the influence of their
preceptor, but their doggerel verses show the general belief
about these aspects of playhouse conduct. The first boy wrote,
in part:

> When on a sudden some one cries:
> Pickpocket! And attracts all eyes;
> Men, women, boys, cry toss him o'er!
> Thy art thou ne'er shalt practice more:
> Amidst this hubbub, and this din,
> Fiddles and fiddlesticks come in.
> Seated in slips with practis'd art,
> The town lass wins the sailor's heart. . . .

The same incidents were described in these lines by the
second boy:

> Now all is husht, and now a song,
> Wide spreads a laugh through all the throng,
> But if pickpockets intervene,
> We risk a broken leg I ween.
> For oft the noisy voices roar,
> Toss o'er the rascal, toss him o'er:
> Then oranges in clusters fly,
> And quids half chew'd rough tars supply:
> The music next with pleasing strains,
> Close to the ear the soul detains,
> While painted nymphs in slips appear,
> And some unthinking youths ensnare; . . .

The average theatregoer seems to have taken pickpockets
and prostitutes so much for granted that they in no way
seriously interfered with his complete absorption in the
drama upon the stage.

What did interfere were riots and kindred disorders common to both early and late century audiences. Because of the
colorful publicity surrounding them, these did much to characterize theatregoing as hazardous in the extreme. We must

remember, however, that such demonstrations occurred only at widely separated intervals. In between, conduct at the playhouses ran a fairly even course. The first number of *The British Theatre* congratulated management and audiences upon their conduct, saying that "...except the tumult occasioned by the opposition to the French dancers in 1755, and the commotions excited by a few angry individuals in 1763, who insisted on constant admission at half-price, the reign of these theatrical monarchs Garrick and Lacy has been an uninterrupted series of harmony and tranquility."[24] The following schedule of more serious disturbances at Drury Lane will serve to show their infrequency:

1743. Two-day riot resulting from a party feud between Macklin and Garrick.

1750. Riot against Woodward for satirizing Foote in Otway's *Friendship in Fashion*.

1755. Six-day riot against *The Chinese Festival*.

1763. Two-day riot at Drury Lane, Garrick's share in the general Half-Price Riots.
Unusually violent first night of Mrs. Griffith's *The Platonic Wife*.

1770. Three-day riot against Hugh Kelly's *A Word to the Wise*.

1776. Four-day riot against Bate-Dudley's *The Blackamoor Wash'd White*.

Not all of these disturbances can be blamed upon the general public. The Macklin-Garrick fracas involved packing the house with "orders" as protection against the Macklin partymen.[25] Thomas Davies described the situation.

The patentee [Fleetwood], who trusted more to the arm of flesh than the ablest defence of the greatest writer, was now determined to try the courage of his friends of Hockley in the Hole. They and their associates were distributed in great plenty in the pit and galleries, armed with sticks and bludgeons, with positive orders from their commanding officer to check the zeal of

Macklin's friends by the weightiest arguments in their power. When the curtain drew up, the playhouse shewed more like a bear-garden than a theatre-royal. The sea in a storm seemed not more terrible and boisterous than the loud and various noises which issued from the pit, galleries, and boxes.[26]

What is interesting in this account is the contrast Davies draws between the audience of this particular evening and the usual conduct at a theatre royal. The same is true of the Woodward incident at the revival of Otway's *Friendship in Fashion*. From Cross's Diary we learn that Woodward aroused the ire of theatre professionals by his mimicry of Samuel Foote. The incident only approached riot proportions in the destruction of playhouse property after the galleryites had been offended by the introduction of soldiers. Cross's entry reads:

Mr. Woodward did ye part of Malagone in which he took off Mr. Foote & wou'd have many of ye Actors but the Audience grew so outrageous, that he was forc'd to desist ye 4th & 5th Acts were much hooted . . . it was given out again, wch so enrag'd the Audience yt they call'd loudly for Garrick, but as he was not this Night at the House, they pull'd up the Benches, tore down ye Kings Arms, & wou'd have done much more mischief had not Mr. Lacy gone into the Pit, & talk'd to 'em, what they resented was giving out a piece again after they had damn'd it — the Gallery resented ye Guards being sent in.[27]

In fact, of the seven disturbances listed, only the prolonged rioting over *The Chinese Festival* and the Half-Price Riots involved the general public in any real sense. The former came about from a mixture of patriotic enthusiasm and class-consciousness, the latter from latent dissatisfaction with Patent management and the very real economic issue involved in restricting admissions to the theatre.

Detailed accounts of both major riots are too well known to bear repetition.[28] But attention should be directed to the degree to which class consciousness increased the proportions

of the earlier disturbance. Without this element it is doubtful
if *The Chinese Festival* would have caused more than the
usual patriotic damning of an evening's bill. Davies writes:

The inhabitants of the boxes, from the beginning of the dispute,
were inclined to favour the exhibition of the Festival, and very
warmly espoused the cause of the managers against the plebeian
part of the audience, whom they affected to look down upon
with contempt. The pit and galleries became more incensed by
this opposition of the people of fashion, and entered into a
strong alliance to stand by each other, and to annoy the common
enemy. Several gentlemen of rank being determined to conquer
the obstinacy of the rioters, they jumped from the boxes into
the pit with a view to seize the ringleaders of the fray. The
ladies at first were so far from being frightened at this resolu-
tion of the gentlemen, that they pointed out the obnoxious
persons with great calmness. Swords were mutually drawn, and
blood shed. . . . The contest between the boxes and the other
parts of the house was attended with real distress to the
managers, for they knew not which party they could oblige
with safety. One would not give way to the other, and they
seemed to be pretty equally balanced: at last, after much mutual
abuse, loud altercation, and many violent blows and scuffles,
the combatants fell upon that which could make no resistance,
the materials before them. They demolished the scenes, tore up
the benches, broke the lustres and girandoles, and did in a
short time so much mischief to the inside of the theatre, that
it could scarce be repaired in several days.[29]

It is also significant, as Fitzgerald points out, that in the
attack upon Garrick personally, the chief rioters "inflamed
the mob without doors to join them to attack Mr. Garrick's
house in Southampton Street." [30] That such a disturbance
should spread to the streets outside the playhouse is normal.
To argue that a great audience went almost *en masse* into
Southampton Street to break Garrick's windows is absurd.

Reference has already been made to the economic aspects
of the Half-Price Riots as they affected the humbler lot of

metropolitan playgoers.[31] But another factor should be mentioned in defense of Garrick's audiences. The managers of Drury Lane had broken with custom in 1762 by banishing stage seats and enlarging the auditorium.[32] Granting the courage and good judgment of Garrick in introducing this long-needed reform, the abolition of half-prices a few months later was more than the public could be expected to bear with patience. And this was a period in which Garrick's personal popularity was waning.[33] That public sentiment could join itself to a small faction headed by Francis and Fitzpatrick is proof of a sincere concern over theatrical inflation even by those who knew they were patronizing a performance for which full charges had never before been questioned. Their accumulated resentment triumphed over management's claim that the "house charges" had increased from £34 to £90 a night.[34]

The other instances of rioting at Drury Lane may be explained in terms of "party," both critical and political. They bear little relation to the feelings of the bulk of the audience. Davies says of the first night of Mrs. Griffith's *The Platonic Wife* (Drury Lane, January 24, 1765) that,

The audience, under the influence of a few tremendous criticks (though not very formidable persons, except on account of their extreme want of candour) who took upon themselves the trouble of judging for all the rest of the spectators, treated this comedy . . . with uncommon severity. . . . The criticks were so exceedingly clamorous, that the writer gave up her play for lost. Holland and Powell, who acted the principal parts in it, and had not been used to the noise of catcalls, hisses, groans, and horse laughs, the most powerful instruments in the exploding of a play, were so much intimidated, and so forgetful of their duty, as to thrust their heads on the stage from behind the curtain, and to entreat these merciful gentlemen, called the Town, to put an end to the play that very night, that they might be no longer exposed to such terrible mortifications. But the absurd counsel of these actors did not prevail; the good-natured part of the audience, esteeming this opposition and uproar to be a kind of cruel interlude, acted by these very gay gentlemen at the expense of the authour, managers, and actors, insisted upon the play having the chance of a new tryal.[35]

Here is one instance at least to prove Fielding's point that "our Betters . . . take the utmost Care to preserve their Decency in their Inferiors, and are a Kind of Deputies to the Censor in all public Places. . . . And it is, perhaps, the Awe of the Mob alone which prevents People of Condition, as they call themselves, from becoming more egregious Apes than they are." [36] Of like nature must have been the uproar over *The Blackamoor Wash'd White,* which lasted four evenings. A contemporary critic explains the confusion of the audience as to the actual import of the violence.

There were violent disturbances on the third and fourth nights, occasioned, originally, as it was thought, by some gentlemen elevated with liquor interrupting the actors, without designing to interrupt the representation. But the last night set the matter in a different point of view; these very gentlemen insisting on the opera being withdrawn. On both of these nights there were many skirmishes between the contending parties upon the stage; and on the last night Mr. Garrick appeared twice, and Mr. King once before they could appease the opponents by assuring them that the piece was withdrawn.[37]

As for the three-day rioting occasioned by Kelly's *A Word to the Wise,* the same critic explains that the opposition came from

a party who seemed resolved at all events to damn it; a report having been circulated that there were several political strokes in this comedy against the supporters of the Bill of Rights, which appeared quite destitute of foundation; and which, indeed, from the severe inspection that dramatic productions undergo by the managers, was altogether impossible.[38]

Once more we see the very slender connection between these disturbances and the majority of the audience. In calling attention to them, we must not fail to note the many years of playgoing in which these spectators must have behaved very well indeed.

The reaction of theatre patrons in time of panic and disaster had not changed by the end of the century, if it ever changes. If the lady who thought she detected smoke pouring from beneath the Drury Lane stage caused a panic in 1727 in which "a pregnant woman was pressed to death, and several persons severely injured" before her error was discovered,[39] the fire at Sadler's Wells late in the century caused the death of many persons by trampling and suffocation.[40] On one occasion at least, according to Henry Fielding, the audience maintained its poise by virtue of its absorption in the stage activities. He tells of a trip to Covent Garden when that theatre "by four o'clock one may truly say was cramm'd from Top to Bottom." Two gentlemen attempting to find themselves seats in the middle gallery decided to clear the house:

Then, with a broad Grin upon his Face, he thrust his empty Head into the Gallery Door, and cried out Fire; which on his repeating, a Lady at the Door rebuked him in such a Manner as made him, ignorant as he was, sensible of his Folly. He looked up in her Face, damn'd her for a grave Bitch, turned upon his Heel, and went down Stairs laughing, only to conceal his Confusion. Happy it was for hundreds, that their Attention was too much fixed on their Entertainment, to suffer them to be susceptible of this false Alarm.[41]

Turning now to a consideration of audience behavior according to the seating arrangements, credit must go first to the middle gallery. Thornton says,

Those who pay their two shillings at the door of the middle gallery, seem to frequent the theatre purely for the sake of seeing the play: though these peaceful regions are sometimes disturbed by the incursions of rattling ladies of pleasure, sometimes contain persons of fashion in disguise, and sometimes critics in ambush.[42]

The greatest fault of these auditors

is their frequent and injudicious interruption of the business of the play by their applause. I have seen a bad actor clapped two minutes together for ranting, or perhaps shrugging his shoulders, and making wry faces: and I have seen the natural course of the passions checked in a good one, by these ill judged testimonies of their approbation.

Nevertheless, their behavior must have been above reproach, though Dolly Snip described them as "Folks that laugh and cry, just as they feel." [43]

Of the "Mob" which inhabited the upper gallery, Fielding observed the boisterous qualities of its "trunk-makers" and yet dubbed them "our Betters."

I readily allow, that on certain Occasions the Gentlemen at the Top of the House are rather more vociferous than those at the Bottom: But to this I shall give three Answers; First, that the Voice of Man is stronger and louder than that of Beaus. Secondly, that on these Occasions, as at the first Night of a new Play, the Entertainment is to be considered as among the Audience, all of whom are Actors in such Scenes. Lastly, as these Entertainments all begin below-stairs, the Concurrence of the Galleries is to be attributed to the Politeness of our Betters who sit there, and to that decent Condescension which they show in concurring with the Manners of their Inferiors.[44]

Speaking in the character of the Busy Body (1763), Garrick addressed his patrons as

My friends above there — honest John and Nancy!
How well their secrets with their passions suit,
Hearts full of love, and pockets full of fruit,
Each jolly sailor thus his mistress grapples,
They look, and laugh, and love, and — eat their apples.[45]

and Thornton asks them not

to shatter the gallery panels without amending our taste; since their thwacks, however vehement, are seldom laid on with sufficient judgment to ratify our applause. It were better, therefore, if all the present twelve-penny critics of this town, who preside over the diversions in the upper gallery, would content themselves with the inferior duties of their office; viz. to take care that the play begins at the proper time, that the music between the acts is of a due length, and that the candles are snuffed in tune.[46]

Those who have commented upon playhouse behavior have few kind words for the *beau monde*. Whether they seated themselves in boxes, or (before 1762) disported upon the stage, the conduct of the forward members of this circle was the scorn of critics and "the Mob" alike, and was perhaps the major factor underlying almost every theatrical disturbance. The indefensible behavior of stage spectators need not delay us here, except to remark upon the persistence of their privileges. Immediately upon assuming management, Garrick began his long battle for a clear stage by announcing that admissions would no longer be taken behind the scenes.[47] And at the peak of that first season Lord Hubbard's party damned Garrick's production of *The Foundling* ostensibly because "it ran too long, and they wanted variety of Entertainments." But according to the prompter, "the main cause of their anger, in spite of their Excuses, was their Being refus'd admittance behind the Scenes." [48]

So great were the forces of fashion and theatre economy that fifteen years were required to accomplish a more or less complete reformation, and that only by an extensive enlargement of Garrick's auditorium and the increasing use of the complicated machinery for spectacular productions. Something of the frustration experienced during these years of struggle between management and the fashionable public is described by *The Connoisseur* in 1754.

There is no part of the house from which a play can be seen

to so little advantage as from the stage; yet this situation is very convenient to a fine gentleman. . . . But notwithstanding all these advantages accruing to our fine gentleman, I could heartily wish they would leave a clear stage to the performers; or at least that none should be admitted behind the scenes. As these gentlemen are readily dressed, they might help to swell the retinue of a monarch, join the engagement in a tragedy-battle, or do any other little office that might occur in the play, which requires but little sense and no memory. But if they have not any genius for acting, and are still desirous of retaining their posts by the side-scenes, they should be obliged to take a musket, bayonet, pouch, and the rest of the accoutrements, and stand on guard quietly and decently with the soldiers.[49]

Richard Cross says that the audience resentment at gentlemen crowding behind the scenes stopped the farce for half an hour one evening — "I drew lines with Chaulk, but Miss Norn's applying publickly to Cap: Johnson, desiring he wou'd retire, He did, & ye farce went on with great Applause." [50] On another occasion the audience was thrown into gales of laughter when, "As ye Curtain was rising for ye farce a Gentleman's sword was taken out of ye Scabbard & carry'd up with ye Curtain & there Hung to ye terror of those under it (least it shou'd fall) & ye Mirth of ye rest of ye audience — a Scene man fetch'd it down." [51]

The Fine Lady in *Lethe* and the wealthy tradesman's daughter valued their seats in the boxes. But Bonnell Thornton begged such persons "not to call off the attention of others; nor interrupt the dialogue on the stage by a louder conversation of their own," and added that "The silent courtship of the eyes, ogles, nods, glances, and court'sies from one box to another, may be allowed them the same as at church; but nothing more, except at coronations, funeral processions, and pantomimes." [52] Thornton addressed a like plea to

the gentlemen who draw the pen from under their right ears

about seven o'clock, clap on a bag-wig and sword, and drop into the boxes at the end of the third act, to take their half-crown's worth with as much decency as possible; as well as the bloods, who reel from the taverns about Covent-Garden near that time, and tumble drunk into the boxes.

Those who were next in social importance sat in the pit and pursued a conduct scarcely more admirable. Their fabulous criticisms were vociferously given, to the vast entertainment of the galleries. Mrs. Parsons expressed the fervent hope that it was during an intermission that

Boswell, one night, entertained the Drury Lane audience "prodigiously" by lowing, in the pit, like a cow. *"Encore* the cow!" cried the galleries, till, finally, the Reverend Dr. Hugh Blair found it necessary to restrain his young friend's "very inferior" imitations of other animals by the caustic recommendation, "My dear sir, I would *confine* myself to the *cow!"* [53]

It was in the pit too that Garrick noted the conduct and critical fervor of that arch enemy Fitzpatrick, the hero of *The Fribbleriad:*

> Then from his bosom forth he drew
> A crow-quill pen — "Behold, for you
> And your revenge, this instrument!
> From hell it came, to me 'twas sent:
> Within is poison, sword, and all;
> Its point a dagger dipt in gall.
> Keen ling'ring pangs the foe shall feel,
> While clouds the hand that stabs conceal.
> With this, while living, I'll dissect him;
> Create his errors, then detect them;
> Swell tiny faults to monstrous size,
> Then point them out to pur-blind eyes.
>
> . . . .
>
> Attended with some noisy cit,
> Of strong belief, but puny wit,
> I'll take my seat, be rude and loud,
> That each remark may reach the crowd;

> At Lear will laugh, be hard as rocks,
> And sit at Scrub like barbers blocks:
> When all is still, we'll roar like thunder;
> When all applaud, be mute, and wonder! . . ." [54]

Evidence to underscore our estimate of the behavior of eighteenth century audiences is to be found in the comments of foreign visitors. Of the German visitors to English theatres quoted by John A. Kelly, sixteen had something specific to say concerning audience behavior.[55] Their accounts range from 1696 to 1800; and of the sixteen, eight were favorably impressed, three adopted a noncommittal attitude, and only five were condemnatory — and all of these five were visitors to the London of 1774 and later! Kelly notes that all visitors to the year 1763 "were either silent or complimentary as to the behavior of the audience," while later witnesses were divided in their opinions.[56] In a summary of the impressions of von Archenholz (1775), a man whom he describes as the one "who did most in his country to present a complete picture of England to the German public," [57] Kelly notes the visitor's amazement at the complete absorption of Englishmen in a tragedy performance by Mrs. Bellamy: "The actress herself was overcome by a sense of tragedy and had to be carried off the stage unconscious. And the audience, too, unable to endure the strain, departed, so that the piece had to be finished without the leading lady, before a handful of unusually hard-boiled spectators." [58]

In sketching the behavior of these eighteenth century audiences we have attempted to prove only one point — that the earlier spectators were not the undesirable playgoers we have been led to consider them, and that later audiences were not as refined as some would have us believe. Perhaps the whole problem is one of separating the actions of these people into two simple categories — what happened *before* and what happened *after* the rise of the curtain. The former can be dismissed as a problem for the police authorities; the latter is seriously involved in the production of dramatic literature. If we stand upon this division of the evidence, whatever the superficial differences between early and late eighteenth century playgoers, the case is clear. These people went to theatres to see and to hear. And see and hear they did to their entire satisfaction. We can approve the report of von Archenholz: "When the play begins, all noise and bombardment ceases, unless some especial provocation gives rise to further disturbances; and one is bound to admire the quiet attentiveness of such an estimable folk." [59]

MR. DANGLE deplored the changed taste of English audiences in unequivocal terms. "The worst alteration," he complained, "is the nicety of the audience. No double entendre, no smart inuendo [*sic*], admitted; even Vanbrugh and Congreve obliged to undergo a bungling reformation!" [1] His lament highlights the paradoxical fate of altered and adapted plays staged under the compulsion of critical dogma in support of the Sentimental movement. Garrick's audiences demanded reformation; they knew what they wanted. But reformation was not always a resounding success at the box office. It is often difficult to distinguish between what would pass this moral censorship and that grossness of which the public was supposed to be intolerant. Before we attempt to evaluate the quality of the theatrical public in Garrick's time it will be well to examine some typical alterations.

Of the sixty-four altered plays produced at Drury Lane from 1747 to 1776, four were by George Colman the Elder; two each by Isaac Bickerstaffe, Francis Gentleman, and John Hawkesworth; seventeen by authors making only a single production; eighteen of unknown authorship; and nineteen by David Garrick as actor-manager. [2] Among the eighteen productions by unknown authors there must be other plays unacknowledged by Garrick, and most certainly plays reworked by house dramatists and play doctors such as Bickerstaffe. These men wrote under direct order of the management and often from a "fable" supplied by Garrick. Let us make no mistake about it, Garrick's leadership and influence in catering to public taste was quite real. For twenty-nine years his word was law at Drury Lane, and the wailing of those who accused him of exploiting his own successful alterations to avoid producing new plays and sharing the profits only served to emphasize the strength of a patentee's position as arbiter of taste. If we limit this chapter to a consideration of Garrick's adaptations, it is upon the assumption that we are measuring also the aim and quality of the other plays altered for Drury Lane audiences. And while it is necessary to analyze in considerable detail the changes Garrick made in the old plays, we shall avoid confusion by selecting from original and altered versions of plays those passages which best answer three simple questions of taste: *What was altered? Why did it have to be altered? How did the altered play fare at the box office?*

Remembering his much-puffed devotion to the poet, we will not be surprised to find that eleven of Garrick's nineteen alterations are from Shakespeare.[4] These have been subjected to detailed investigation by Professor G. W. Stone, Jr., who defends Garrick's handling of Shakespearean plays against those who have questioned the actor's sincerity as a "restorer" of the original text.[5] Stone frequently draws attention to the demands of Drury Lane audiences. He reminds us, for instance, that Londoners had attended over two hundred performances of D'Avenant's "improved" version of *Macbeth* in the forty-one years before Garrick's appearance. Describing the audiences as "custom-bound," he adds: "The task which lay before Garrick was a more difficult one than we realize today. He had to restore Shakespeare's text, yet please an audience whose taste had long been formed."[6] This idea is expanded later in a study of *King Lear* as "the dilemma of an eighteenth-century mind caught between an ideal liking for Shakespeare and a canny understanding of box office appeal."

Garrick started with Tate, but ended with a play much closer to Shakespeare. Thoroughly apprised of the mainsprings of tragic appeal as Pity and Fear, he alternately dissolved his audience in tears and froze them with horror (if we can credit the hyperbole of mid-century comment). But pity won, for Garrick saw in *King Lear* a Shakespearean play which could surpass competition from all writers of pathetic tragedy and could command the emotional pleasure of tears more success-fully than sentimental comedy. Tapping the strong vogue for the pathetic and sentimental, Garrick skillfully met public desire for those dramatic types in his production of *King Lear,* and without much sacrificing the sacredness of Shakespeare's text.[7]

The problem of shifting public taste is summed up by Garrick himself:

There are no hopes of seeing a perfect stage, till the public as well as the Managers get rid of their errors and prejudices — the reformation must begin with the first. When the taste of the public is right the Managers and Actors must follow it or starve. I speak of those who understand something of their busi-ness — there are and have been Managers & Actors who are so naturally blind that they cannot find the right way tho' the finger of ye Publick point it out ever so strongly to 'Em.[8]

From Stone's studies we soon discover that Garrick's Shake-spearean productions created their own peculiar problems for an adapter working under the searchlight of contempo-rary scholarship and tremendous public interest. For this reason the Shakespearean alterations will not serve our purpose as well as plays of lesser dramatists.

To the eight remaining alterations we turn then. Arranged chronologically as produced at Drury Lane, they are: Jon-son's *Every Man in His Humour* (1751); Fletcher's *The Chances* (1754) and *Rule a Wife and Have a Wife* (1756); *Isabella* — altered from Southerne's *The Fatal Marriage* (1757); *The Gamesters,* from James Shirley's *The Gamester* (1757); *The Country Girl,* from Wycherley's *The Country Wife* (1766); Dryden's *King Arthur; or, The British Worthy,* subsequently referred to as *Arthur and Emmeline* (1770); and Tomkis' *Albumazar* (1773). The two last-named will not claim our attention, the Dryden work because it is chiefly a musical piece, and that of Tomkis because the alterations are not significant. While the same might be said of Garrick's alteration of *The Fatal Marriage,* it will be considered briefly as the lone representative of tragedy in the group.

Every Man in His Humour

The Jonson comedy *Every Man in His Humour* is the only one of the six alterations to have received anything like close attention heretofore. It has been treated so exhaustively by three scholars that little needs to be added here.[9] In the latest study of the adapted comedy, R. G. Noyes pointed out that Garrick "contented himself . . . with removing traits of obsolescence, indecencies of expression no longer tolerable, obscure allusions, and puns. He made as few structural changes as possible." [10] Alterations occur particularly in the fourth act and allow Garrick to expand the story of the cuckolding of Kitely at the expense of obsolete low-comedy types such as Cob.

We shall find this the characteristic approach of Garrick in preparing the other plays under consideration. As a good adapter, although he recognized the necessity for alteration if the plays were to be countenanced by his audiences, he attempted as far as possible to keep faith with the originals. Noyes says that he "rearranged rather than rewrote" as much of the original scenes as were relevant to his purposes. We shall see that it is only rarely that the actor in him betrays the author into such offenses against the artistic conscience as prompted Genest's peevish judgment, that "Garrick's alterations of old plays are highly judicious when he does not attempt too much — when he goes beyond a certain point, he only exposes himself — he knew he could act, and he fancied he could write." [11]

In the case of *Every Man in His Humour* the resulting production was a triumph. The altered comedy was per-

formed 16 times in its first season (1751–52) and remained
a favorite in the Drury Lane repertory for 22 seasons. Garrick played the Kitely role in all but one of its 82 performances.

The Chances

To the casual observer Garrick's alteration of Fletcher's
comedy *The Chances* (Drury Lane, November 7, 1754) is
merely a bowdlerized version of the adaptation by George
Villiers, Duke of Buckingham (Drury Lane, December,
1682). Genest describes how the idea for its further alteration arose in the King's whimsy and infers that Garrick
rushed it into immediate production. He negligently terms it
a mere revival "with slight alterations, which consisted
chiefly in omitting some exceptionable expressions of the
Duke of Buckingham." [12] Now while it is certainly true that
it follows the Duke's altered plot structure rather closely,
study will show that Garrick made careful preparation and
derived his comedy indeed "judiciously" from the better
elements of *both* Fletcher and Buckingham. Another view
but recently advanced implies that Garrick's contribution to
this second alteration consisted largely of characterizations
"tinged with 'sensibility,' " heroines who deliver "sentiments
on 'humanity,' 'honour,' 'innocence,' and 'nobleness.' " [13]
Quite true! The characters in Garrick's alteration do utter
such sentiments, and of such Garrick undoubtedly approved.
He knew his audiences and took their taste into account.
But this sensibility is developed by Garrick from lines and
situations already present in both Fletcher and Buckingham
versions. The alteration is more carefully executed than
either of these views would suggest.

Garrick followed the altered plot structure devised by
Buckingham. It consisted in the omission in its entirety of
Fletcher's Act V (at the home of Vecchio, the schoolmaster
and supposed conjurer), its replacement by a new conclud-

ing act taking place in the streets, and in altering events in
Act IV leading to the new denouement.[14] Raising the moral
stature of the Second Constantia from "whore to Antonio"
to that of his "mistress" and relating the character of the
Bawd to the heroine as a "mother," Buckingham expanded
both characterizations greatly, introducing them as early as
Act IV, scene 1. The "Mother" has sold her daughter to
Antonio for five hundred gold pieces and absconded with the
purchase price. The Second Constantia flees her "protector"
and places herself in the keeping of Don John. While the
Mother stops at a tavern, John takes the girl to his lodgings.
There the two are surprised by Don Frederick, who thinks
his friend is locking up the First Constantia and violating
his service to the Duke. In an attempt to satisfy the Duke's
party as to the identity of the girl, Don John permits old
Antonio to enter the house. Whereupon the Second Constantia is forced to flee the establishment by a back way, her
erstwhile owner in hot pursuit. This misunderstanding continues into Act V until chance brings Frederick face to face
with the Mother and her Kinswoman and the realization that
there are *two* Constantias. Don John and the Second Constantia are confronted by an outraged Antonio, but effectively silence that worthy when the girl dares him to confess
the unsavory nature of their past relationship. In return for
his reluctant agreement not to trouble the young couple
longer, they promise to recover Antonio's gold pieces. With
the reunion of the Duke and the First Constantia, the
promise of a union between Don John and the Second Constantia (the real heroine of Buckingham's comedy), and the
pardon and satisfaction of both Don Frederick and Don
Petruchio, the comedy is brought to a close.

Garrick recognized in the Buckingham version alterations
that were to his own taste and proceeded to build his comedy
on this framework. He referred constantly, however, to the
original by Fletch... Such minor structural changes as he

made in the Buckingham play will be noted as we examine
the use of materials from both earlier versions.

Changes in Act I include the discarding of two brief
scenes (iv and x), the omission and rearrangement of
individual speeches, and additional dialogue. Scene i is the
same in all versions, and Garrick omits some 17 lines from
Fletcher to 5 from Buckingham. His own additions are
limited to unimportant lines, including in this instance the
usual "tag-lines" with which he liked to link a scene to the
one which was to follow. Often such concluding lines and the
opening lines of the next scene are added with telling effect
for the audience's understanding of the plot. Here, however,
the lines are of no importance except in their advantage to
the actor leaving the stage. Don Frederick promises to meet
Don John for their usual evening walk within the hour,
after he has completed "a few devotions."

John: Devotions, Frederick! Well, I leave you to them:
       Speed you well: but remember —
Fred: I will not fail. (*Exeunt*)

In scene ii Garrick, intending to omit scene x of the older
versions, transposes a 9-line fustian speech of the Duke and
puts it into the mouth of fat old Antonio. In the discarded
scene the Duke's words had instilled a noble courage in his
comrades who feared to be caught within range of the wrath
of Constantia's brother Petruchio. Now it appears very ap-
propriately in the characterization of a blustering fat man
who fancies himself the soul of courage and a true libertine.
When others would caution Petruchio against inflaming the
Duke's faction, that worthy insists upon continuance of his
feud and dares them to side with him. To this old Antonio
replies:

       Dare!
       Say we were all sure to die in this venture
       As I am confident against it, is there any

> Amongst us of so fat a sense, so pamper'd,
> Would choose luxuriously to lie a-bed,
> And purge away his spirit? send his soul out
> In sugar sops, and syrups? Give me dying,
> As dying ought to be, upon my enemy:
> Let them be all the world, and bring along
> Cain's envy with them, I will on.

Garrick knew how his audiences would relish such a speech from a character who was the despair of his surgeon, who, with his body racked with pain from a sword wound, affected a fondness for "the war-like tune, John Dory" and screamed at his physician, "I have a dozen rascals to hurt within these five days. Good man-mender, stop me up with parsley like a stuffed beef, and let me walk abroad." [15] Two other speeches of one line each are salvaged from scene x and given to Petruchio and Antonio.

Garrick's scene iii utilizes scenes v and vi of the other versions, scene iv (containing a brief soliloquy by Don Frederick as he searches for Don John) having been discarded. While it is not worth while to list all the changes Garrick wrought in the materials of these scenes, the long soliloquy by Don John (scene vi) affords a fine opportunity to demonstrate the taste of the eighteenth century audiences. The adapter was forced to eliminate indecencies of expression and compress the original, and yet to retain the genuine spirit of Fletcher's text. As Buckingham followed Fletcher verbatim in this 48-line monologue, I quote the earlier text. Lines and individual words in italics represent what Garrick discarded to please his audience.

> *Enter Don John.*
> Was ever man so paid for being curious?
> Ever so bob'd for searching out adventures,
> As I am? did the Devil lead me? must I needs be peeping
> Into mens houses where I had no business,
> And make myself a mischief? *'Tis well carried;*

I must take other mens occasions on me,
And be I know not whom: most finely handled:
What have I got by this now? *what's the purchase?*
A piece of *evening Arras* work, a child,
Indeed an Infidel: this comes of peeping:
A lump got out of laziness; good white bread
Let's have no bawling with ye: s'death have I
Known wenches thus long, all the ways of wenches
Their snares and subtilties? *have I read over*
All their School learnings, div'd into their quiddits,
And am I now bum-fidled with a Bastard?
Fetch'd over with a Card of five, and in mine old days,
After the dire massacre of a million
Of Maiden-heads? caught the common way, i'th' night too
Under another name, to make the matter
Carry more weight about it? well Don John,
You will be wiser one day, when ye have *purchas'd*
A beavy of these Butter-prints *together,*
With searching out conceal'd iniquities,
Without commission: why, it would never grieve me,
If I had got this Ginger-bread: *never stirr'd me,*
So I had had a stroak for't: 't had been Justice
Then to have kept it; but to raise a dayrie
For other mens adulteries, consume my self in *candles,*
And scowring works, in Nurses Bells and Babies,
Only for charity, for meer I thank you,
A little troubles me: the least touch for it,
Had but my breeches got it, had contented me.
Whose e're it is, sure 't had a wealthy Mother,
For 'tis well cloathed, and if I be not cozen'd,
Well lin'd within: to leave it here were barbarous,
And ten to one would kill it: a more sin
Then his who got it: well, I will dispose on't,
And keep it, as they keep deaths heads in rings,
To cry memento to me; no more peeping.
Now all the danger is to qualifie
The good old gentlewoman, at whose house we live,
For she will fall upon me with a Catechism

Of four hours long: *I must endure all;*
For I will know this Mother: Come good wonder,
Let you and I be jogging: your starv'd trebble
Will waken the rude watch else: all that be
Curious night-walkers, may they find my fee. (*Exit*)

We turn now to Garrick's version. Lines and individual
words in italics here represent his additions and alterations.

Enter Don John, with a Child, crying.
John: Was ever man so paid for being curious;
    Ever so bobb'd for searching out adventures,
    As I am! Did the devil lead me? Must I needs be peeping
    Into men's houses, where I had no business,
    And make myself a mischief?
    What have I got by this now?
    A piece of *pap and caudle-work* — a child:
    This comes of peeping!
    What a figure do I make now! good white bread
    Let's have no bawling wi' ye. 'Sdeath! have I
    Known wenches thus long, all the ways of wenches,
    Their snares and subtleties,
    And am I now bumfiddled with a bastard?
    Well, Don John,
    You'll be wiser one day, when you have *paid dearly*
    For a collection of these butter prints.
    'Twould not grieve me to keep this gingerbread,
    Were it of my own baking: but to beggar
    Myself in caudles, nurses, coral, bells, and babies,
    For other men's iniquities!
    What shall I do with it now?
    Should I be caught here dandling this pap-spoon,
    I shall be sung in ballads;
    No eyes are near — I'll drop it,
    For the next curious coxcomb. How it smiles upon me!
    Ha! you little sugar-sop! 'tis a sweet baby;
    'Twere barbarous to leave it: ten to one 'twould kill it;
    Worse sin than his who got it. Well, I'll take it,
    And keep it as they keep death's head, in rings,

To cry memento to me, "No more peeping!"
Now all the danger is to qualify
The good old gentlewoman, at whose house we *lodge;*
For she will fall upon me with a catechism
Of four hours long. Come, good wonder,
Let you and I be jogging; your starv'd treble
Will waken the rude watch else. All that be
Curious night-walkers, may they find my fee! (*Exit*)

Omitting some 20 lines from Fletcher and adding 10 of his own, Garrick has managed to convey the spirit and purpose of this monologue without offense and has saved about 11 lines in playing time.

In scene iv (scene vii of the other versions) Garrick cuts objectionable lines from Frederick's brief soliloquy, and yet by retaining one sentence manages to secure the flavor of the original. It is interesting to note also the dialogue between Frederick and the First Constantia. Here is the first instance of Garrick's use of lines found in both earlier versions for which he is credited with having tinged the characterizations with sensibility. The First Constantia flees to the man she believes is her husband the Duke, only to discover that it is Don Frederick. "Are you a gentleman?" she asks in desperation. When Frederick assures her on this point, the dialogue continues:

> *Con:* As ever you lov'd honour,
>   As ever your desires may gain their ends,
>   Do a poor wretched woman but this benefit,
>   For I am forc'd to trust you.

> *Fred:* You have charm'd me:
>   Humanity and honour bid me help you;
>   And if I fail your trust . . .

The scene in its entirety comes from Fletcher's text and is used by both Buckingham and Garrick!

Scene v (scene viii in the other texts) is noteworthy as an example of the closeness with which Garrick followed variations between the two earlier versions. In building the character of Antonio he could not resist the temptation to restore lines of Fletcher. A gentleman rebukes Antonio for being "too bloody." The old fellow replies that this is the very month for opening veins and wants to know why they are met together if not for the Duke's blood. "Would you make the cause a cudgel-quarrel?" he cries, only to be interrupted by Petruchio. But before this interruption Garrick restores the rest of Antonio's speech.

> On what terms stands this man? is not his honour
> Open'd to his hand, and pickt out like an Oyster?
> His credit like a quart pot knockt together,
> Able to hold no liquor? clear but this point.

The sixth and closing scene of Act I is an alteration of scene ix in Fletcher's text. Changes here consist of the omission of indelicacies of expression, and the addition of brief "asides" for Don John describing the effect of wine upon his Landlady and 13 lines at the close of the act. Nothing is more puzzling than the distinction drawn between what is morally admissible upon the stage at Drury Lane and those gross indelicacies, indecencies, so deplored by Garrick's critics. The line is finely drawn indeed in this scene; for Garrick has carefully omitted most of the speech of the Landlady beginning:

> Well, well son *John,*
> I see ye are a wood-man, and can chuse
> Your dear, though it be i' th' dark, . . .

in which she states her philosophy of philandering young men. At the same time he has added a closing speech for Don John which rivals in suggestiveness all that has been deleted. The Landlady has agreed to see to the child and Don John is left alone upon the stage.

John: Away! So, so; I thought the wine would do its duty:
  She'll kill the child with kindness: t'other glass,

> And she had ravish'd me. There is no way
> Of bringing women of her age to reason,
> But by this: girls of fifteen are caught
> Fifty ways; they bite as fast as you throw in;
> But with the old cold 'tis a diff'rent dealing,
> 'Tis wine must warm them to their sense of feeling. (*Exit*)

Knowing Garrick's personal affection for the spirit of the old comedies and his wariness in dealing with his contemporaries in the audience, we must suppose that, while he dared not trust Mrs. Clive's relish of the Landlady's robust humor, with his own personal magic he knew he could be more audacious.[16]

There is no structural change to be noted in Act II. It begins with Fletcher's Act I, scene xi, but otherwise follows closely both versions throughout. Again lines are omitted for the usual reasons of indelicacy and obsolescence, the greatest number being about 20 lines from Fletcher's scene iii. This is the dialogue in which Don John mistakenly informs his friend that the First Constantia is the "kind" lady of wealth whose report has excited them to their nocturnal prowlings. Additional dialogue introduced into this act is of interest, especially in scenes ii and iii. In the former occurs an example of the way in which the adapter often interlaces the older texts with his own dialogue in order to produce the accelerated pace his audience demanded of comedy. Don John is wheedling Don Frederick into permitting him a glimpse of the woman he has established in their lodgings. The Fletcher text (followed by Buckingham) appears on the left and Garrick's alteration on the right:

John: I am answer'd:	*John:* I'm answer'd;
But let me see her though: leave the door open	But let me see her though.
As ye go in.	*Fred:* I can't.
Fred: I dare not.	*John:* Leave the door open as you go in.
John: Not wide open,	*Fred:* I dare not.
But just so, as a jealous husband	*John:* Not wide open, but a little, a very little,
Would level at his wanton wife through.	So as a jealous husband

Fred: That courtesy,
If you desire no more, and keep it strictly,
I dare afford ye: come, 'tis now near morning. (*Exeunt*)

Would level at his wanton wife through.
Fred: That courtesy,
If you desire no more —
John: No more.
Fred: And keep it strictly —
John: Upon my honour.
Fred: I dare afford you. Come, 'tis now near morning.
John: Along, along, then, dear Frederick. (*Exeunt*)

In scene iii the changes in the long speech by Don John to Don Frederick after the latter has introduced him to the girl as a "modest man" are significant for what has been omitted in the name of delicacy and also for a single line added by Garrick at its close. This line is an attempt to preserve the rakish spirit imperiled by Garrick's deletions: "Oh! damn your water-gruel honour!" As a canny manager Garrick was adept at dramatic "fence-sitting." His own delight was in the "old comedy," and when he dealt a blow in favor of its spirit, he toned it down by lines which frown upon the license of what has been uttered. After the "modesty" speech Garrick allows the First Constantia and Don John to soothe the ruffled sensibilities of his audience with

> *Con:* To you, and your humanity, a hapless,
>   Helpless creature, begs for safety. Oh! grant
>   Me your protection; to your honours, sirs,
>   I fly, as to the altar, for a refuge.
>   Be your nobleness
>   My sanctuary, and shield a woe-sick heart
>   From all its terrors and afflictions. (*Kneeling*)
> *John*: Pray, rise. (*Kneels*) I can't bear it.

These are Garrick's lines, and with them he seeks to take the curse from the licentious lines which have gone before. The sentimental had its uses; although even here it is but an elaboration of what is inherent in Fletcher's characterization. On the other hand, when Garrick has emasculated the dialogue to the limit of his artistic conscience, he will blithely

add a speech such as the one put in the mouth of the servant
Peter in scene ii.

> *Peter:* My saint-like Don has hired a chapel
> In the corner there, for his pious uses;
> Where I, against my will, watch, fast, and pray.

and another portion of his audience is satisfied.

The closing scene of Act II (Fletcher's scene iii) is the
same in all versions. Here again we note the judiciousness
with which Garrick borrows dialogue and intersperses it with
his own. In fact the closing passage between Don John and
Don Frederick is an intricate mosaic of lines by all three
writers. Of the 22 which make up the scene, 11 belong to
Fletcher, 4 are Buckingham's, and 6 others were added
by the manager. It is to this passage also that we are
indebted for a clear statement of the adapter's philosophy as
opposed to all those belonging to the sentimental school. It is
an exquisite rebuke to the Philistine element in Drury Lane
audiences. Don John assures his friend that they have found
the lady of their wayward dreams; she is both "handsome"
and "kind" and that is enough to satisfy him. Don Frederick
will not believe her dishonest, although John insists "she's
no saint." Then Garrick inserts the following exchange:

Fred: How can you talk so?
John: Because I think so. Now you think so, and talk otherwise; therefore, I am the honester, though you may be the
modester man.

It is the Buckingham text which is followed throughout
Act III, including the transposition of Fletcher's Act IV,
scene ii, to Act III, scene vi, and the original Act IV, scene
i, to Act III, scene vii. In scene ii Garrick manages to
improve upon Buckingham by retarding the entrance of
Antonio until the Surgeon has had time to discover his
patient's physical condition and mental attitude. The Land-

lady's characterization of her two young lodgers as she gossips with the First Constantia in scene iii is taken from Buckingham's cutting of the original text. But now the characterization is confined to Don John. Garrick is forced to cut Fletcher's startling encomium, "the most incomprehensible whore-master — twenty a night is nothing," but he retains the line immediately following, "Whose chastity he chops upon he cares not," and explicitly limits the Don's accomplishments to "Bastards . . . he has now a hundred of 'em."

Lines referring to Don Frederick's "modesty" are given to Don John throughout the remaining scenes of this act for added humor. As we have already noted, the change effected by Buckingham in using the scene in which Antonio discovers the loss of his gold and the flight of his mistress (Fletcher IV, ii) as scene vi of this act was approved by Garrick as affording a better climax. The same is true of Fletcher's Act IV, scene i, with which the third act closes. The Duke and Petruchio meet the two friends before their lodgings, only to be told that the Landlady and her gentle charge have fled.

Buckingham and Garrick begin Act IV with a new scene set before a tavern. Here the important plot change begins with the introduction of the Second Constantia and her Mother ("mother-in-law" in Garrick's version). It is at this point too that direct charges have been leveled against Garrick's additional dialogue. It is supposed, together with his cutting of Buckingham's text, to have sentimentalized the characterization of the Second Constantia.[17] It is true that in the girl's speeches about her relationship with old Antonio and her desires for a new life Garrick has modified both language and situation. But we may counter by saying that he also amplifies the facts already at hand in Buckingham's dialogue. A comparison of a single speech will show my point in terms of the audience.

(Buckingham)

2nd Con: This sinning without pleasure I cannot endure; to have always remorse, and ne'er do any thing that should cause it, is intolerable. If I loved money too, which I think I don't, my mother she has all that: I have nothing to comfort myself with but Antonio's stiff beard; and that alone, for a woman of my years, is but a sorry kind of entertainment. I wonder why these old fumbling fellows should trouble themselves so much, only to trouble us more. They can do nothing, but put us in mind of our graves. Well, I'll no more on't; for to be frighted with death and damnation both at once is a little too hard. I do here vow I'll live for ever chaste, or find out some handsome young fellow I can love; I think that's the better.

(Garrick)

2 Con: I have a great mind to leave this fantastical mother-in-law of mine, with her stolen goods, take to my heels and seek my fortune; but to whom shall I apply? Generosity and humanity are not to be met with at every corner of the street. If any young fellow would but take a liking to me, and make an honest woman of me, I would make him the best wife in the world: but what a fool am I to talk thus? Young men think of young woman now-a-days, as they do of their clothes: it is genteel to have them, to be vain of them, to show them to everybody, and to change them often; when their novelty and fashion is over, they are turned out of doors, to be purchased and worn by the first buyer. A wife, indeed, is not so easily got rid of: it is a suit of mourning, that lies neglected at the bottom of the chest, and only shows itself now and then, upon melancholy occasions. What a terrible prospect! However, I do here swear and vow to live for ever chaste, till I find a young fellow who will take me for better or for worse. La, what a desperate oath have I taken!

Let us not be deceived by the adapter's cleverness in altering this character and situation for his audience. The Second Constantia is to be allowed quite a bit of latitude as the act (and indeed as the scene) progresses; for the adaptation must retain the spirit of the original. And so the adapter is beforehand with his critics. In their proper places are the sentiments of "generosity and humanity." But note that he is at pains to show that these are not the usual ways of the world and draws a rueful picture of "for better or for worse," a picture quite in keeping with Restoration humor. Note too the mockery with which he derides his fine sentiments: "La! what a desperate oath have I taken!" With such a sop to audience taste, the adapter is now free to indulge himself with double entendre the moment the girl meets Don John. The concluding lines of this scene (with Garrick's altered lines in italics) are revealing as to the method used in pleasing an audience. Don John gazes for the first time upon the unveiled girl.

    2 Con: Well sir, what say you now?

    John: Nothing, I'm so amazed, I'm not able to speak. Pr'ythee, my sweet creature, *don't let us be talking in the street, but run home with me, that I may have* a little private *innocent conversation with you.*

    2 Con: No, sir, no private dealing, I beseech you.

    John: 'Sheart, what shall I do? I'm out of my wits. Harkye, my dear soul, canst thou love me?

    2 Con: If I could, what then?

    John: Why, then I should be the happiest man alive! (*Kissing her hand*)

    2 Con: Nay, good sir, hold — remember the conditions.

    John: Conditions! what conditions? I would not wrong thee for the universe!

    2 Con: Then you'll promise?

    John: What, what? I'll promise anything, everything, thou dear, sweet, bewitching, heavenly woman!

    2 Con: To make me an honest woman?

    John: How the devil, my angel, can I do that, if you are undone to my hands?

    2 Con: Ay, but I am not; I am a poor innocent lamb, just escaped from the jaws of an old fox.

    John: Art thou, my pretty lamb? then I'll be thy shepherd, and fold thee in these arms. (*Kisses her hand*)

    2 Con: Ay, but you must not eat the lamb yourself.

    John: I like you so well, I will do anything for thee, my dear delightful incognita! I love you so much it is impossible to say how much I love thee! My heart, my mind, and my soul, are

*transported to such a degree, that — that — that — d——n it,
I can't talk; so let us run home, or the old fox, my lamb, will
overtake us. (They run out)*

Here let us note two points. The girl demands as her
"condition" that the Don make an honest woman of her.
With this direct statement the adapter appears to have satisfied the morally exacting part of his audience. But note also
that there is no such forthright commitment on the part of
the fast-talking young gentleman. Nor will he be permitted
a definite stand in the matter until his curtain speech of
Act V. It is true that in the very next scene, as Don John is
locking her up, the girl reminds him that he has given his
word of honor. To which Don John replies: "And my
love — and when they go together, you may always trust
them." But when Frederick berates him for keeping "a
woman thus against her will, that thou knowest is in love
with another man too," and solemnly inquires, "Dost think
a judgment will not follow this?," Garrick amends Buckingham's dialogue to read: "Good, dear Frederick, do thou
keep thy sentences and thy *sentiments, which are now out
of fashion,* [italics mine] for some better opportunity. . . ."
When Don John insists the girl would not be to Frederick's
taste, it is because ". . . thou art all for flames and darts, and
those fine things! *now I am for pure, plain, simple love without any embroidery;* I am not so curious, Frederick, as
thou art." [Italics mine.]

Buckingham's version ends Act IV with the flight of the
Second Constantia and old Antonio in pursuit. Garrick continues the act for one more scene (the first part of Buckingham's Act V, scene i). The First Constantia fleeing from the
constabulary meets Don John who is frantically searching
for the Second Constantia. When he learns that it is his
Landlady who has been taken up by the constables, not his
girl, Don John rushes off leaving the First Constantia to flee
from the onrushing Antonio. Garrick follows Buckingham

faithfully, even to retaining Antonio's tag line, "A plague confound all whores!"

Act V begins with a continuation of Buckingham's scene used to close Act IV. The only changes are the omission of two speeches of the Mother and Kinswoman describing the "careless way" of the Second Constantia, and the omission of three speeches after the entrance of Frederick identifying the Bawd as a "Mother" and which describe the relations between old Antonio and his young mistress. The opening monologue of the Second Constantia in scene ii is expanded to permit a contrasting of old and young lovers, but the meaning and situation remain unchanged from the earlier text. The Shopkeeper's lines are given to the servant Peter and the scene expanded for comic effect. When Don John turns from the terrified servant to discover the girl at his side, Garrick returns to the Buckingham text. Thirteen speeches of comic love-making are added following the girl's question: "I would fain know, whether you can be kind to me." Once again we note the careful treatment of the material to retain the Restoration flavor.

> *John: Look in your glass, my charmer,* and answer for me.
> 2 *Con:* You think me very vain.
> *John:* I think you devilish handsome.
> 2 *Con:* I shall find you a rogue at last.
> *John:* Then you shall hang me for a fool; take your garters, and do it now, if you will. (*Sighing*)
> 2 *Con:* You are no fool.
> *John:* Oh, yes, a loving fool.
> 2 *Con:* I have better security.
> *John:* What's that, my angel?
> 2 *Con:* The tenderest affection for you now, and the kindest behaviour to you, for evermore.

These are Garrick's lines which seem to mark him as the creator of this sentimental heroine. But again this is but an elaboration of what is to be found in the earlier versions.

The lines lead quite naturally into Buckingham's dialogue in which the two young people swear lovers' vows. Then Garrick adds his own characteristic line for Don John evading a direct promise of marriage and accentuating the humor of the entire exchange.

John: We'll love as long as we live, and then we'll die together; and there's an end of both of us.

The unraveling of the plot gets under way with the entrance of Antonio with the First Constantia. After Don John and the girl come to terms with Antonio, the dialogue added by Garrick is indicative of the abrupt concession in comic spirit which an adapter had to make for his audience. When the Second Constantia declares that she is resolved to have all his love or none,

John: Well, well, my dear little covetous rogue, thou shalt have it all — thus I sign and seal — (*Kisses her hand*) and transfer all my stock of love to thee, for ever and for ever.

2 Con: I accept it, in the warmest spirit of love and gratitude.

This is but a prelude to John's resolve to "never more think of any other woman, for her sake," and Frederick's taunt that "it was but this morning that women were such hypocrites that you would not trust a single mother's daughter of them." To which Don John replies:

Ay, but when things are at the worst, they'll mend; example does everything, Frederick, and the fair sex will certainly grow better whenever the greatest is the best woman in the kingdom; that's what I trust to.

From this point Garrick follows Buckingham to the end of the act, adding only a curtain speech for Don John in which sentiment triumphs momentarily, only to be gently derided by the adapter's parting thrust:

> A match, my girl! — Come, let us all away,
> And celebrate THE CHANCES of this day;
> My former vanities are past and gone,

> And now I fix to happiness and one,
> Change the wild wanton for the sober plan,
> And, like my friend — become a *modest* man.

Again the careful hand of the adapter was rewarded by audience approval. This blending of just enough of the sentimental to enable the old comedy to be tolerated resulted in one of Garrick's greatest acting triumphs and a run of 13 performances in the first season (1754–55). *The Chances* remained in the repertory for 8 seasons and achieved a total of 32 performances.

Rule a Wife and Have a Wife

On March 25, 1756, Garrick produced his alteration of another Fletcher comedy, *Rule a Wife and Have a Wife*.[18] Little wonder that he took no pains to identify himself as the adapter — not because it was poorly done and scorned by his audiences, but because the changes in Fletcher's text are such as might have been worked out in the rehearsal periods prior to revival. Only one structural change is evident, the omission of Fletcher's Act V, scene i, a brief scene in which Leon shows his wife Estifania's letter warning them of Cacafogo's infatuation. Otherwise, there are no such extensive revisions as in the alteration of *The Chances*. New material added is limited to a few words or phrases to replace the lines cut for reasons of indelicacy or obsolescence. Indeed, the fact that changes were limited almost entirely to such line omissions (the longest being 10 lines in Act IV, scene ii) shows that the adapter recognized in the Fletcher text a superb piece of stagecraft — something his audience would applaud. The original characterizations and the climactic development of the comedy, added to the fact that the underplot involving Perez and Estifania is interwoven with main events to achieve a unity seldom realized in the older comedies, provided Garrick with an acting piece to which he need only apply the blue pencil to prepare it for an audience.

Although some of the overfrank lines describing the wanton appetites of Margarita are omitted, the lady still emerges in alteration as a neurotic voluptuary intent upon creating a mask of respectability to cover her relations with the Duke and others. As for the role of Leon, which Garrick intended for himself, the only lines of importance omitted were those pertaining to the hero's figure. In Act I, scene v, Cacafogo attempts to provoke the stupid youth; as he strikes Leon, both Alonzo and Juan exclaim:

Alon: You struck too low by a foot, sir.
Juan: You must get a ladder when you would beat this fellow.

Such lines could not be spoken with Garrick representing Leon and still be accepted by his audience. The same is true of Margarita's lines in Act II, scene iii, and Act III, scene i, in which Leon is described as "a strong fellow," and "a portly presence." Thomas Davies alludes to this embarrassment in reviewing Garrick's performance in the comedy.

Though Garrick's person did not present us with the true figure of Leon, and he was obliged to curtail several lines which described him as the author intended him to be in representation, yet his performance was so much in truth and nature, that the spectators wanted neither height nor bulk. He wore the disguise of folly, to intrap the cautious Margaretta, so exactly and humourously, that he presented the complete picture of a Wittol. When he put on the man of courage, and asserted the honest rights of a husband, no one of a more brawny or sinewy figure could have manifested more fire or beautiful animation.[19]

The adapter's hand can be seen in the judicious cuts employed in the closing scene of Act V. With a fine sense of timing, he realized that the bawdy joke upon the frenzied Duke and the effects of Cacafogo's voice from the nether regions could not be prolonged as in the original and still be accepted by a Drury Lane audience. We have seen too how those audiences preferred acceleration of pace for comic effect in the alteration of *The Chances*. Once a point was well established Garrick refused to jeopardize it by extension. With vigorous cutting he managed to heighten the intensity of the scene, to avoid a great part of the embarrassing business of the teasing of Medina's Duke, and yet to retain the full flavor of the old comedy — something which the later hands of James Love and J. P. Kemble failed to accomplish when they rewrote almost the entire scene.[20] These later alterations only serve to point up the gulf between the comic sense of Garrick's audiences and that of the next generation.

Unlike *The Chances, Rule a Wife and Have a Wife* was not such an immediate sensation. Only six performances were given the first season (1758–59). Audiences, however, gradually overcame their objections to the basic indecencies of the plot through the spirit of Garrick's portrayal of Leon and they gradually accepted it as a standard repertory play. Once established, *Rule a Wife and Have a Wife* outdistanced the record of *The Chances* and was played for a total of 50 performances in 17 seasons.

The two altered plays we are to consider next were brought out at Drury Lane not only in the same season but also in the same month. *Isabella; or, The Fatal Marriage* was produced in its altered state (including an epithalamium composed for the occasion) on the night of December 2, 1757. Twenty days later, December 22, *The Gamesters* appeared.

Isabella; or, The Fatal Marriage

The Southerne tragedy in its original state had appeared on two benefit programs in the season 1749–50 and again for a benefit the following season.[21] It was then discarded until Garrick's alteration and Mrs. Cibber's acting of the title role gave it new life. In its altered state [22] Southerne's tragedy has been unified by the omission of all of the comic underplot, the cast of characters has been reduced from 16 to 10 speaking roles, and the whole (so we are told) could then be performed in two hours and thirty-three minutes.[23]

Garrick's Act I (Southerne's Act I, scenes i and iii, in part) takes place before the house of Count Baldwin. With the underplot involving the antics of Fernando and his family out of the way, the adapter plunges at once into the tragic story of Isabella. From Southerne's Act I, scene i, Garrick extracted 12 lines of dialogue between Villeroy and Carlos and linked them to scene iii of the original by 20 lines of his own writing. Garrick's Carlos sends Villeroy off-stage to greet the approaching Isabella with a second offer of marriage. Then Carlos is given a soliloquy informing the audience of the reasons for his unrelenting hatred of Villeroy, a matter not sufficiently clear in the original drama.

> There is an evil fate that waits upon her,
> To which I wish him wedded — Only him:
> His upstart family, with haughty brow,
> (Tho' *Villeroy* and myself are seeming friends)
> Looks down upon her house; his sister too,
> Whose hand I ask'd, and was with scorn refus'd,
> Lives in my breast, and fires me to revenge. —
> They bend this way —
> Perhaps, at last, she seeks my father's doors;
> They shall be shut, and be prepar'd to give
> The beggar and her brat a cold reception.
> That boy's an adder in my path — they come,
> I'll stand a-part, and watch their motions. (*Retires*)

The original scene iii begins at this point and with the omission of a part of one speech by the garrulous servant Sampson is followed faithfully to its close. Garrick adds one of those inevitable tag-lines beloved by tragedy queens, "Then heav'n have mercy on me!"

Act I closed with Count Baldwin's rejection of his daughter-in-law and Garrick links it to Act II, scene i, by two new speeches given to Villeroy and Carlos. The former rehearses the Count's cruelty toward the little family and Carlos replies that his father looks upon Isabella as "Biron's

fate, that hurried him to death." Carlos then takes up the
Southerne lines on the "advantages" to Villeroy and Isabella
of her re-marriage. Garrick closes the scene with three additional lines for Carlos in which the villain gloats over the
simplicity of Villeroy and plans another stage in his campaign against his sister-in-law. Scene ii, at Isabella's house,
is taken verbatim from the original. Isabella capitulates to
Villeroy after he has promised never to ask her to put off
her widow's weeds. Garrick's Act II ends at this point.

Southerne's tragedy began Act III with a comic scene, at
the end of which the characters departed for the wedding at
Isabella's house. But Garrick, having omitted the comedy,
uses this opportunity to introduce an entirely new episode as
his scene i and to add to the audience understanding of the
background of the tragedy. Count Baldwin and Carlos are in
family conference, and the father has just heard that Villeroy
and Isabella were married the preceding night.

> *Baldwin:* Misfortune join 'em!
> And may her violated vows pull down
> A lasting curse, a constancy of sorrow
> On both their heads — I have not yet forgot
> Thy slighted passion, the refus'd alliance;
> But having her, we are reveng'd at full.
> Heav'n will pursue her still, and *Villeroy*
> Share the judgments she calls down.
> *Carlos:* Soon he'll hate her;
> Tho' warm and violent in his raptures now;
> When full enjoyment palls his sicken'd sense,
> And reason with satiety returns,
> Her cold constrain'd acceptance of his hand,
> Will gall his pride, which (tho' of late o'erpower'd
> By stronger passions) will, as they grow weak,
> Rise in full force, and pour its vengeance on her.

The Count would have his younger son profit by the example
of his brother's fate, while Carlos hypocritically hopes he

can assuage the sorrows of his father by his own obedience.
Garrick then supplies a speech for the Count which is the
first of several scattered throughout the remainder of the play
intended to redeem Count Baldwin in the eyes of the
audience.

Baldwin: With tears I thank thee, Carlos —
    And may'st thou ever feel those inward joys
    Thy duty gives thy father — but my son
    We must not let resentment choak our justice;
    'Tis fit that *Villeroy* know he has no claim
    From me, in right of Isabella — *Biron,*
    (Whose name brings tears) when wedded to this woman,
    By me abandon'd, sunk the little fortune
    His uncle left, in vanity and fondness:
    I am possesst of those your brothers papers,
    And now are *Villeroy's,* and shou'd ought remain,
    In justice it is his; from me to him
    You shall convey them — follow me, and take 'em. (*Exit*
    C. Baldwin)

Garrick objected to the unnatural and abrupt change in the
characterization of the Count in Southerne's Act V, scene iv,
and tried to provide for this change by anticipating it at the
first opportunity. Perhaps he also felt that the villainy of
Carlos was sufficiently black for this tragedy without piling
further guilt upon the old Count. In his closing speech, however, Carlos gives us an opportunity to observe the adapter's
use of the language of sentimentalism to administer a sharp
rebuke to sentimentalists in the audience. Carlos privately
determines to deliver Biron's papers to the new husband only
when they will serve his own dark schemes and adds,

      . . . What a paradox
      Is man! my father here, who boasts his honour,
      And ev'n but now was warm in praise of justice,
      Can steal his heart against the widow's tears,
      And infant's wants; the widow and the infant

> Of *Biron;* of his son, his fav'rite son,
> 'Tis ever thus weak minds, who court opinion,
> And, dead to virtuous feelings, hide their wants
> In pompous affectation —

The lines were written by Garrick, to be sure, but this is the attitude of Carlos the rake as we see him in action in the comic underplot of Southerne's original play. When Garrick cut the comic scenes he gained a heightened effect in his stagecraft, but only at the sacrifice of realism in the characterization of Carlos.

Scene ii is the point at which the greatest amount of alteration was necessary. Garrick managed to cut the underplot characters from the list of wedding guests and used some of their dialogue with considerable success, notably in the lines of Frederick which are spoken by Carlos. Only one structural change was necessary, the deferring until the following scene of the episode in which Villeroy receives word of his brother's illness and leaves his bride. Musical entertainments are introduced as in Southerne and the scene closes with the announcement of the bridal supper.

Here the adapter wisely ordered a new scene, one set in another room of the house. His scene iii begins with a dialogue between Sampson and Isabella's Nurse upon their favored position in Villeroy's service. Then he brings on Villeroy and Isabella for the letter episode postponed from the earlier scene. By so doing the adapter not only makes certain that the matter of the scene will be rescued from the confusion of the bridal festivities, but also that the audience will note the effect of the news upon Isabella. In Southerne's drama no such opportunity was given. The scene ends as Carlos enters to say that the guests have departed and Villeroy leaves him as the "protector" of his bride. Garrick adds closing lines for Isabella in which she voices her foreboding but resolves to keep her "honest obligation" to Villeroy.

Act IV, scene i (Southerne's IV, ii), begins with the

arrival of Biron and his companion Belford before Isabella's street-door. Slight changes of less than a line are made in Southerne's text, but Garrick adds some lines to build audience anticipation of Biron's entry into the house. After the exit of Belford Biron knocks on the street-door and says,

> The long expected moment is arriv'd!
> And if all here is well, my past sorrows
> Will only heighten my excess of joy;
> And nothing will remain to wish or hope for!

The servant invites him to enter, but he pauses once more to say,

> Now all my spirits hurry to my heart,
> And every sense has taken the alarm
> At this approaching interview!
> Heav'ns! how I tremble! (*Exit into the house.*)

Scene ii follows Southerne (IV, iii) closely, with few line changes and only seven lines of additional dialogue. After the lovers have recognized each other and Biron inquires about his father and his child, Isabella leaves him to order entertainment. Into his speech on Isabella's deserving "goodness" and the villainy of fathers Garrick injected two lines and a stage direction in the sentimental vein:

What is your trash, what all your heaps of gold,
Compar'd to this, my heart-felt happiness? (*Bursts into tears*)

Scene division and dialogue in Act V are taken from Southerne. In the first scene, when Isabella distracted tries to stab the sleeping Biron she rushes from the room. Southerne's text has Biron speak thus:

> . . . Death had been most welcome,
> From any Hand but hers; she never could
> Deserve to be the Executioner,
> To take my Life; nor I to fall by her.

Garrick cut these lines and replaced them with the following:

. . . Horrors come fast around me;
My mind is overcast — the gath'ring clouds
Darken the prospect — I approach the brink,
And soon must leap the precipice! O, heav'n!
While yet my senses are my own, thus kneeling
Let me implore thy mercies on my wife,
Release her from her pangs; and if my reason,
O'erwhelmed with miseries, sink before the tempest,
Pardon these crimes despair may bring upon me. (*Rises*)

In scene ii a speech is added for Biron when mortally
wounded, and in scene iii, to a speech already provided by
Southerne for the expiring husband, Garrick adds not only
instructions concerning delivery of Biron's letter to Count
Baldwin, but also,

. . . — my Isabella:
Cou'dst thou but hear me, my last words should bless thee.
I cannot, tho' in death, bequeath her to thee. (to *Villeroy*)
But cou'd I hope my boy, my little one,
Might find a father in thee — O, I faint!
I can no more — Hear me, Heav'n! O support
My wife, my *Isabella* — bless my child!
And take my poor unhappy — (*Dies*)

In deference to the sensibilities of the audience the scene
showing Pedro stretched upon the rack is cut, but references
to an off-stage torture are included in the dialogue. Two
further cuts by the adapter occur before the close of the
tragedy; the final couplet is removed from the dying speech
of Isabella,

The Waves and Winds will dash, and Tempests roar;
But Wrecks are toss'd at last upon the Shoar.

and the following lines from Count Baldwin's final address
to Biron's little son,

There's not a Vein but shall run Milk for thee.

That such omissions were an improvement no one will

deny. But we cannot be so certain that they would have been deleted had they belonged to Garrick's own role. Perhaps in this instance it really *is* Mrs. Cibber to whom we should be indebted, as Garrick so modestly stated in the Advertisement to the printed play:

when the passions are violent and the speeches long, the performers must either spare their powers, or shorten their speeches — Mrs. Cibber chose the latter, by which she has been able to exert that force and expression, which have been so strongly felt and so sincerely applauded.[24]

Public approval was registered in 14 performances the first season (1757–58) and assured it of a place in the repertory for eight seasons, a total of 26 performances. It became a standard vehicle for another great star, Mrs. Siddons, who played it well into the next century.

The Gamesters

The alteration of James Shirley's comedy *The Gamester* was brought out at Drury Lane on December 22nd, 1757, under the title of *The Gamesters*. As in the case of the alteration of *The Chances,* the adapter had before him two versions of the comedy. In addition to the original, Garrick could have availed himself of Charles Johnson's *The Wife's Relief; or, The Husband's Cure* (Drury Lane, November 12, 1711).[25] But to Garrick's mind Johnson as an alterer of old plays was not a second Buckingham, and he refused to consult *The Wife's Relief*.[26] Genest says, "Garrick properly calls his play the Gamesters, Wilding being as much a Gamester as Hazard — he has very judiciously restored the original names, and Shirley's own language in the scenes which he retains — in other respects his alteration does him no credit." [27] Our present task, however, is not so much to pass judgment upon the worth of the adaptation, but to discover just what was altered and why it had to be done.

In regularizing this comedy the adapter cut all of the serio-comic underplot involving Sir Richard Hurry, the two girls Leonora and Violante, and their lovers Delamore and Beaumont, reducing the cast of characters from 24 to 15.[28] Except for changes due to the omission of these comic characters there are no structural changes in Act I. The dialogue is Shirley's and Garrick has been content to make only small changes in expression necessitated by the demands of his audience. Once again we shall observe, as in *The Chances,* how the adapter tries to keep faith with the spirit of his original and yet to keep from offending contemporary taste.

The first encounter between Wilding and his wife provides us with examples of two different methods of dealing with this problem. The first is the more obvious one of cutting the most indelicate expressions. Mrs. Wilding has been standing behind her husband in the street and overhears part of his solicitation of Penelope. When her spouse is left alone with her, not knowing exactly how much she has overheard, he immediately takes the offensive. He rues the day, he tells her, when he married Mistress Wilding. In Shirley the lines run thus:

> I married thee for thy soul's sake, not thy body,
> And shall as soon get children on't; and yet
> I do not hate thee, witness, I dare kiss thee,
> Hold thee by the hand, and sleep in the same house;
> And in thy bed sometimes something has been done
> Within the memory of man; but —

Garrick's omissions make the same speech read,

> I married thee for thy soul's sake, not thy body;
> Yet I do not hate thee. Witness, I dare kiss;
> Hold thee by the hand, sleep in the same house,
> Nay, in the same bed sometimes; but —

An instance of the second method occurs only three speeches later. In the Shirley play Wilding accuses his wife

of jealousy and says that such emotion becomes no modest
woman who loves her husband. "Some wife," he cries, "will
bid her husband's leverets welcome," and he proceeds to paint
a vivid picture of the domestic triangle. Now Garrick cannot
use this embarrassing speech unless he alters it. This is
effected by shifting the subject out of the singular and into
the plural ("Some wives"), and as social comment it becomes
acceptable to his audiences in all its former suggestiveness.
A few speeches later the same device is used to make the
situation even more palatable. When Mrs. Wilding promises
to cease being jealous, her husband becomes even more
explicit. By the simple expedient of inserting one additional
sentence — "I'll try you then" — the adapter is free to retain
all of the following lines.

> *Wilding*: But if I bring home a mistress —
> *Mrs. Wild*: I'll be patient.
> *Wilding*: What if there be one
> 　　Already, that does please me? will you not
> 　　Repine, and look awry upon's, when we
> 　　Make much of one another?
> *Mrs. Wild*: So you will but sometimes smile on me too:
> 　　I'll endeavour.
> *Wilding*: Well said, this may do good upon me; as
> 　　I find you prompt in this, I may consider
> 　　Other matters; to tell you true, I like
> 　　Your kinswoman.
> *Mrs. Wild*: How!
> *Wilding*: How; why as a man shou'd like her.

In Shirley the impatient Wilding is all but ready to introduce
Penelope as his mistress then and there; in Garrick's version
the implication will be tolerated by his audience as long as
it is assured the whole business is but a "testing" of the
wife. The motive is quite clear in lines Garrick adds for
Wilding after the departure of his wife.

But let me see, why do I use this wife of mine thus terribly?

she gave me all — ay, that all's the devil! my desires are satisfied, and I have got not a grain of inclination left: — vanity is
the thing — in eating, music, wine, or women; nothing but
variety gives the palate to them all: now, my wife is always in
the same tune, the same dish, the same dull bottle of port; and,
to sum up all, the same woman — 'twill never do —

A foretaste of the manner in which Shirley's plot is to be
manipulated is given in the speech of Hazard after parting
from Wilding.

Hazard: I wish I could get this *Penelope* out of his hands.
She's a charming girl, and though she has not quite money
enough to be made a wife of, by one of no fortune, yet she has
too many good qualities to be made a strumpet of, by such a
fellow as *Wilding* — he will not succeed surely —

And yet such a betrayal of the spirit of Shirley's comedy is
absolutely necessary if the adapter is to be allowed to retain
the comic bawdry of the play as a whole.

In Act II, scene i, Garrick again follows the original with
minor cuts, word omissions, and the addition of a few lines.
Mrs. Wilding's words to Penelope, "Your love, by gift made
mine, I give my husband. Do you love him?" The scene
proceeds verbatim to the episode of the diamond ring which
Wilding presents to Penelope. Here Garrick sends Wilding
off-stage to get it (" 'tis in my drawer above, I'll fetch it
strait") and provides the girl with a brief speech which is
characteristic of the contemporary handling of the suggestive
while seeming to disapprove the indelicacy.

Penelope: Indeed Mrs. *Wilding*, this is going a little too far
for you — there is something so like reality in all I have been
doing, that I am more than half in a fever already — this
playing with fire is a very foolish thing, but tho' I burn my
fingers I must go thru' with it.

Wilding's final speech is cut by Garrick as indecent (which
it is) and he continues the Wilding-Penelope dialogue for

five more speeches. Penelope promises to wear the diamond until she can "oblige" Wilding and is sure she will "not prove ungrateful." Garrick also prolongs the scene by having Wilding insist upon leaving his page behind, that the boy may run to the tavern for his master the moment Mistress Wilding leaves the house. When Penelope frowns on this suggestion and promises to meet him, he breaks out in a closing speech which leaves no doubt as to his meaning.

Events in the tavern scene (scene ii) which follows are rearranged somewhat. Garrick omits the episode in which Hazard makes sport of the fiddler; instead he has Hazard call for "the gamester's apology," a song certain to be popular with the audience and calculated to cheer the melancholy gamester of the comedy, Littlestock. Wilding's entrance follows the song, and the scene progresses as in Shirley to the entrance of a Drawer announcing the approach of Old Barnacle and his Nephew. At this point, however, Garrick adds a brief episode in which a note is delivered to Wilding, by which the audience can guess that Mistress Wilding has gone from home even before Wilding's cry of victory. Hazard proceeds to caution Wilding against obtaining his pleasure "at the expence of every virtue," to which that hearty replies:

Wilding: What, a moralizing gamester! ha, ha, ha, 'tis envy, Will, attacks thee in the shape of conscience: and was I, like the foolish dog in the fable, to catch at the shadow and drop my tit bit, thou would'st be the first to snap it up — but I have no time to laugh at thee — I must away — the wench calls, and I must fly. (*Exit*)

Hazard: This affair perplexes me — How little do we know of woman! had I had fortune enough to have ventur'd upon marriage, I would have fixt upon this cousin of his, preferable to the whole sex — but the devil is in them, and will peep out one time or other — I don't know why, but I am vex'd at this affair — I'll never go to *Wilding's* house again.

After this addition the adapter returns to his original to introduce Old and Young Barnacle and Dwindle for the mock quarrel scene. The extension of this scene with new dialogue provides Garrick with opportunity to inveigh against the habits of gaming and to point up audience expectancy as to the outcome of Wilding's next encounter with Penelope. The closing dialogue is an excellent example of climax to whet the appetite of the audience for events in the next act.

Sellaway: A love-matter! let him but hear the rattling of the dice, and it will bring him from the arms of the finest woman in the kingdom.

Hazard: Pooh, pooh! you carry this too far.

Sellaway: I know him in this particular better than you, Hazard — when he is in the circle of the gaming-table, 'tis all magic, he has not power to move; and I challenge the devil to bait his hook with a stronger temptation to draw him out of it — besides, among ourselves, what was once with him occasional pleasure, is now become a necessary occupation: *Jack Wilding* has made a large gap in the widow's jointure.

Hazard: Pshaw! rot your gossiping, don't abuse the generous wine you have been drinking, by mixing such scandal as this with it — stay till you get with your mistresses over their ratafia, and when you're maudling open the sluices of slander; — However we'll try the experiment; I'll meet you in the evening, and we'll write to him from the field of battle, and see to which his courage most inclines: From love to gaming we'll his heart intice, But woman will prevail, —

Sellaway: ——— I say the dice.

In Act III, scene i, the adapter is able to follow Shirley's text closely, cutting a few indelicacies but retaining most of them by use of the same device we noted in Act I, scene i. When Wilding swears eternal love for Penelope and promises to find her a husband to maintain some semblance of propriety, Shirley's Penelope asks, "When I am married?" But the alteration reads, "When I am to be married?" Thus Garrick aims to take the edge off the immoralities expressed and is free to retain most of Shirley's text except the grossness of Wilding's, "And the assurance that thou hast two fathers before thou hast a child, will make thee spring more active in my arms." Again we wonder at the taste of the audience. It will permit an adapter to retain a line like, "'Tis my ambition to make a cuckold — the only pleasure o' th' world," but refuse to accept a line such as, "I would not wish to enjoy thee now, but in the hope of t'other harvest, and to make thy husband hereafter cuckold." It is interesting to note also that to the closing line of this speech, "that imagination sweetens the rest, and I do love it mainly," Garrick adds another "mainly," which in the speaking must have made up in suggestiveness for the deletions made earlier in the scene.

At this point Garrick adds a new episode in which Wilding plays the hypocrite and announces to his wife that Penelope's influence has reformed him. When a servant announces that the gamesters await him, Mrs. Wilding wishes to send word that her husband has forsaken the old haunts. But Wilding proposes to wean rather than tear himself from his friends and sends word that he will attend them.

In scene ii Garrick had to provide for the changes in plot structure and accordingly had to cut the display of typical gaming patrons (a Lord, a Knight, and a Country Gentleman) in the original. Hazard, alone, ponders his disappointment over Penelope's seeming wantonness and confesses that he cares for her. Again this change in Hazard's character allows the adapter to retain the *double entendre* of both men after the entrance of Wilding and the speech beginning, "No, no; but I swell with imagination." New dialogue is of course required for their discussion of the Nephew of Barnacle as a prospective cuckold for Penelope. A final change is made as the adapter reverses the details of the scene in which the gamesters meet again with Young Barnacle. Garrick gives the reading of the Coranto to Wilding, who then imposes upon the credulity of the youth.

Perhaps the chief virtue of this alteration is the additional scene which Garrick now includes before ending his Act III. The midnight assignation was confined to expository dialogue in the original version, but Garrick realized the advantage of representing it upon the stage. By showing the scene in all of its guilelessness, the audience would readily accept the indelicate plot in its fullest flavor. There are more lines against the passion for gaming and others in which the wife's trickery is applauded as a "scheme of virtue." Hazard and Mrs. Wilding touch in the darkness, the latter stamps her foot as a prearranged signal for the entrance of Penelope with lights, and the ladies take advantage of Hazard's embarrassment to force his promise of assistance against the husband. The three then plot to deceive Wilding into thinking himself cuckolded and his innocent wife the victim of his own grossness.

Act IV begins with a new scene in which Old Barnacle comes to inquire of Mrs. Wilding whether there has been progress in the proposed match between Young Barnacle and Penelope. The alteration advances the incident further than the original by bringing Penelope on to confound Young Barnacle and the surly Dwindle. The youth departs in a fury.

For his scene ii Garrick reverts to Shirley's Act IV, scene i, the meeting of Hazard and Wilding next morning. In scene iii Garrick provides additional dialogue for Mrs. Wilding to inform her husband of her own "plot" and of his supposed cuckolding. If there were any doubt as to why such concessions were made to the audience — the changed characterization of Hazard, the representation of the true facts surrounding the midnight assignation, and other minor alterations — the freedom and obvious relish of these lines will be sufficient answer. The adapter inserted them to expand a situation which in the original is certainly frank enough. Italicized words represent Shirley's text.

Mrs. Wild: Not to bed, all night! — think again, my dear — your mem'ry may fail you.

Wilding: What do you mean? — I say I have not been to bed to-night — and had you any eyes but jealous ones, you'd see by mine I have not slept tonight.

Mrs. Wild: Look at me, husband.

Wilding: So I do — there! there! — What mummery's this?

Mrs. Wild: Now tell me — do you feel no small compunction at thus looking in my injur'd face?

Wilding: A pox upon these stale expostulations; must I ever be dinn'd with 'em? and can't my reformation work a change in you? — thou art the strangest woman. —

Mrs. Wild: Soft, soft, my good husband — did you not meet *Penelope* last night?

Wilding: No, I met no *Penelope* last night.

Mrs. Wild: And were you not to meet her? — speak, my dear.

Wilding: Prithee, let me alone, my head aches.

Mrs. Wild: No, no, 'tis my head that aches — did you not pass the night, the live-long night, in wanton, stolen embraces?

Wilding: *Refuse me if I did.*

Mrs. Wild: You did not lie with Mrs. *Penelope*, my kinswoman?

Wilding: Cuckold me if I did. I swear —

Mrs. Wild: Come, come, don't swear — *but 'twas no fault of yours, no fault, no virtue — but this is no time to expostulate these actions — in brief, know 'twas my plot.* (*Smiling*)

Wilding: What plot?

Mrs. Wild: Yes, yes, my plot, my dear. (*Smiling*)

Wilding: My plot, my dear! what do you smirk and giggle at? — Leave your ideot tricks, and tell me what you mean!

Mrs. Wild: You are so tasty — but I shall please you.

Wilding: Shall you? I wish you would —

Mrs. Wild: Thus then — I have with sorrow long *observ'd*

which way your warm affection mov'd, and found 'twould be
in vain with open pow'r t'oppose you; I therefore work'd by
stratagem — I got the secret of your meeting, and I *wrought
so with my honest cousin, to supply her wanton place, that with
some shame, at last, I might deceive your hard heart into kindness.*

*Wilding: That, that again, sweet wife; and be a little Serious
— Was it your plot to excuse your cousin, And be the bed-
fellow?*

Mrs. Wild: 'Twas *indeed,* my dear. [Italicized in alteration]
Wilding: 'Twas *in hell,* my dear. [Italicized in alteration]

. . . .

Wilding: . . . and did you really contrive the plot yourself?
Mrs. Wild: I did.
Wilding: You lie — I contriv'd some part of it — and can
you prove all this to be true?
Mrs. Wild: I can — witness those tender joys, which tho'
not meant for me —
Wilding: O damn your description! I am satisfied.

Very little alteration occurs in the first scene of Act V
except the usual cuts for reasons of taste. The adapter does,
however, make Hazard insist upon Wilding's confirming the
account of Penelope's portion before witnesses. Acreless,
Littlestock, and Sellaway are selected for this purpose. The
scene between Old Barnacle and Hazard appears almost
verbatim in Garrick's version; the Nephew is reduced to his
old status once more and agrees not to press his claim for
Penelope. As the scene closes they all prepare to go to
Wilding's house.

Alteration of the final scene of the comedy begins at once.
Mrs. Wilding urges Penelope to take Hazard in marriage.

Mrs. Wild: His gaming is accidental — A younger brother,
and bred to no business, naturally leads to the dice for his supplies — I know he is tir'd of the company he has kept; his
honour is as yet unimpeach'd, and with your fortune, what can
either of you want, or desire further?

With such advice she turns the girl over to Hazard's wooing, and the alteration follows the original with few deletions. Soon after Wilding's entrance Garrick adds a few lines in which the audience is informed that a lawyer and "papers" are within, that a contract has been signed and sealed by which Wilding has relinquished all rights as Penelope's guardian to Hazard. The additional lines expanding the comedy of Wilding's budding cuckold's horns are broad and coarse.

> *O. Barnacle*: You have it there, Mr. *Wilding*. (*Pointing to his head*)
> *Wilding*: The devil! — Do you see 'em? Have they broke the surface?
> *O. Barnacle*: I mean Mr. *Hazard's* business.
> *Wilding*: I mean that too — My head's a torment to me.
> *Nephew*: What would you give me now, Mr. *Wilding,* to be of the nation without heads?

Except for such cuts as were necessary because of the omission of the underplot, the alteration follows Shirley's scene almost to its close. But a new ending is provided. Penelope asks pardon of Old Barnacle and his nephew for casting her lot with Will Hazard. Wilding appears to rejoice that matters are no worse and actually refers to "our bridal day," urging Mrs. Wilding to begin "new joys with these our happy cousins." Hazard forswears "harlot fortune" and the dice, to which Sellaway jeeringly replies: "The sinner preaches, *Wilding;* but his lectures will make few penitents." And this line will have to stand for the adapter's own apology for penning the closing lines of this comedy. Wilding not only reforms but faces life with her he calls his "prudent pilot," who promises to steer him away from that fatal shore

> Where a friend's ruin is by friends enjoy'd,
> And ev'ry virtue is by turns destroy'd.

Garrick's alteration deeply offended a certain part of his audience. So much we learn from a letter addressed to him by Dr. Warburton a month after the initial production at Drury Lane. Garrick had written of his great concern, for the Bishop replied

. . . We have read over the altered Play with much pleasure. The occasional strokes up and down, of the nature of those in the excellent prologue, make us honour you greatly. If you did not give offense, you would not deserve applause.

The miscarriage of the first nights, from the cause you mention, was very natural. It was not the virtue of the audience which took offence at a supposed adultery; it was not their vice which was disappointed when they saw none committed; it was their vanity which was shocked, in finding themselves outwitted by the poet. They had sat long enough in their suspense to be secure in their sagacity, that Wilding had been really cockolded; and to find themselves mistaken at last, was enough to put them out of humour.[29]

The good Doctor knew his audiences! He also put his finger upon the real fault in this alteration, as indeed of all Garrick's alterations — the divided allegiance with which he approached the old plays. On the one hand was a strict ideal of what constituted a true *vis comica;* on the other was his conception as manager of what the Drury Lane patrons wanted. It is but another example of what we have already quoted from Professor Stone in relation to the Shakespearean alterations, "the dilemma of an eighteenth-century mind caught between an ideal . . . and a canny understanding of box-office appeal." [30] In his anxiety to protect himself as a manager while preserving the salty humor he valued in Shirley's comedy, Garrick *had* to deceive his audience. And when he had succeeded all too well, he attempted an orderly retreat in the closing scene of Act III. The result was disastrous. His confused audience refused to follow him, disbelieving what it saw, and consequently failed to accept the events of the last two acts in complete good faith. In altering *The Chances* and *Rule a Wife and Have a Wife* he had succeeded in walking this theatrical tight-rope; in *The Game-sters* his audience found him out at half-price time and remained hostile for the rest of the evening. After seven performances in the first season (1757–58) Garrick dis-carded the comedy. He revived it, however, in 1772–73 — but not for himself. His friend Tom King played Wilding 13 times that season, three times in 1773–74, and once again in 1774–75.[31]

The Country Girl

If author and manager warred within Garrick over Shir-ley's plot, what a battle must have raged about the year 1766 when he set himself the task of altering William Wych-erley's *The Country Wife!* The original comedy no longer held the stage at Drury Lane, in fact had not since the season of 1752–53 when one performance was given during the benefit months. In all, only three performances had been played in the nineteen years since Garrick had assumed man-agement.[32] Perhaps the comedy gained in interest for Gar-rick after one of his actors, John Lee, introduced his alter-ation at a benefit on April 26, 1765. Lee had reduced the play to a two-act farce and retained the title of *The Country Wife.* As an afterpiece it achieved six performances that sea-son and two others toward the close of the next.[33] Of the quality of Lee's farce we may judge from Genest's account.

he omits Horner, Sir Jasper, and Lady Fidget, etc. — Dorilant falls in love with Mrs. Pinchwife instead of Horner — the 1st act is taken with slight alterations from Wycherley — the 2nd act begins with the scene in which Harcourt enters as a parson — then follows the scene in which Mrs. Pinchwife writes her letter — Pinchwife gives it to Dorilant — he throws it on the ground — Sparkish reads it aloud — Pinchwife is in a rage — Alithea advises him to allow his wife all reasonable liberties — Pinchwife immediately acquiesces — nothing can be more flat than the concluding scene, nor more unsuitable to Pinchwife's character than his conduct in it — Mrs. Pinchwife's escape in Alithea's clothes is totally omitted.[34]

Garrick's five-act alteration was produced at Drury Lane October 25, 1766, under the title of *The Country Girl* and achieved a popular success at once, 14 performances before the season closed.[35] Following the suggestion of Lee, Garrick omitted the characters of Sir Jasper Fidget and the four ladies of his coterie and also the Quack Doctor and Dorilant, retaining an economical cast of nine characters.[36] In alteration Wycherley's Master Horner becomes a genial uncle, Harcourt, whose more adventurous amours are now undertaken by a nephew Belville. This lad is in love with old Moody's (Pinchwife's) "country girl" Miss Peggy (Mrs. Margery Pinchwife), and inevitably Harcourt is paired with Alithea. Sparkish and Lucy the maid are retained from the original play.

Except for about twelve speeches in Moody's first scene, which are directly borrowed from Wycherley, the entire business and dialogue of Act I is new, although adapted from material found in the original. The scene is still Harcourt's lodgings (Horner's), but now uncle and nephew are discovered offering one another consolation in matters of love. Belville is "miserably" in love with a country girl named Peggy, but he is in great fear that she is already married. Harcourt derides him gently for his "unfashionable weakness — modesty." But soon the uncle is confessing that he too is in love, that his mistress is "just going to be married to another," and that strangely enough she lives in the same house as Belville's beloved! Enlarging upon his exposition, Harcourt relates how his friend Sparkish is engaged to wed Alithea and characterizes him as a fop and a bore to be circumvented at all costs. These confidences are interrupted by a servant who describes the strange visit of Harcourt's old friend Moody, a country gentleman. Moody has promised to return. This allows Harcourt and Belville to inform the audience more thoroughly concerning the relationship between Moody and Peggy. The girl's father at death had made old Moody her guardian. Moody has set his heart on marrying Peggy for her portion and has raised her as a "country girl." Belville describes his "Romeo and Juliet" courtship in the country which is continuing now that old Moody has brought his ward to town. In fact Belville's kissing his hand to Peggy from the new tavern window that looks upon the back of her house has already aroused the ire of her guardian and no doubt accounts for his impending visit to Harcourt.[37]

The entrance of Sparkish interrupts the two at this point. He confirms Belville's worst fears — Moody has been seeking the youth who made love from the tavern window. He is determined to keep Peggy from the notice of city gallants and promises to return with his ward to the country as soon as he settles some legal affairs. According to Sparkish the old man has convinced the girl that they are already married by the breaking of a sixpence. At Harcourt's suggestion Sparkish accepts his offer to supply a twin brother as parson for his coming wedding with Alithea. He retires with Belville the moment Moody's second visit is announced, cautioning Harcourt to "Remember that he is married, or he'll suspect me of betraying him."

The scene which follows paraphrases that between Pinchwife and Horner in the original, with about twelve speeches taken directly from Wycherley. Harcourt speaks of Belville as "a poor sheepish lad" who has seen Alithea at the opera and fallen in love with her. But to Moody the boy is "a wolf in sheeps' clothing," and he parts from Harcourt in a rage. Harcourt indulges in the following lines which close Act I.

Harcourt: Ha, ha, ha! poor Jack! what a life of suspicion does he lead! I pity the poor fellow, though he ought and will suffer for his folly. — Folly! — 'tis treason, murder, sacrilege! When persons of a certain age will indulge their false, ungenerous appetites, at the expense of a young creature's happiness, dame Nature will revenge herself upon them, for thwarting her most heavenly will and pleasure. (*Exit*)

It was to this Act in particular Genest must have been referring when he wrote,

> . . . the Country Wife was so indecent that Garrick was obliged to make considerable alterations; he has removed all the exceptionable parts, but he has in a great measure destroyed the vigour of the Original — the spirited character of Horner is reduced to a walking Gentleman — the scenes which Garrick has substituted for those which he has omitted, are insipid to the last degree.[38]

Certainly Act I as it stands in Wycherley would not have been tolerated by Garrick's audiences. But with the indecencies cut away he not only loses the key to all humor in the plot but is faced with insurmountable problems in the unfolding of his tale. Act I is in fact so cluttered with antecedent materials that even poor Sparkish is smothered beneath the load of exposition Garrick piles upon him.

We must recognize also at the outset that once again we are dealing with an adapter who strives mightily to keep his left hand from knowing what his right is doing. The result in terms of the audience is unpleasant and almost as unsavory as the situation it is supposed to correct. Wycherley's Pinchwife tries his best to keep his London friends from the knowledge that he has married an extremely pretty girl. Restoration audiences laughed at his cuckolding by Horner. In his anxiety to keep adultery out of his version Garrick hit upon the expedient of drawing the situation in reverse: he gives his audience a situation in which a solid citizen has counterfeited marriage with a young maiden.

> *Sparkish:* . . . I fancy the brute, her brother, has a mind to marry his country idiot at the same time.
> *Belville:* How, country idiot, sir?

Harcourt: Hold your tongue. (*Apart to* Belville) I thought he had been married already.

Sparkish: No, no, he's not married, that's the joke of it.

.   .   .   .   .

Belville: I thought you said, just now, that he was not married; is not that a contradiction, sir? (*Harcourt still makes signs to* Belville.)

Sparkish: Why, it is a kind of one; but considering your modesty, and the ignorance of the young lady, you are pretty tolerably inquisitive, methinks; ha, Harcourt! ha, ha, ha!

Harcourt: Pooh, pooh! don't talk to that boy, tell me all you know.

Sparkish: You must know, my booby of a brother-in-law hath brought up this ward of his (a good fortune let me tell you), as he coops up and fattens his chickens for his own eating; he is plaguy jealous of her, and was very sorry that he could not marry her in the country, without coming up to town; which he could not do on account of some writings or other; so what does my gentleman? He persuades the poor silly girl, by breaking a sixpence, or some nonsense or another, that they are to all intents married in heaven; but that the laws require the signing of articles, and the church service to complete their union: so he has made her call him husband, and bud, which she constantly does; and he calls her wife, and gives out she is married, that she may not look after younger fellows, nor younger fellows after her, egad; ha, ha, ha! and all won't do.

Belville: Thank you, sir. What heavenly news, uncle! (*Aside*)

Harcourt: What an idiot you are, nephew. (*Apart*) And so then you make but one trouble of it, and are both to be tack'd together the same day?

Sparkish: No, no, he can't be married this week; he d——ns the lawyers, for keeping him in town. . . .

Such is the reformation demanded by the audiences at Drury Lane, and we may well inquire whether such a reversal of the circumstances does actually launder the situation found in Wycherley. The answer will become apparent as we consider the later acts of this alteration and the effect a more faithful rendering of Wycherley's text will have upon an audience provided with the background of this new relationship.

Cutting a few lines of obsolescent or indelicate nature and omitting the business of the husband's peeping, Garrick begins Act II with Wycherley's Act II, scene i. Alithea and Peggy plead with old Moody to allow Peggy the liberties of the town. In the girls' account of the pleasures of London we note that Garrick carefully deletes Alithea's line about conversation in the boxes at the theatre. Sparkish soon enters bringing Harcourt and Belville. The nephew is introduced to Moody and humbly apologizes for his supposed liberties in addressing Alithea. The two retire leaving Harcourt, Sparkish, and Alithea to play the scene as in Wycherley. Moody returns and the dialogue follows the original verbatim to the point at which the Wycherley text introduces Lady Fidget and her companions. Here Garrick ends his scene with the appearance of a Countryman to tell Moody that his lawyers have arrived "with a green bag full of papers." An interesting glimpse of playhouse behavior is provided by the changes Garrick has made in the original lines of Alithea and Sparkish. Bracketed words represent Wycherley's dialogue; italicized words show Garrick's additions.

Alithea: I will not go, if you intend to leave me alone in the box, and run [into the pit] *all about the house,* as you used to do.

Sparkish: Psha! I'll leave Harcourt with you in the box to entertain you, and that's as good. If I sat in the box, I should be thought no [judge but of trimmings] *critic. I must run about, my dear, and abuse the author.* Come away, Harcourt, lead her down. *B'ye, brother.* (*Exeunt* Harcourt, Sparkish and Alithea)

Having omitted the arrival of the Fidgets to carry Margery to the playhouse, Garrick's scene ii is taken from Wycherley's Act III, scene i. Alithea's lines are given to the maid Lucy, whose role is expanded by a lengthy dialogue with Peggy. Garrick has Peggy tell her own version of the marriage contract with Moody. He is determined to get this point across to the audience. Then Lucy confides the news of Belville's passionate love and his hope that Peggy will meet him in the Park that night. Moody enters and the scene is again that of Wycherley to the end of the act. The husband is persuaded to allow Peggy to walk in the Park in boy's clothes, business which the manager carefully provides for in Lucy's line, "When you were with your lawyers last night, Miss Peggy, to divert me and herself, put 'em on, and they fitted her to a hair."

Act III, scene i, is set in the Park (Wycherley's Act III, scene ii), where Belville awaits the arrival of Peggy. He informs his uncle that he has impressed old Moody with a supposed infatuation with Alithea, but that he hopes to meet Peggy at this spot. The two men are discovered by Sparkish, who is bursting to tell how his latest musical composition has been burlesqued by the poets. "I never am ask'd twice, and so have at you," cries the fop, and begins to sing his song "Twang, twang" as his friends steal away.[39] But soon they reappear to announce the arrival of Moody and his family. The scene then follows the original closely to the end.

In scene ii we note that the adapter has profited by the lesson so recently learned in altering Shirley's *The Gamester*. Again he takes the opportunity to show his audience that no immoralities take place by representing on-stage what Wycherley had left to the imagination of his public. But this time the adapter is taking no chances with audience disapproval. His lovers are confined to an indulgence of rapturous dialogue the quality of which may be judged by Belvilles' speech: "No disguise could conceal you from my heart: I pretended not to know you, that I might deceive the dragon that continually watches over you; but now he's asleep, let us fly from misery to happiness."

Again Peggy recounts the details of her marriage contract

and Belville explains the deceit of her guardian. The young couple has just decided to marry without Moody's consent, though for Peggy it means marriage with a younger son and consequently half a fortune, when old Moody appears. He is in no humor to grant Belville's request that he be permitted to "show the young spark Rosamond's pond." "Whatever I think he ought to see," cries the outraged Moody, "I shall show him myself. You may visit Rosamond's pond, if you will; and the bottom of it, if you will." And off he goes with Peggy under his arm.

The brief scene with which Garrick begins Act IV is taken from Wycherley (Act IV, scene i), with the omission of a great part of the author's comments upon the marriage state as expressed by Lucy. The maid, however, pleads the case of Harcourt with Alithea until Sparkish and his friends are announced. Since she disapproves of the Sparkish-Alithea alliance, Lucy declares she'll take her advice where it will be more welcome. "Miss Peggy is bent upon mischief against her guardian, and she can't have a better privy-counseller than myself," she confides to the audience as the scene ends.

Although much of Wycherley's Act IV, scene ii, is omitted, the general pattern of events is followed, including the letter scene, which is reproduced verbatim. Such is not the case, however, in scene iii, for here the adapter is faced with the task of avoiding and replacing the notorious "china-scene" of Wycherley. He begins the action (set in Belville's lodging) with a council of war between Lucy and Belville. The maid has come to inform him that Miss Peggy agrees to fly from Moody's house at her first opportunity. But before she can leave Belville's rooms Lucy is trapped by the sudden arrival of her master. Hastily Belville thrusts her into a closet as Moody enters bearing his wife's letter. The ensuing dialogue is taken from the corresponding scene in Wycherley to the entrance of Sparkish. When the fop arrives he is bursting with news of his jilting by Alithea.

Sparkish: Nay, nay, you shall hear my story out. She walk'd up within pistol-shot of the church, then twirl'd round upon her heel, call'd me every name she could think of; and, when she had exhausted her imagination, and tired her tongue (no easy matter, let me tell you), she call'd her chair, sent her footman to buy a monkey before my face, then bid me good morrow with a sneer, and left us with our mouths open in the middle of a hundred people, who were all laughing at us! If these are not tantrums, I don't know what are.

All this is too much for the closeted Lucy, whose laughter is mistaken by Sparkish for that of his erstwhile mistress. When Belville refuses to let him see the person in hiding, the fop departs in high dudgeon. Whereupon Lucy emerges from the closet to express her amusement and pleasure at the turn of events, especially the ingenuity displayed by Miss Peggy in the delivery of her letter.

Two scenes from Wycherleys' play (Act IV, scene iv, and Act V, scene i) are used by Garrick for the first scene in Act V. He closely follows the original Act IV, scene iv, to the entrance of Sparkish. Moody surprises Peggy at work upon her second letter to Belville and demands to know its conclusion and destination. As he draws his sword to threaten the girl the dialogue is shifted to that of Wycherley's Act V, scene i, unifying the dramatic situation and pointing up the humor of the letter episodes. Throughout the remainder of the scene the alteration adheres to the original, except for the stage business called for at its close. Wycherley requires Margery to give her hand to Pinchwife and then in the darkness to steal to his other side to be led off to Horner's lodgings as Alithea. Evidently fearing that the audience might refuse to believe in so obvious a trick, Garrick had to sacrifice the humor in Wycherley's situation to business which would be more natural. His Peggy simply moves in disguise across the stage and exits weeping. Moody, thinking she is still within the other room, locks the door and departs in great satisfaction.

At this point Garrick leaves the Wycherley text behind and provides an entirely new closing scene for the comedy. Set in the Park before Belville's house, it begins with the entrance of Sparkish in drunken disorder as the disguised Peggy is about to reach Belville's door. The girl is rescued from his annoying attentions by the sudden arrival of old Moody and enters the dwelling. As a footman is about to close the house door, Moody stops struggling with Sparkish long enough to send word to Belville that he gives whole-hearted assent to his marriage. As Sparkish taunts Moody with the fact that Belville really desires Peggy, and as Moody taunts his opponent with his jilting, to their mutual astonishment Harcourt enters leading Alithea as his bride. Realizing the trick played upon him, Moody pounds upon Belville's door. The footman reappears on the balcony to announce that a wedding is in progress, and soon the bride and groom appear to make sport of the old man. Miss Peggy cries,

How dare you look me in the face, bud? Have you not given me to another, when you ought to have married me yourself? Have you not pretended to be married to me, when you knew in your conscience you was not? And have you not been shilly-shally, for a long time? So that if I had not married dear Mr. Belville, I should not have married at all; so I should not.

To which Moody replies,

I am stupified with shame, rage, and astonishment. My fate has o'ercome me; I can struggle no more with it. (*Sighs*) What is left me? I cannot bear to look, or be looked upon. I will hurry down to my old house, take a twelve-months provision into it, cut down my drawbridge, run wild about my garden, which shall grow as wild as myself; then will I curse the world, and every individual in it; and when my rage and spirits fail me, I will be found dead among the nettles and thistles, a woeful example of the baseness and treachery of one sex, and of the falsehood, lying, perjury, deceit, impudence, and damnation of the other. (*Exit*)

After Sparkish has congratulated both couples Miss Peggy speaks the closing lines as epilogue.

Unlike the alteration of Shirley's *The Gamester,* Garrick's production of *The Country Girl* was an immediate hit. There were 14 performances of the comedy in the first season (1766–67) and the management continued it in repertory for six seasons, a total of 28 performances. We have noted the adapter's concern over the reception which his audiences accorded the Shirley comedy, and we have seen how he profited by that experience in *The Country Girl.* In the latter he gave the audience what it liked and wanted to see, and the result was gratifying in terms of the box office.

In the course of the fifteen-year period covered by these alterations we have seen the increasing demands placed upon an adapter trying to please the growing sensitivity of the audience. In the early treatment given *Every Man in His Humour* and the respect shown the two Fletcher comedies in alteration we saw how successfully the balance was maintained between the spirit of these old comedies and prevailing audience taste. Kitely, Don John, Leon — these became three of Garrick's really great comedy roles. They could always be relied upon to draw crowds to Drury Lane. But there is a limit beyond which alteration could not go, and we have seen how the audience prevailed over the good sense of the adapter. In each succeeding production the omissions and the language of sentimentalism which made up the greater part of the additions were significant indications of the direct influence exerted by the box office. For Garrick, the conflict reached the breaking point in his alteration of *The Gamester.* In *The Country Girl* it is resolved in the complete capitulation of the author to the manager.

Horace Walpole may represent the taste of many theatregoers in Garrick's time when he declares himself opposed to certain of the old plays on grounds of taste. Writing of the work of Beaumont and Fletcher, he said,

To produce a good play from one of theirs, I believe the only way would be, to take their plan, draw the characters from nature, omit all that is improbable, and entirely rewrite the dialogue; for their language is at once hard and pert, vulgar and incorrect, and has neither the pathos of the preceding age nor the elegance of this. They are grossly indelicate, and yet have no simplicity. There is a wide difference between unrefined and vicious indecency: the first would not invent fig-leaves; the latter tears holes in them after they are invented.[40]

This was the majority verdict from the audience concerning most of the old plays by the close of Garrick's management at Drury Lane. Alteration was a practical necessity, and only occasionally can the voice of the opposition be heard. Listening to the protests of those who affected good taste, we are reminded of the comment which Sheridan placed in the mouth of Mr. Sneer: "Our prudery . . . is just on a par with the artificial bashfulness of a Courtesan, who encreases the blush on her cheek in an exact proportion to the diminution of her modesty."[41]

The difficulty of the task confronting the adapter is shown best perhaps by the fact that of the 64 altered plays produced during Garrick's management only 24 were successful at the box office. It was indeed, as Mr. Dangle said, "a bungling reformation!"

v. Bon Ton

Tonight our Bayes, with bold, but careless tints,
Hits off a sketch or two, like Darly's prints.
Should connoisseurs allow his rough draughts strike 'em,
'Twill be Bon Ton to see 'em, and to like 'em.
                    Prologue to Bon Ton, *by George Colman, Esq.*

AUDIENCE taste in any age is difficult to appraise, but none
is more so perhaps than that of eighteenth century London.
Her contemporaries often seem to us to have been occupied
continuously with evaluations of this taste, usually in most
uncomplimentary terms. Articles deploring the "Present
State of the Stage," the fate of which is determined by an
ignorant and tyrannical patronage, are almost as numerous
as the short-lived newspapers and periodicals in which many
of them appeared. What such criticism lacked in addition to
perspective was an honest recognition of the fact that it spoke
for particular groups which it had nominated as the sole
arbiters of taste. Theophilus Cibber in his "Preface to the
Town" wrote:

This Phrase (the Town) has been made frequent Use of without any determinate Meaning; and is often considered in a
vague, or partial Sense; — ask an Author, or an Actor,
separately, what is meant thereby? Each will tell you ('tis
probable) that, "by the Town is meant, the Judging Few." —
as They will style their Friends; — that is, in other Words,
those, who approve, and cry up their several Performances: —
Ask the theatrical Managers, they will give that as the Sentiments of the Town, which, perhaps, is only what they wish to
have said; such Chat as is ecchoed, and re-ecchoed, by their
particular Intimates, or theatrical mercenaries: — But to drop
them, — I think, the Town may be supposed to include all

Degrees of Persons, from the highest Nobleman, to the lowly
Artisan, etc., who, in their different Stations, are Encouragers
of dramatic Performances: — Thus all persons, who pay for
their Places, whether Noble, Gentle, or Simple, who fill the
Boxes, Pit, and Galleries, in a theatrical Sence, form the Town.[1]

The younger Cibber need not detain us with gossip of playhouse politics, but in his forthright statement that the taste
of the "Town" is determined at the box office in terms of
all paying patrons is the key to any right appraisal. The
majority of playhouse patrons in any age attends in blissful
ignorance of prevailing fashions in criticism, desires only to
be caught up for a few hours in the magic of dramatic entertainment, and judges all it sees and hears upon the fascina-
tion of those hours.

The difficulty of contemporary appraisal is reflected in the
confusion in the minds of authors, actors, and management.
In 1735 Henry Fielding openly confessed that he could not
measure it and humorously described the plight of an author:

> If wit he aims at, you the traps can show;
> If serious, he is dull; if humorous, low.
> Some would maintain one laugh throughout a play,
> Some would be grave and bear fine things away.
> How is it possible at once to please
> Tastes so directly opposite as these?[2]

Twenty years later Warburton was complaining of the
fickleness of Garrick's audiences and hinting at the probable
fate of a tragedy by Home:

I hope and make no question, but that "Agis," under your direction, will better deserve the applause of the public than "Douglas." But dramatic writers are often used like ladies of pleasure:
they are received with rapture and enthusiasm by the public on
their first appearance, but on farther acquaintance are received
very coolly, though they have indeed by this time greatly
improved themselves in the *art of pleasing*.[3]

There was even a marked difference between the audiences

of the several theatres. Thomas Davies recalled that Delane's success as Alexander the Great "brought him from Goodman's fields to the more critical audience of Covent-garden." [4] When Garrick rejected Victor's tragedy *Altamira* in 1766, it was with a very practical suggestion.

I gave my advice like a friend, and I pointed out the only method by which Mr. Victor could have any chance to reap advantage from the performance; but, it seems, I must be pressed into the service and solicited to contradict myself. Previous to Mr. Faulkner's seeing the play, I gave my sincere sentiments upon it, and which I still maintain, viz. — that "Altamira" will have a better chance of succeeding at Covent Garden than with us, and that I am certain that "Cleone," "Virginius," "The Double Mistake," and many others, would not have been well received at Drury-lane. [5]

A week later the disappointed author expressed his chagrin and enlarged upon the manager's meaning.

after the interview with Mr. Garrick, then the expected consequences was to be sent . . . that on a serious reading, though the tragedy was something better for the alterations, yet there was something dangerous in the fable that would not escape an audience inclined to severity, and such are the audiences at Drury-lane; therefore the only change for lenity was at Covent Garden, where pieces of little merit have been received with favour. [6]

That Garrick was correct in thus distinguishing between audiences at the two Patent theatres in this particular period his disappointed treasurer knew only too well and estimated the criticism of his tragedy accordingly.

The testimony of Henry Woodward in the litigation which enveloped Covent Garden under the management of Colman, Powell, Rutherford, and Harris is eloquent in the glimpse it affords of dwindling spectators and its implications as to the quality of those patrons who remained loyal to the new management. After declaring that the "time of the company and

the chief expence of the Theatre" has been squandered by
Colman on "plays which instead of novelty had been ex-
hibited so often at Drury Lane Th[eatre] as to be stale and
Dull long before they appeared at Cov[ent] G. [arden,]"
Woodward further testified:

when the representatives of John Rich Esq sold the Patents &
concerns of Cov G Th . . . there were many plays & operas
that generally & respectively brought full houses which Col by
his cond^t soon red^d to four in number . . . Love in a Vill Maid
of the Mill Busy Body & Every Man in his humour & even
each of those Col hath worn down to the unprofitable state of
being scarc[sic]able to produce a saving house for often a play
in which Powell had been advertis'd to act for some time if it
so happened that the Boxes were not well taken or that there
was a prospect of an indifferent house that Powell or some
other person that he could prevail upon was alledged to have
been taken ill the night prevly which necessarily changed the
play(,)the public being thus disap^d the exigence was gen^{ly}
supplied by acting at such short notice one of the before mentioned pieces. & it occurred so often that at length they lost
their power in drawing audiences(;) and which falling off in
attraction is of great loss not only by destroying a valuable
exhibition but also by hurting the minds and sowering the tem-
pers of usefull persons.[7]

Despite the formal pretension of his public utterances,
Garrick shared Fielding's sense of frustration in estimating
the taste of his audiences. His well-known lines in the Epilogue to Arthur Murphy's *All in the Wrong* (Drury Lane,
1761) distribute the degrees of spectator comprehension as
follows:

What shall we do your different tastes to hit?
You relish satire (*to the pit*) you ragouts of wit — (*to the
  Boxes*)
Your taste is humour and high-season'd joke. (*First Gallery*)
You call for hornpipe, and for hearts of oak. (*Second Gallery*) [8]

The gallery taste in farce is described by Sophia in Act I of *The Male Coquette* as she wears "the breeches."

Sophia: I presume, Sir, you never was out of *England* — (*Picking her teeth*)

Tukely: I presume, Sir, that you are mistaken. — I never was so foolishly fond of my own country, to think that nothing good was to be had out of it; nor so shamefully ungrateful to it, to prefer the vices and fopperies of every other nation to the peculiar advantages of my own.

Sophia: Ha, ha! well said, old England, i'faith — Now madam, if this gentleman would put his speech into a farce, and properly lard it with roast beef, and liberty, I wou'd engage the galleries wou'd roar and haloo at it for half an hour together. — Ha, ha, ha.[9]

And yet in the preceding chapter we noted times when Garrick felt the public pulse, only to learn that he had been deceived. This was a struggle between the "author" and the "manager" within him. Certainly as a manager bowing to what he sensed to be the public taste he had his difficult moments. Such a one must have been that in which he received his brother George's report on the promising first-night of Joseph Reed's tragedy (March 28, 1767). It brought the strongly-worded reply from the manager: "And does '*Dido*' please? Good God! — and will they come twice to see it? Good God! it is time to leave the stage, if such a performance can stand upon its legs. Good God!"[10]

But after all this is a private opinion expressed to a brother. Against it we should place his answer to John Cleland, whose tragedy *Titus Vespasion* (printed 1754) he rejected. Cleland had written to complain of Garrick's policies regarding new scripts as follows:

Nor did I ever once entertain a spark of resentment against you for your rejection of that luckless play, in which I aimed at a medium between the frigidity and flightiness of the sonorous jargon of our modern tragedies, and the ridiculously familiar chit-chat of Fontenelle, which is almost as unnatural, since great dramatic situations require greatness of language. But then buskins are not stilts. Beside, you took care to give me ample revenge. You brought on "Boadicea," "Barbarossa," and how many more, only fit to make an ice-house of a summer theatre, if there was such a thing as taste existing.[11]

And for once the manager's guard was down! His reply is most illuminating:

Why do you raise the ghosts of Boadicea and Barbarossa to haunt me? If I had not performed the first, I should have been a very shallow politician; and if I had not received the last, I should have suffered as a manager, for no tragedy had more success.[12]

That Garrick had quite definite ideas as to what constituted good drama we already know. When called upon he could reduce his ideal of comedy, for instance, to the simple formula used in rejecting one of Mrs. Sheridan's plays. Addressing her current champion, Mrs. Benjamin Victor, he wrote,

that there were characters in the Play I allow'd but I thought they were not well employ'd: I felt the scenes languid for want of an interesting fable, & that Spirit of dialogue or Vis comica which was to be found in many Scenes of the Discovery. . . . How could Mrs. Sheridan imagine that I wanted the passions to be interested? I should as soon expect to have my laughter raised in a tragedy — I said indeed that the Comedy wanted interest, but not of ye *Passions* — I meant a Comic interest, resulting from ye varying humours of the Characters thrown into spirited action & brought into interesting Situations, naturally arising from a well constructed fable or Plot — This, with a good Moral, deduc'd from ye whole, is all I wish or look for in a *COMEDY*.[13]

Such a definition is almost as perfect in its simplicity as that of Goldsmith, who wrote, "The term 'genteel comedy' was then unknown amongst us, and little more was desired by an audience than nature and humour, in whatever walks of life they were most conspicuous," [14] or that of Samuel Foote when he asked, "Don't Folks come to a Play to laugh? And if that End be obtained, what matters it how?" [15]

Although as a manager Garrick produced some thirty-five sentimental plays ranging from Edward Moore's *The Foundling* (1747–48) through the works of such authors as Whitehead, Cumberland, and Kelly, to Mrs. Cowley's *The Runaway* (1775–76), his own sympathies were not with the ventures and he hoped to wean his audiences from the type. On occasion he publicly lashed at the taste for the sentimental, as in the scene between Sir Macaroni and Lady Fuz in *A Peep Behind the Curtain*. The Lady and Sir Toby her husband have brought Sir Macaroni to a morning rehearsal at Drury Lane.

> *Lady Fuz:* (*Looking about with a glass*) My dear Sir Toby, You may be as sarcastical as you please; but I protest a playhouse is a prodigious odd sort of a thing, now there is nobody in it — is it not, Sir Macaroni?
> *Sir Mac:* O yes, and a prodigious odd sort of a thing when 'tis full too. I abominate a playhouse; my ingenious countreymen [*sic*] have no taste now for the high season'd comedies; and I am sure that I have none for the pap and loplolly of our present writers.
>
> .   .   .   .   .
>
> *Sir Mac:* A play house in England is to me as dull as a church, and fit only to sleep in.[16]

In *The Theatrical Candidates* Tragedy taunts her rival Comedy with

> *Tragedy: You* can be wise too: nay, a *thief* can be!
>   Wise with stale sentiments all stol'n from me:
>   Which long cast off, from my heroic verses,
>   Have stuff'd your motley, dull sententious farces:
>   The town grew sick!
> *Comedy:* For all this mighty pother,

> Have you not laugh'd with one eye, cry'd with t'other?
> *Tragedy:* In all the realms of nonsense, can there be
>   A monster like your comic-tragedy?
> *Comedy:* O yes, my dear! — your tragic-comedy.[17]

It is true that Garrick could write to John Hoadly saying, "I rejoice that you wept at y West Indian," [18] but it is equally true that he could address Charles Jenner in the hope

> that You would think of giving a Comedy of Character to ye Theatre one calculated to make an Audience Laugh than cry — the Comedie Larmoyant is getting too much ground upon Us, & if those who can write the better Species of ye Comic drama don't make a Stand for ye Genuine Comedy & vis comica the Stage in a few years, will be (as Hamlet says) like Niobe all tears.[19]

In *A Peep behind the Curtain* Garrick satirizes not only the extravagancies of Italian opera, as he did in writing,

> They say, a certain dame they Op'ra call,
>   Monopolizes all your favors.
> When passions' storms should rise, Signoras squall,
>   And wit and humour's moved to quavers.[20]

but also the taste of the town for musical entertainments in general.

> *Author:* I make Orpheus see in my hell all sorts of people, of all degrees, and occupations; ay, and of both sexes: that's not very unnatural, I believe; there shall be very good company too, I assure you; *High Life below Stairs,* as I call it, ha, ha, ha! you take me — a double edge — no boys play — rip and tear — the times require it — *forte* — *fortissime* —
>
> *Patent:* Won't it be too *forte?* — Take care, Mr. Glib, not to make it so much above proof that the boxes can't taste it; take care of empty boxes.
>
> *Author:* Empty boxes! I'll take care that my Cerebrus alone shall fill the boxes for a month.[21]

Such instances probably prompted John Hoadly to declare that "The stage, by your means, and the good taste you have introduced, is not so much the subject of real satire and burlesque, as you found it thirty years ago; though galloping down hill apace, with the help of those false syrens who should assist it, Music, Painting, Mechanics, etc." [22] Hoadly suggesting a burlesque sketch for Thomas King wrote Garrick assuring him that "There may be some satire against the bad taste of the town, that even listen after Foote's intended puppet-show, and the other more costly puppet-show of both the managers." [23]

As for the ever-popular pantomime, while Garrick realized the necessity for it in terms of his box office, he publicly expressed the hope that this form might eventually take third place in importance in the repertory. When *The Theatrical Candidates,* Tragedy and Comedy, ask the audience to choose between them, Harlequin comes bounding upon the stage to interpose his suit.

Harlequin: O yes, we're three!
   Your votes and int'rest, pray, for me! (*to the pit*)
Tragedy: What fall'n so low to cope with thee?
Harlequin: Ouy, Ouy!
Comedy: Alas, poor We! (*Shrugs her shoulders and laughs*)
Harlequin: Tho' *this* maid scorns me, *this* with passion flies out,
   Tho' *you* may laugh, and *you* may cry your eyes out;
   For all your airs, sharp looks, and sharper nails,
   Draggled you were, till I held up your tails:
   Each friend I have above, whose voices so loud is:
   Will never give me up for two such dowdies;
   She's grown so grave, and *she* so cross and bloody,
   Without my help your brains will all be muddy:
   Deep thought and politics so stir your gall
   When you come here you should not think at all;
   And I'm the best for that; be my protectors!

In Harlequin's song which immediately follows we have the situation explained.

> Shou'd Harlequin be banish'd hence,
> Quit the place to wit and sense,
> What wou'd be the consequence?
>> Empty houses,
>> You and spouses,
> And your pretty children dear,
>> Ne'er wou'd come,
>> Leave your home,
> Unless that I came after . . .

But finally Mercury returns bearing Apollo's decision (and Garrick's hope?).

> You, Tragedy, must weep, and love, and rage,
> And keep your turn, but not engross the stage!
> And you, gay Madam, *gay* to give delight,
> Must not, turn'd prude, encroach upon her right:
> Each sep'rate charm: *you* grave, *you* light as feather,
> Unless that Shakespear bring you both together;
> On both, by nature's grant, that conq'ror seizes,
> To use you *when,* and *where,* and *how* he pleases.
>> For you, Monsieur! (*to Har.*) whenever farce or song
> Or sick or tir'd — then you, without a tongue,
> Or with one if you please — in Drury Lane,
> As Locum Tenens, may hold up their train.
>> Thus spoke Apollo — but he added too,
> Vain his decrees until confirm'd by you! [24]

A final glance at Garrick's impressions of audience taste is afforded by one of his notes on the art of acting. Here he is interested in the contrast between the acceptance accorded actors as opposed to writers, between acting and the play performed.

It is very strange that the bulk of an audience will be satisfied and applaud very indifferent Acting, when they seldom excuse very indifferent new performances. What can be the reason? Is it that the presence of an Actor creates a kind of regard which is wanting in the performance from the author's ever keeping out of sight. The clapping of hands in an audience is a kind of Dram-Drinking — the actor's spirits are raised for the present and if he is not very well fortified in understanding (which is not often the case) he is ever craving after it: which in the end will destroy him.[25]

When we consider the opinions of men outside the bounds of theatrical management, who were at the same time authors or critics, we find their views to be similar to those of Garrick and Fielding but on the whole more gloomy. John Brown, whose work *An Estimate of the Manners and Principles of the Times* (1757) passed through seven editions in its first year, found a ray of hope for audiences which responded to Garrick's management.

Let us then search the theatre for the remains of a manly taste; and here, apparently at least, it must be acknowledged, we shall find it. A great genius hath arisen to dignify the stage, who, when it was sinking into the lowest insipidity, restored it to the fulness of its antient splendour, and, with a variety of powers beyond example, established *Nature, Shakespeare,* and *himself.*[26]

Dr. Brown is careful to limit audience appreciation of such a renaissance, however, to the "judicious few."

But as the attractions of the theatre arise from a complication of causes, beyond those of any other entertainment; so while the judicious critic admires *his original excellencies,* it may well be quetsioned, whether the crowd be not drawn by certain secondary circumstances, rather than by a discernment of *his real powers.* Need we any other proof of this than the conduct of his fashionable hearers, who sit with the same face of admiration at Lear, an opera, and a pantomime?[27]

Thomas Davies, who quotes from the Estimate, calls this passage "an unaccountable mixture of praise and censure on the actor and his auditors, where truth is hazarded, and satire ill applied." He is quite certain that Garrick's performance of *King Lear* was justly appreciated by the audi-

ence, "even to the shedding of tears," and that these
spectators were not "equally affected with an opera or a
pantomime!" [28] And yet there must have been a considerable
element of truth in Brown's statement. Consider the lines
written by Garrick "to Lady Glyn upon her laughing at
King Lear,"

> Why would you cruel Lady Glyn,
> At Old Lear's Madness smirk & grin,
>   And harrow up poor David,
> He cares not, when the house is cramm'd,
> Tho he by all the Wits is damn'd,
>   If he by you is saved!
>
> By the Same Means, were you but kind,
> You might both vex, & charm my mind;
>   Tis what my wishes drive at;
> For if by Fashion I'm decreed,
> In publick by your Smiles to bleed,
>   They'll heal my wounds in private. [29]

or the following lines from his *Epilogue to Virginia* (1754),

> May I approach unto the boxes, pray —
> And there search out a judgment on the play?
> In vain, alas! I should attempt to find it —
> Fine ladies *see* a play, but never *mind* it —
> 'Tis vulgar to be moved by *acted* passion,
> Or form opinions, 'till they're fixed by fashion. [30]

Thomas Wilkes was another who deplored the taste and
capacity of Garrick's audiences, but he placed the blame upon
the middle classes.

The state of the Stage in this kingdom is truly unhappy, the
common people have strange notions of its want of importance.
These notions it is scarcely possibly to remove: for where popular prejudice has reigned so long as to obtain the sanction of
hereditary right, reason languishes in a state of captivity; the
intellects are manacled; judgment driven into exile. In this

case, great must be the abilities that can awake the slumbering senses, break the fetters of prepossession, and so far clear the mind, that every object may be viewed in a distinct and impartial light.[31]

Most of these writers agreed that their theatres should be instruments for instruction in public morality. The following is typical of their pronouncements:

If the stage should be really what the generality of our polite writers tells us it ought to be, a school of agreeable morality, it naturally follows that those plays are the best which afford us the most pleasing instruction, and that it is neither a strict adherence to the severity of critical discipline, nor a slavish imitation of the antients, which can possibly constitute the excellence of dramatic literature.[32]

Such standard doctrine is qualified, however, by Thomas Davies, who marks a distinguishing feature of English audiences as contrasted with their French neighbors.

The Frenchman, when he goes to a play, seems to make his entertainment a matter of importance. The long speeches in the plays of Corneille, Racine, Crebillon, and Voltaire, which would disgust an English ear, are extremely pleasing to our light neighbours: they sit in silence, and enjoy the beauty of sentiment, and energy of language; and are taught habitually to cry at scenes of distress. The Englishman looks upon the theatre as a place of amusement; he does not expect to be alarmed with terror, or wrought upon by scenes of commiseration; but he is surprised into the feeling of those passions, and sheds tears because he cannot avoid it. The theatre, to most Englishmen, becomes a place of instruction by chance.[33]

Thus the theorizing of the critics must be taken with the proverbial "grain of salt," and we may suppose that Hugh Kelly's lines in the *Epilogue to A Word to the Wise* reflect the true conditions as suggested by Davies.

Modish Divines, at Court and in the City,
Are in their pulpits hum'rous, gay, and witty —

They've now chang'd hands, the stage and pulpit teaching,
Sermons are plays, and plays are merely preaching —
A Word to the Wise, a pretty pert adviser!
As if 'twere possible to make you wiser:
Yet as each here may think the poet labours
Not to teach him, but to instruct his neighbours:
As the bright tenants of that splendid row
Sneer on the pit, for beings much below:
And these in turn, as things in order move,
Toss up the sneer to those who mount above:
The gods look down, and let their pity fall
On front, side, green, stage-boxes, pit and all.[34]

A further group of witnesses remains to be heard from before we permit the audiences to speak for themselves. Once again the group will include some critics and authors, but for the most part it will consist of the testimony of individuals who set down their impressions from attendance at the theatres as spectators.

The earliest of these is the author of a letter "On the Present State of the Theatre" in 1747. He describes himself as a "Gentleman in Town" who writes to "his Friend in the West" to tell of the triumph of Rich in filling his roster at Covent Garden with the famous four — Quin, Garrick, Mrs. Cibber, and Mrs. Pritchard. He concludes by saying,

The Consequence has been, that the Stage was never, in my Memory, so fashionable; not even in the Time of Mrs. *Oldfield's* highest Fame. A good Taste both of Acting and of Plays themselves, is much more general than I ever expected to have seen it; and those who are skilled in such Matters, tell me, that Rich will be a greater Gainer this Season than has been known for these many years; and that too, without the Assistance of almost a single Dancer. In short, he has put the Opera out of Countenance; and even endangered the Empire of Whisk [pantomime] itself.[35]

Here is one instance at least in which the hope of an earlier

pamphleteer was partially realized. In 1744 another scribbler
had inquired,

Which would be more likely to gain you a full House Tomor-
row, the *Fair Penitent,* for Instance, with Mrs. *Cibber,* Mr.
Garrick, and Mr. *Sheridan,* as the Town thinks they have a
Right to see them all three together; this Play alone, I say, or
the *Alchymist,* as you have it now perform'd, with one of your
Pantomimes? Who is there but wou'd crowd to see the one, and
who, I had almost said, wou'd even be hired to sit out the
other? Here then, Sir, lies a plain and open Method for you
to get good Houses and good Credit, to receive at once People's
Money and their Thanks.[36]

Such must have been gratifying news to friends in the country, whose confusion was to be described in later years by
George Colman when he wrote,

There are many modern compositions seen with delight at the
theatre, which sicken on the taste in the perusal; and the honest
country gentleman who has not been present at the representation, wonders with what his London friends have been so
entertained; and is as much perplexed at the *Town-manner* of
writing as Mr. Smith in the Rehearsal.[37]

"Theatricus," writing in the *London Chronicle,*[38] reviewed
the "revolutions of the stage" from 1700 to 1763 and gave
Garrick credit for having reestablished some semblance of
taste in the theatre. He remembered the days, however,
when farce was "seldom used" and considered it to be "the
gleanings of the Drama." He agreed with John Dryden that
the generality of those now in possession of the stage are
"a compound of extravagancies, fit only to entertain such
people as are judges of neither men nor manners," and in
particular scorned Macklin's *The True-born Irishman.* Finally, he considered Pantomime to be one of the principal
factors in the vitiated taste of the Town.

Perhaps as good a sample of the impression made upon
an individual spectator as we shall find is that summarized
in doggerel verse and printed in *The Gentleman's Magazine*

(January, 1767) under the title "Upon the new Performances exhibited at the two Theatres this Winter." The
author invites the public to weigh with him the season's
productions at both Patent theatres. "Of *Quantity* we've had
enough," he cries, "the *Quality* must mark the stuff."

> *Imprimis* — at Old Drury Lane Royal,
> Have they to Shakespeare been so loyal?
> They gave us for a charming piece
> (But Poets *swans* are always *geese*)
> *A whore of Wycherley's lewd pen
> Chang'd to a flabby *Magdalen.*
> To answer this at t'other house,
> The mountain labour'd with a mouse.
> What money, patience, time, it cost us,
> To see dull plays, with duller *Faustus:*
> At which, as wit with Drury scarce is,
> They fir'd at once two pot gun farces:
> ‡One was too *high,* and one too § *low:*
> *Buckborse* wrote this, and that *Rousseau.*
>
> *Beard* for a while seem'd much afraid,
> 'Till out he brought *Th' Accomplish'd Maid:*
> At whom, old Slyboots, General G——k,
> Push'd, with his bouncing *Earl of Warwick:*
> But such a *Maid,* and such an *Earl!*
> A flimsy bully, piss-tail girl!
> Take 'em, thou ghost of *Edmund Curl.*
>
> But now have at your eyes and ears;
> The high-puff'd *Cymon* next appears:
> Earth, heav'n, and hell, are all united,
> The upper gall'ry, so delighted!
> They sing, they dance, they sink, they fly!
> For *scenes, show, dresses,* all defy:
> And then the *wit* and *humour* — stay —
> We'll talk of *them* another day;
> With both, the *School for Guardians* stor'd,
> You'd sware 'twas written by a Lord:

---

* The Country Girl   ‡ The Cunning Man   § Neck or Nothing

So fine the *wit,* so fine the *plot,*
You have 'em, and you have 'em not:
The *plot* and *wit* make such a pother,
You cannot see the one for t'other:
Like ghosts they're here, and now they're there;
'Tis *M——y* now, and now *Moliere:*
'Tis, 'tis neither, *English, French,*
And all to serve a pretty wench. . . .

Some of the German visitors quoted by Kelly [39] would have agreed heartily with the sentiments of this spectator. In the eyes of one German the English repertory at both Patent houses was weak "not only in comedy, but in the other lighter types of plays as well." [40] Another said that if a Shakespearean play was produced, it had to be brilliantly staged and interspersed with songs, dances and other divertissements between the acts in order to keep the audience awake: "I have seen various Shakespeare plays performed before audiences which were conspicuously bored, although a Garrick or a Woodward employed his talents to make them pleasing." [41]

If, therefore, this necessarily brief survey of contemporary opinion regarding audience taste has accomplished little else, it ought to have made us conscious once again of the supreme truth, commonsense justice and finality of Dr. Johnson's summing-up in the familiar lines,

Ah! let not censure term our fate our choice,
The stage but ecchoes back the public voice;
The drama's laws, the drama's patrons give,
For we that live to please, must please to live.[42]

Now we are ready to turn to the judgments pronounced by the audiences themselves over the twenty-nine-year period of Garrick's management of Drury Lane, judgments made by no rule save the simple enjoyment of an evening's entertainment. Allardyce Nicoll in the two volumes of his *History* which cover this period [43] has surveyed the London theatre repertoires by selecting certain theatrical seasons at regular intervals and discussing the plays represented there according to type. Unfortunately no complete list had been compiled for the period. Genest's entries were extensive but in no way accounted for the full production schedule. It was not until the publication by Dougald MacMillan of the *Drury Lane Calendar* in 1938 that an exhaustive statistical appraisal of Drury Lane productions became possible. While the *Drury Lane Calendar* leaves much to be desired, especially in its omission of many entr'acte features, entertainments, (which had at times a drawing power not to be underestimated), it does represent the full history of main attractions over the twenty-nine years of Garrick's management. MacMillan himself suggests the method of the present survey and uses it briefly in his Introduction to the *Calendar* to summarize production history.[44]

The complete repertory of Drury Lane as compiled from the *Drury Lane Calendar* will be found in Appendix C. It is intended as a statistical survey of the taste of eighteenth century audiences. A similar survey for Covent Garden Theatre is based upon the incomplete entries in Genest's *Some Account of the English Stage*. The latter will not be used at any point in our discussion, but its tabulations should be of interest for purposes of comparison. The tables in the Appendix are designed to include the original date of composition, the number of seasons the play remained in repertory, the greatest number of performances in a single season and the date of that "best" season, the total number of performances given during Garrick's management, and the number of performances (if any) in which the Manager's own acting could be expected to have been the drawing power at the box office.

Fixing our thought for the moment upon the productions achieving the greatest number of performances in the twenty-nine-year period, the general popularity of the types is clearly defined and represents what we have already anticipated. Four pantomimes head the list, three by Henry

Woodward and one by Garrick. The most popular one was Woodward's *Queen Mab* which outdistanced all the others by 52 performances. Two farces, Ravenscroft's *The Anatomist* (1697) and Garrick's *Lethe* (1740), Garrick's spectacle *The Jubilee* (1769), and the ballad-opera *The Devil to Pay* (1731) all come before the first dramatic effort of any real worth, Shakespeare's tragedy *Romeo and Juliet* (in Garrick's version) which totaled 142 performances in 25 seasons. In other words, until we arrive in descending scale at this tragedy, audience preference is overwhelmingly in favor of the afterpieces of the repertoire.

Among the productions attaining 75 or more performances the figures for the types vary only slightly — tragedies 8, comedies 12, farces 7, musicals 5, and pantomimes 7. We should distinguish, however, between those attractions which were popular for a season or several seasons and those which became a more permanent part of the repertoire. After all, the longevity of a piece in the theatre is a more convincing test in matters of audience taste.

The following tabulation will serve as a summary of the statistical evidence to be found in Appendix C.

Dramatic Production at Drury Lane, 1747–1776

Type of Play	Total Produced	Number Successful	Old Plays and Alterations	Number Successful	New Plays Produced	Number Successful
Tragedy and History	84	60	48	32	36	28
Comedy	113	77	73	51	40	26
Farce	91	33	25	10	66	23
Ballad— Opera and Other Musicals	49	34	11	8	38	26
Pantomime and Spectacle	39	27	12	6	27	21

Thus if we assume that 9 or more performances marked the difference between current success or failure, we note that, of the 84 tragedies and histories brought forward by Garrick, 60 could be termed successful and had a better than average chance of gaining a place in his repertoire. Of the 60, we see that 32 were stock plays, revivals, alterations or adaptations, while 28 plays written and produced within the limits of his management were also successful.

Thirty-three authors are represented in the successful dramas, but 23 of them are limited to a single winning entry. Of the remainder, Shakespeare of course leads with 13 dramas, followed by John Home with 5, Nicholas Rowe and Arthur Murphy with 3 each, and Otway, Southerne and Hill, Brown, William Whitehead, Francklin, and Dow with 2 each. Of the Shakespearean plays 9 are tragedies and 4 are chronicle plays. Among the tragedies we note that although his *Romeo and Juliet* was played 142 times in 25 seasons, his *Hamlet* no doubt equaled it in popularity in that its 116 performances span all 29 years of the management, with Garrick's appearance in the title role limited to 56 times. The least popular were *Timon of Athens* (Richard Cumberland) and *Coriolanus,* both of which passed the 9-performance mark but were dropped in their initial season; *Antony and Cleopatra; Henry V.* In order of popularity the plays were: *Romeo and Juliet* and *Hamlet; Richard III* and *Macbeth; King Lear; Othello* and *Cymbeline; Henry VIII; Henry IV, Pt. 2; King John; Henry IV, Pt. 1; Timon of Athens; Coriolanus; Antony and Cleopatra; Henry V.* All tragedies were presented in altered versions with the exception of *Othello* and *Coriolanus* and, in part, *Hamlet.*[45]

Although John Home follows Shakespeare in the number of successful Drury Lane productions, both Rowe and Murphy outdistanced him in performances and in the number of seasons in which their offering appeared. Only two of Home's tragedies extended beyond a single season: *Douglas* ran for seven seasons and *Agis* for two. On the other hand, we must place Rowe far ahead of Arthur Murphy. Rowe's *The Fair Penitent, Jane Shore,* and *Tamerlane* remained in the repertoire for 23, 24, and 28 seasons, respectively. Audience preference was decidedly in favor of the older tragic writers. Otway's *The Orphan* and *Venice Preserv'd,* and even the production of Congreve's *The Mourning Bride* (79 performances in 24 seasons), outrank Rowe's pieces in popularity. Together with Southerne's *Oroonoko* and *The Fatal Marriage* the plays of these writers achieved more performances and remained in the repertoire longer than any contemporary works excepting those of Aaron Hill. Two of Hill's adaptations, *Zara* (1735) and *Merope* (1749), rank with the older writers' record. *Zara* had 64 performances in 23 seasons and *Merope* 59 in 15 seasons.

Arthur Murphy outranked contemporary authors not only in the number of productions but also in performances and in lasting power. Little difference is to be noted in the record between the popularity of *The Grecian Daughter, The Orphan of China,* and *Zenobia,* except that Garrick's acting of Zamti accounted for half of the total performances of *The Orphan of China.* This tragedy remained in repertoire two years longer than the others. In order of their popularity, then, we may group the tragedy writers as follows: Shakespeare; Otway; Hill and Rowe; Southerne; Congreve; Murphy; Francklin, Whitehead, and Brown; Home; Dow.

Tragedy, however, was not the most popular type of entertainment for eighteenth century audiences despite the outstanding performances of Garrick, Barry, and the "tragedy queens" of the age. A glimpse at the total repertoire will give us an interesting sidelight on how management tried to meet the problem. If we consult the *Drury Lane Calendar* we shall see that Garrick's regular policy was to "prop-up" his tragedies, especially the new ones, quite soon after their first appearance. The comparative strength of any tragedy may be judged by the number of performances it achieved before a significant and time-tested afterpiece was added as its companion. Dr. Johnson's tragedy, *Mahomet and Irene* came out at Drury Lane on February 6, 1749. It was a comparative failure even though it managed to attain the required nine performances. The drama managed six performances on its own, the sixth being a benefit night for Johnson. But with the seventh night, February 16, the highest ranking afterpiece of all, Ravenscroft's *The Anatomist* (157 performances in 19 seasons), was added. The next night it was Garrick's own comedy *The Lying Valet* (106 performances in 23 seasons), and on the ninth and final evening for the Johnson tragedy it was Fielding's *The Virgin Unmask'd* (58 performances in 14 seasons). Even with the help of these vital pieces of entertainment the Johnson tragedy was doomed.

Or let us take for an example the very successful production of Aaron Hill's *Merope* which was brought out in the same season as Johnson's play. The first season saw 11 performances in all; but after the ninth night the tragedy was reinforced by coupling it with Charles Coffey's *The Devil to Pay* (143 performances in 28 seasons) for the tenth, and a command performance for the Prince and Princess of Wales secured the final night for *Merope* alone. In its second season, 1749–50, *Merope* was given twice by itself, but for the remaining seven times Garrick supported it with *The Lying Valet, The Savoyard Travellers* (two nights), *The Anatomist, The Chaplet* (two nights), and *Lethe*. The third season saw three performances of *Merope*, two of them with successful afterpieces and the third with a performance of the second most popular pantomime in the history of the management, Woodward's *The Genii* (207 performances in 12 seasons). But by the fourth season, 1753–54, *Merope* needed something more. It was then advertised to be given "with a procession and sacrifice after the manner of the ancients," [46] and it was played twice with *Lethe* and a final time with Foote's *The Englishman in Paris*. Of the advertisement MacMillan says, "Though the procession and sacrifice were already features of *Merope,* beginning with this season they are advertised in playbills and newspapers more prominently than before." [47]

The tragedies of Shakespeare were "propped-up" even sooner. Garrick's production of *Romeo and Juliet* opened November 29, 1748. Its second performance on December 1 was advertised as performed "with a new masquerade dance," [48] and for the remaining 18 performances that season the record shows the afterpieces to have been *The Lying Valet, The Intriguing Chambermaid* (three times), *The Virgin Unmask'd* (three times), *The School Boy* (two times), *The King and the Miller of Mansfield* (two times), *The Anatomist* (three times), *The Lottery, The Devil to Pay, Lethe,* and a spectacle *The Triumph of Peace.*

The partiality of English audiences for comedy is shown in the fact that the number of comedies which were successful almost equaled the total tragic production good and bad. Out of 113 comedies 77 met with the approval of Drury Lane audiences. Of this number, 51 were plays current in the repertoire inherited by Garrick, or revivals in altered or adapted form; 26 of the comedies were composed and produced during his management; 35 authors in all are represented, with 17 having only one success to their credit. As in the case of tragedy, Shakespeare again heads the list with nine comedies. He is followed by Colley Cibber with seven; Vanbrugh with five (including the Cibber-Vanbrugh comedy *The Provok'd Husband*); Congreve and Foote with four each; Farquhar, Jonson, Mrs. Centlivre, Garrick, Colman, and Cumberland with three each; and Dryden, Fletcher, Steele, Bickerstaffe, Kelly, Murphy, and Moore with two each.

Of the Shakespearean comedies we note that *Much Ado about Nothing* far surpassed all others in popularity. It was played 105 times in 27 seasons with Garrick in the leading role in all but one performance. Even the least popular of the comedies, however, remained in the repertoire for more than a single season. *All's Well that Ends Well* was played nine times in three seasons; *The Winter's Tale* had 25 performances in five seasons; and *Measure for Measure* bettered both these marks with 22 performances in seven seasons. Arranged in order of their popularity they are: *Much Ado about Nothing; The Tempest* (in various altered states, including operatic versions) and *As You Like It; The Merchant of Venice; Twelfth Night* and *The Merry Wives of Windsor; Measure for Measure; The Winter's Tale* (several altered states); *All's Well That Ends Well*.

Colley Cibber's collaboration on the Vanbrugh play outdistanced the six comedies he wrote by himself. *The Provok'd Husband* was performed 82 times in 26 seasons. While he is surpassed in individual comedies by the record of Vanbrugh and that of Congreve, in sheer number of productions Cibber holds the lead. His plays easily fall into order of their popularity: *The Provok'd Husband; The Careless Husband; The Double Gallant* and *Love Makes a Man; Love's Last Shift; She Wou'd and She Wou'd Not; The Refusal*. Individual plays of Vanbrugh and Congreve which enjoyed wider favor with audiences than those of Cibber will of course include *The Provok'd Wife* (95 times in 29 seasons), *The Confederacy* (25 times in 12 seasons), *The Relapse* and *The Mistake* (10 seasons each); and Congreve's *The Way of the World* and *Love for Love* will match all but one of Cibber's plays in performances and number of seasons. *The Old Bachelor* and *The Double-Dealer* were also retained in the repertoire for three and seven years, respectively. Of his contemporaries only Samuel Foote ranks with the older comic writers in number of pro-

ductions, but not in the lasting qualities necessary to gain a
similar place in the repertoire.

In the group represented with three plays each Farquhar
and Ben Jonson lead the others. The former's *The Beaux
Stratagem* was played 100 times in 26 seasons, his *The
Recruiting Officer* 42 times in 18 seasons, and *The Incon-
stant* 20 times in nine. Two of Jonson's comedies became a
permanent part of the repertoire; *Every Man in His
Humour* was played 82 times in 26 seasons and was closely
followed by the 74 performances of *The Alchymist* in 24
seasons. George Colman's adaptation of Jonson's *Epicoene*
was well received by the critics, but it had only nine performances in two seasons. All three of Mrs. Centlivre's
comedies were constant favorites, *The Wonder* being first,
The Busie Body second, and *A Bold Stroke for a Wife*
third in popularity. Garrick, Colman, and Cumberland represent their contemporaries in this group. The collaboration
of the first two in the comedy of *The Clandestine Marriage*
resulted in one of the most popular plays of the management
(87 performances in 11 seasons), while Garrick's *The Lying
Valet* achieved 106 performances in 23 seasons, and Colman's *The Jealous Wife* was played 75 times in 15 seasons.
All of these signify an audience approval which was lasting,
one not as sensational perhaps as that accorded Richard
Cumberland's *The West Indian* (63 performances in six
seasons), but one which certainly outweighs his other pieces,
The Fashionable Lover and *The Choleric Man*.

Fletcher, Dryden, and Steele represent earlier writing in
the next group. Of these Steele easily outdistanced the others
with *The Conscious Lovers* (96 performances in 28 seasons). His *The Funeral* held its own with Dryden's *Amphi-
tryon* and *The Spanish Fryar,* but was overshadowed by the
success of Garrick's playing Leon in Fletcher's *Rule a Wife
and Have a Wife* (50 performances in 17 seasons). With the
exception of Arthur Murphy, none of the contemporary

writers in this group could match their elders. Murphy's *The Way to Keep Him* and *The Old Maid* won a steady following, 65 performances in 16 seasons and 44 in 11 seasons respectively. Kelly is represented by *False Delicacy* and *The School for Wives;* Bickerstaffe by *The Hypocrite* and *'Tis Well 'Tis No Worse;* and Edward Moore by *The Foundling* and *Gil Blas.*

Authors making an outstanding record with one production include Benjamin Hoadly, whose *Suspicious Husband* probably ranks first in audience popularity in all the repertoire (126 performances in 29 seasons); Henry Fielding, whose *The Miser* was played 26 times in 17 seasons; Joseph Addison with *The Drummer,* and George Villiers, Duke of Buckingham, with *The Rehearsal.*

Another indication of audience preference for comedy over tragedy is the fact that, although Garrick still had to resort to reinforcement of his productions by coupling them with a successful afterpiece, this "propping-up" did not have to begin as soon in the production history of comedies. Let us glance at the performance records of some new comedies. Edward Moore's *The Foundling* was produced February 13, 1748, and ran for 12 performances without the aid of an established afterpiece. It was withdrawn, however, after 11 nights, and two other productions were interposed between the eleventh and twelfth nights of Moore's play. After an evening of *King Lear* with *The Lying Valet* and one of *Hamlet* with *The Double Disappointment, The Foundling* could again be played by itself. But with the thirteenth night *The Dragon of Wantley* had to be added, which appeared again on the fourteenth night. For the fifteenth and final presentation that season the afterpiece was *The Lying Valet.* The next year only three performances were given, each accompanied by an afterpiece of approved standing — *The Virgin Unmask'd, The Lying Valet,* and *The Lottery.*

The history of one of Garrick's most successful plays,

The Clandestine Marriage, is interesting in this respect. It was brought out on February 20, 1766, and ran for 13 consecutive performances. During the initial performances it was bolstered on one evening (the fourth) by a command performance, but no afterpiece was necessary until the eighteenth night. At this time it was billed for two final evenings with Henry Woodward's pantomime *Fortunatus* (158 performances in 14 seasons). Next season it began its run by advertising a new epilogue and Bickerstaffe's popular musical *Daphne and Amintor* (61 performances in seven seasons), and in the two following performances was coupled with James Love's pantomime *The Hermit.* The next three presentations coincided with the first run of Charles Burney's musical *The Cunning Man,* after which Woodward's pantomime *Queen Mab* became its running mate for three nights. Seven additional nights billed the following afterpieces: *The Cunning Man, High Life Below Stairs, Linco's Travels* and *Daphne and Amintor, Flora, Linco's Travels* and *Queen Mab, The Virgin Unmask'd, Linco's Travels,* and *Flora.*

Perhaps because of over familiarity on the part of audiences already partial to Shakespeare, the Shakespearean comedies had to be "propped-up" even sooner than his tragedies. *Much Ado About Nothing,* the most popular of Garrick's productions of Shakespearean comedy, was brought out November 14, 1748, and played for only two nights before an afterpiece was added to prolong the run for six additional evenings. In the eight performances of the comedy remaining that season, only once was it billed alone.

A note upon the Sentimental Comedy as a type is relevant at this point before proceeding to a consideration of minor forms of entertainment at Drury Lane. Although the enthusiasm of audiences at times ran high for this type of comedy, especially in the successes of Cumberland and Kelly and the continuing popularity of Steele's *The Conscious Lovers* and the works of Cibber, Whitehead and others, and despite the fact that Garrick did not hesitate to foster the type when it suited his purposes, the fact remains that under Garrick's management Sentimental Comedy was not a ranking type in his repertoire. We have noted his private views upon it and will not be surprised to find that out of the total of 376 productions during his management only 35 plays can be cited as definitely of the Sentimental school, including domestic tragedies such as Lillo's *The London Merchant,* Moore's *The Gamester,* and others. Of these 35 sentimental plays, by the standards we have used thus far, only 25 can be qualified as successful. Heading the list in number of performances and longevity in the repertoire are Garrick's *The Lying Valet* (106 performances in 23 seasons) and Steele's *The Conscious Lovers* (96 performances in 28 seasons). Two of the most sensational comedies of this type, Cumberland's *The West Indian* and Hugh Kelly's *False Delicacy,* attained their performance ratings in a very few seasons. In estimating audience taste for this type we must assume that certain sentimental plays were favored, not because they were sentimental but because they actually were good plays in their time. Professor Nicoll is right when he cautions,

While we note the numbers of sentimental comedies written and produced . . . we must always bear in mind two things: that there was ever an undercurrent of amused cynicism in regard to these sentimental plays as well as a certain amount of quite definite opposition, and that the repertoire-lists of the theatres show that sentimental dramas by no means formed the bulk of the playhouse fare.[49]

Certainly this was the case at Drury Lane under Garrick's management.

We have already seen the importance of the farce as an afterpiece in eighteenth century theatres. When all seemed lost it often saved the day for the manager, and once in a while enabled him to maneuvre a worthy but undistinguished drama into temporary favor. Thomas Davies in an anecdote concerning Quin and Garrick gives us a glimpse of the importance with which their contemporaries invested the farce. He is reviewing the production history of Garrick's *Miss in Her Teens* when he writes,

This petit-piece was acted a great number of nights. Mr. Quin was called upon to play some of his characters during its representation. He complied at first, but soon after repented: he swore that he would not hold up the tail of any farce. "Nor shall he," said Mr. Garrick, when he was told what Quin had said; "I will give him a month's holidays." He picked out of the prompter's list of plays all such as could be acted without Quin, and were not supposed to have any internal strength to draw company of themselves. To these Miss in her Teens was tacked every night for above a month, or five weeks. Quin would sometimes, during the run of the farce, pay a visit to the theatre; but on being told that the house was crowded, he would give a significant growl, and withdraw.[50]

Miss in Her Teens was the exceptional farce, it seems, for out of the 91 pieces Garrick produced during his management only 33 could be deemed successful, and 10 of these were inherited from the previous repertoire or were alterations of older comedies. Eight others were of his own authorship. If we included with the farces those "preludes" and "interludes" in which the farcical element is predominant, Garrick provided more successful pieces of this type for Drury Lane than any other author. When he assumed management he brought along his already successful *Lethe* (1740), which was destined to reach 154 more performances in 23 seasons, *The Lying Valet* (1741) which had 106 performances in 23 seasons, and *Miss in Her Teens* (1747) rivaling *Lethe* in popularity with 125 performances in 26 seasons. To these he added (in order of their popularity) *A Peep behind the Curtain* (1767), *Catherine and Petruchio* (1756), *The Guardian* (1759), *The Male*

Coquette (1757), *Bon Ton* (1775), *Neck or Nothing* (1766), *The Farmer's Return from London* (1762), and *The Meeting of the Company* (1774).

Ravenscroft's *The Anatomist,* while holding first place in number of performances, is matched by the record of *Lethe.* James Townley's *High Life Below Stairs* was an even greater success than *Miss in Her Teens,* but was closely followed by *The Lying Valet* and Fielding's *The Intriguing Chambermaid.* The writer who most nearly claimed equality with Garrick in this form, however, was George Colman. His *Polly Honeycombe* achieved 86 performances in 12 seasons; his *The Deuce is in Him* followed closely with 78 performances in a like number of seasons; and *The Musical Lady* attained 62 performances in 11 seasons — all three surpassing Garrick's output in popularity excepting *Lethe,* *The Lying Valet* and *Miss in Her Teens.* The only other authors with more than one success to their credit were Fielding and Arthur Murphy. In addition to *The Intriguing Chambermaid* already noted, the former's *Tom Thumb* still had sufficient vitality in Garrick's time to reach 16 performances in five additional seasons. Murphy, on the other hand, had four pieces which met with unusual audience approval. *The Apprentice* and *All in the Wrong* won about the same amount of popularity and importance in the repertoire, while *The Upholsterer* and *The Citizen* were better liked than the majority of their contemporaries in this form. No less than 35 farces were damned upon their first appearance and seven others expired after a second hearing. The impression one gathers from a study of the full list of such pieces is that farce as a type was then, as always, a highly perishable product in the hands of an audience; that only the exceptional old pieces were tolerated by Garrick's audiences; and that most contemporary pieces were quickly rejected by the spectators.

Charles Coffey's ballad opera *The Devil to Pay* not only

heads the list of musical entertainments successful at Drury Lane, but also ranks eighth in number of performances in the entire repertoire. Originally written by Coffey and adapted with the aid of John Mottley, it had been altered by Garrick's time to one act attributed to Theophilus Cibber.[51] Of course there was the perennial favorite "main piece" *The Beggar's Opera,* which achieved 119 performances in 27 seasons. But among the musical afterpieces the Coffey work was the most dependable piece in the prompter's catalogue. Three of Henry Fielding's ballad operas were also certain of a drawing power at the box office: in order of their popular strength they are *The Virgin Unmask'd* (58 performances in 14 seasons), *The Lottery* (51 performances in 13 seasons), and *The Mock Doctor* (39 performances in 13 seasons).

In the field of comic opera the works of Isaac Bickerstaffe, who established the type, stand alone but for the one successful offering of Robert Lloyd, *The Capricious Lovers* (22 performances in three seasons). The popularity of Mungo in *The Padlock* (1768) accounted for 142 performances of this piece in eight seasons. While Bickerstaffe is usually known for his three comic operas, *The Maid of the Mill, Lionel and Clarissa,* and *Love in a Village,* the fact remains that with his own contemporaries his most popular efforts were *The Padlock* and *Daphne and Amintor.* The latter achieved 61 performances in seven seasons, while the most popular of the famous "three" was *The Maid of the Mill* with only 16 nights in six seasons. In order of their popularity then we should group Bickerstaffe's comic operas thus: *The Padlock; Daphne and Amintor; Thomas and Sally* (a musical entertainment) and *The Maid of the Mill; Lionel and Clarissa* and *Love in a Village; The Sultan.* It is interesting to note that Bickerstaffe had only one failure in this form, *The Captive* (based upon scenes from John Dryden's *Don Sebastian*), which was damned at the first hearing.

The only other production of note in this category is the musical entertainment by Moses Mendez, *The Chaplet* (1749), which attained 129 performances in 18 seasons. Garrick's works in this field were successful but short-lived in the repertoire. His operatic farce *May Day* (1775) was a one-season success in its 16 performances, as was his "prelude" *The Theatrical Candidates* (1775) with 17 performances. The "interludes" *A Fairy Tale* (1763, with George Colman), *Linco's Travels* (1767) and *The Enchanter* (1760) were only minor successes.

Thomas Davies in commenting upon the sustained popularity of English pantomimes wrote:

It is a very singular circumstance, that of all the pantomimes which Rich brought on the stage, from the Harlequin Sorcerer, in the year 1717, to the last which was exhibited a year before his death, which fell out in 1761, there was scarce one which failed to please the public, who testified their approbation of them 40 or 50 nights successively. And, in spite of all the rhetoric of Colley Cibber in his Apology for his Life, and some graver critics, the pantomime is a kind of stage entertainment which will always give more delight to a mixed company than the best speaking farce that can be composed.[52]

Certainly we feel that Davies is guilty of understatement, if anything, as we glance at the list of successful pantomimes and spectacular productions of Garrick's time. Although the manager himself told the public he wished it to take third place in their estimation, nevertheless four Drury Lane pantomimes outdistanced every other of the 376 productions in number of performances. In addition to several of unknown authorship the successful ventures in this form are to be credited to Henry Woodward, Garrick, and James Love. Woodward, of course, was a master-fabricator of pantomime, second only to the great "Lun" himself. His *Queen Mab, The Genii, Fortunatus*, and to a lesser extent *Harlequin Ranger,* brought a fortune to Garrick's theatre before he deserted to the rival house. His *Mercury Harlequin* was successful for three seasons, and even *Proteus* attained 33 performances in its one season. Garrick's own pantomime, *Harlequin's Invasion* (1759), surpassed all but *Queen Mab* and *The Genii* in popularity. James Love's best work, *The Witches,* established a record of 103 performances in six seasons. Two other pantomimes by Love are worthy of note, *The Rites of Hecate* and *The Hermit.* Both achieved a distinctive place in audience favor.

That all classes of spectators enjoyed the pantomimes immensely is attested by the performance records; but an interesting note of popular approval is one by the American visitor, Judge Samuel Curwen of Boston, who found the pantomime at Covent Garden in 1781 decidedly not to his taste:

These species of pantomime seem at present greatly in vogue; to arraign the taste is perhaps conceited; but this remark will never come to light, if ever, till I dare say, it will be despised as it is now relished, especially by the more enlightened class; as to the lower, they ever were and ever will be too gross for any entertainment above the lowest humour. I am, I confess, so totally void of all relish for such diversions, that I forbear condemning them, although I consider them as a proof among many others of the depravity of the present day. I would fain call it vulgar, but too many box spectators seem to enjoy it and join the galleries. I can't, however, but believe that all sensible persons do disapprove of these shows as unworthy, but dare not openly avow their opinion.[53]

After approving Mrs. Centlivre's old comedy *The Busie Body* as much exceeding "in point of wit, plot, etc., the, to me, flattish sentimental compositions of the present day, with a few exceptions,"[54] the Judge was nevertheless vastly entertained with "a most grand procession" upon the subject of Freemasonry, which he describes at length and with enthusiasm.

Garrick's capacities, as we have seen in *Harlequin's*

Invasion, were equal to the demands of pantomime at its best. But with Judge Curwen he seems to have preferred to labor over the creation of elaborate musical and dancing spectacles filled with grand processions and using machinery as complicated as that of the pantomime. The most successful of these were *The Jubilee* (1769), the stage representation of ceremonies in honor of Shakespeare held at Stratford-on-Avon the preceding summer, *Cymon* (1767), and *The Institution of the Garter* (1771). Of the background of writing and preparation of these pieces of what Horace Walpole termed "Garrick's gingerbread" [55] we get an occasional amusing glimpse. Here is what Garrick's friend John Hoadly thought of *Cymon:*

I found your scheme of "Cymon" was resolved to be extended to the length of five acts — "I'll speak a prophecy, or ere I go." The character and the scenery, etc. of the rest, may support it through two or three acts at most; but surely nothing full of Urgandas and Merlins can be drawn out longer, to keep a sensible audience pleased. Cymon, the natural Cymon, will be the hero, add what you please; and I could wish that he had none but natural things and objects about him; but as they are, take heed of bending the bow till it loses its elasticity. You are not apt to do that neither, but this struck me so strongly, that I could not help *crying-out.* [56]

In summarizing our findings we may say that Garrick's audiences attended Drury Lane primarily to be amused; that therefore they preferred comedy to tragedy, and, roughly speaking, the older to the newer ones. They supported only such sentimental pieces as proved also to be "good theatre" and made short work of the others. They reserved most of their severest criticism for the farces and afterpieces — these simply had to be highly entertaining. They were most tolerant of the ballad operas, comic operas, and other musical extravaganza. They were most cordial in their endorsement of any pantomime or spectacle. [57] And lest we be tempted from a vantage point of several centuries to condescend, to patronize these eighteenth century audiences for a want of taste, or as one modern writer remarked, "our chief entertainment at eighteenth century theatres has been laughing at them rather than with them," [58] I append the following lines written recently by Mr. Lawrence Perry for the North American Newspaper Alliance:

New York, Feb. 5 — Your reviewer had a tear squeezed out of him in the course of Bernard Reines' new play at the 48th St. Theatre, "Forward the Heart" — and he rather deplores his lack of control. For even the abandoned sentimentalist resents having emotion roused to no good purpose. . . . Nineteen of the current Broadway offerings are musicals or comedies. Six go deeper — two of these holdovers from last season, one of them by a distinguished playwright, another from abroad. Young dramatists say they cannot get their chance; producers complain they lack material and, of course, dat ol' debbil box-office will again be blamed for it all. . . . Personally, we are inclined to absolve the box-office — the playgoing public, generally speaking, is thoughtful and mature in its judgments. They know good plays when they see them — and they want them. . . . The times are serious enough to warrant what is called escape material on the stage — yet sufficiently serious, sufficiently challenging to afford material for better tragic output.

If "Forward the Heart" stays long on Broadway, we will cheerfully eat crow — with, however, such sauce as the observation that it would prove audiences are content to have their heart strings twanged meaninglessly.

The scene is Broadway at 48th Street, New York City, and not that of opening night at Drury Lane or Covent Garden — but the audiences do not seem to differ so very much in what we are pleased to call their "tastes."

THE TWENTY-NINE-YEAR span of David Garrick's management at Drury Lane Theatre embraces such a bewildering
mass of architectural changes, unusual customs and events,
and such a confusion of persons and plays, that one is apt to
feel that its full history will never be told. Certainly we are
conscious of this fact, now that we reflect upon the result of
this investigation of eighteenth century audiences. Of necessity we have been involved in many a mathematical problem
which has ended only in approximation; we have been involved in many diverging lines of inquiry; we have met too
many people and too many plays and alterations of plays,
perhaps, to expect to emerge with anything like the complete
pattern of those years in terms of playgoers. And yet, having
made the attempt, we can hazard some generalizations about
these people with a little more confidence than we had when
we began.

In the beginning we established the probable capacities of
the two Patent theatres in the London of the early eighteenth century. We saw these capacities altered to a point
where 3,704 persons could be accommodated nightly, or a
weekly potential audience of 22,224 persons. From box
office receipts, however, we learned that average attendance
at these theatres could have been only about 8,460 persons
a week by 1742, and that it had increased to 11,874 persons
a week at least ten years before the end of Garrick's regime
— just about the potential audience estimated by Samuel
Foote. In terms of the metropolitan population this meant
that only 17 persons in every 1,000 attended the Patent
theatres with any degree of regularity.

Our investigation of the make-up and distribution of these audiences revealed that, although they were entitled to the claim of being heterogeneous, they were actually limited essentially to the middle class and above; and that the inveterate playgoer from below that rank must have been drawn more and more toward the attractive prices at the minor theatres. As to any particular distinction in behavior between early and late century audiences, we did not find sufficient evidence to warrant berating the one and praising the other. What changes were observed in these spectators could be traced to the evolution of the art of management in the hands of an astute master such as David Garrick, who cleared his stage by enlarging his house, and who, because of his deference to the wishes of the aristocracy and his careful avoidance of what might offend the rest of the audience, was able to make his reforms popular and effective with all but a very few of the spectators.

Of the problems Garrick faced with others as an alterer of plays for these audiences we noted his own deep-rooted affection for the older dramatists and a constant effort to preserve all but the most offensive of their scenes. We noted too the upsurge of sentiment midway in his career and the fate of his dramatic work when he tried to compromise to suit what he thought was the taste of his audiences. But in a study of his repertoire we saw the partiality of those audiences for sentimental plays only in relation to the amusement value of the particular piece before them, that the proportion of plays of this type was exceedingly low in comparison with the bulk of playhouse fare.

At the close of our survey of Drury Lane productions during Garrick's management we were able to characterize his audiences as people who very definitely came for entertainment values and not for discipline in manners or morality, and who judged what they saw accordingly. In general, we saw how these spectators were drawn to the theatre by pantomime and spectacle more than by any other form of entertainment; how they preferred comedy to tragedy, and the plays of Shakespeare to those of any other writers; how they remained faithful year after year to the acting of the old stock plays, refusing to be stampeded into accepting too many of the newer offerings; how when new plays of worth such as *The Clandestine Marriage, She Stoops to Conquer,* or *The Rivals* were produced the "Town" immediately recognized their quality and "followed after" them; in short, how they would, and no doubt did, applaud enthusiastically this *News from Parnassus:*

A true son of Apollo has well observed that the first office of criticism was to beat time to the chorus of the muses, not with clamor and violence to interrupt the song. Let the audiences support the decorum of the theatre. Let the managers procure novelty, by a due encouragement of genius. If new plays of value cannot be had, let them revive the old, but be sparing of alterations. They may lop excrescencies, and remove indecency; but the form in which the fathers of the drama left their works, shew their own frame of thought, and ought to be respected. In a word, let Managers consider themselves at the head of a great warehouse; procure the best assortment of goods, get proper hands to display them; open their doors, be civil to the customers, and, Apollo foretells that the generosity of the public will reward their endeavours.[1]

CHAPTER I: THE ELBOWED CROWD

1. Quoted in *Dr. Campbell's Diary of a Visit to England in 1775*, ed. James L. Clifford (Cambridge, 1947), p. 119.

2. *A.L.S. to Thomas Rackett*, December 2, 1775. Quoted in Sotheby and Company Sale Catalogue, June 19, 1928.

3. *Diary of Richard Cross*, September 26, 1751; Folger Shakespeare Library.

4. *Ibid.*, March 4, 1755.

5. Complimentary or "house" tickets. Thomas Harris, George Colman's fellow-manager at Covent Garden, accused Colman of overdoing the practice. "It is incredible," he writes, ". . . what an enormous burthen it hath been to the partnership: not less than thirty, forty, fifty, and sixty pounds in orders, were generally sent into the Theatre each Night; and on one night in particular, in support of one of your pieces, upwards of one hundred pounds. . . ." Quoted from Harris's letter to George Colman, 1768, in J. P. Malcolm, *Anecdotes of the Manners and Customs of London during the Eighteenth Century*, 2 vols. (London, 1810), II, 257. Colman denied the accusation and reminded his partner that "The people sent to the house on one night in particular did not go at my desire in support of my piece, but at the instance of all the proprietors in support of the house, which was threatened to be pulled down. . . ." (*Ibid.*, p. 267.)

In "A Dialogue in the Shades between James Quin and Tom Weston" (*Town and Country Magazine*, February, 1776, pp. 98–99) the anonymous author alludes to Garrick's practices concerning "orders":

Quin: . . . then I suppose he has been playing to empty seats, and he proposes another trip to Italy to recruit his spirits.

Weston: There were some grounds for your suppositions, for at the beginning of the season he could not fill a house but with paper, and that was a currency that he was not fond of finding in his treasury.

Quin: Very true; I have seen David burn handfuls of his own notes, in the most violent passion, and though unpaid, without committing any fraud.

6. John Genest, *Some Account of the English Stage . . . 1660–1830,* 10 vols. (Bath, 1832). V, 503–04.

7. Percy Fitzgerald, *Life of David Garrick,* 2 vols. (London, 1868), I, 216–17; *A New History of the English Stage,* 2 vols. (London, 1882), II, 67–68, 154, 234, etc.; *The Sheridans,* 2 vols. (London, 1886), II, 2–6. H. Barton Baker, *History of the London Stage,* 1576–1888, New York, 1904.

8. See *The Annual Register,* April 30, 1794; also the notes to this chapter *passim.*

9. G. C. D. Odell, *Shakespeare from Betterton to Irving,* I., 335. See also Percy Fitzgerald, *A New History of the English Stage,* II, 154.

10. Allardyce Nicoll, *A History of Late Eighteenth Century Drama 1750–1800,* pp. 22–23.

11. Elizabeth P. Stein, *David Garrick, Dramatist,* New York, 1938, p. 9.

12. See Hamilton Bell, "Three Plans by Sir Christopher Wren," *The Architectural Record,* XXXIII (1913), 359 ff.

13. Colley Cibber, contrasting the form of Drury Lane in 1739 with the original Wren structure, describes the curtailment of the stage platform by Christopher Rich in 1693 in order to enlarge the auditorium. After recounting the virtues of the original stage, he writes, "To all this a master of a company may say, I now receive ten pounds more than could have been taken formerly in every full house. . . ." See *An Apology for the Life of Mr. Colley Cibber,* ed. R. W. Lowe, 2 vols. (London, 1888), II, 87 ff.

14. *Ibid.,* II, 179–80. Says Cibber, "A current report that the walls and roof of our house were liable to fall had got such ground in the town that on a sudden we found our audiences unusually decreased by it." A survey by Sir Thomas Hewet declaring the building to be sound allayed the public fears and actually stimulated attendance, according to Cibber.

15. According to a letter written by Aaron Hill, November 6, 1733, and quoted by G. C. D. Odell, *Shakespeare from Betterton to Irving,* I, p. 219.

16. Percy Fitzgerald, *Life of David Garrick,* I, 216–17.

17. *Memoirs of the Colman Family,* ed. R. B. Peake, 2 vols. (London, 1841), I, 191.

18. *The Works in Architecture of Robert and James Adam* (Country Life Press, 1931), Pt. V, plates 6, 7.

19. H. Barton Baker, *History of the London Stage, 1576–1888,* I, 97.

20. See *The Annual Register,* April 30, 1794.

21. H. Barton Baker, *op. cit.,* I, 126–27. This figure finds ample support from accounts in Rylands English Ms. No. 1111, John Rylands Library. Six non-benefit performances at Covent Garden in the season 1740–41 achieved a gross of £200 or better: Saturday, October 25, £200; Thursday, October 30, £220; Thursday, November 6, £200; Thursday, November 27, £200; Tuesday, January 13, £200; Saturday, January 24, £200. This was in addition to the usual benefit performances, the largest gross of which was £350 on November 20.

22. See E. W. Brayley, *Historical and Descriptive Accounts of the Theatres of London* (London, 1826), p. 15 and *n.*

23. *The Annual Register,* April 30, 1794.

24. E. W. Brayley, *op. cit.,* p. 15 *n.*

25. London, 1790, p. 87.

26. *A New History of the English Stage,* II, 67–68. H. Barton Baker, *op. cit.,* I, 126–27.

27. The equation's value rests upon two conditions. It requires that the Covent Garden of 1732 have had two galleries as in 1782, which fact is supported by the admission prices announced in the opening-night playbill (see Percy Fitzgerald, *Life of David Garrick,* II, 70). It then requires that the proportion of seatings in pit, boxes, and galleries would not vary greatly in this fifty-year period. On this point George Saunders (*Treatise,* p. 83) is rather definite: "Covent Garden theatre has been built about 60 years; during which time it has not undergone any material alteration, except in the decorations, till the year 1784 [*sic*], when it was judiciously widened under the direction of Mr. Richards, who was confined to the present

walls, and therefore could not extend it as he wished. . . ."
This in the absence of further specific information I have
accepted as a reasonable assumption. Its validity will have to
be tested in the light of the other factual materials used in later
stages of our investigation. Ultimately it must remain tentative
pending discovery of further data.

28. See note 15 above. Aaron Hill referred to Covent Garden
as ". . . . larger by one part in three. . . ."

29. Assuming that the seating categories were the same at
Drury Lane as in Covent Garden. Again a lack of specific
information forces a conjecture. But there is no evidence of
any significant difference between the two theatres except in
their over-all size.

30. Accounts in Rylands English Ms. No. 1111 for the Drury
Lane season 1741–42 support this figure. In a total of 191
performances during this season, only 25 achieved a gross of
more than £150. Of this number, however, 17 were benefit
performances ranging from a low receipt of £150 on three
occasions to a maximum of £240 when the new actor Garrick
played Chamont for the Widow Harper's benefit on May 11;
two were command performances, one of £150 and the other
of £160. The six remaining "ordinary" nights ranged from a
low of £150 to £182 when the elderly Cibber appeared as Sir
John Brute on December 3; two performances by Garrick as
King Lear and Richard III brought £160 and £171, respectively.

31. $\dfrac{1001}{£150} \times \dfrac{X}{£190} = 1,268$ persons.

32. Frederick Howard, Fifth Earl of Carlisle, *Thoughts upon
the Present Condition of the Stage, and upon the Construction
of a New Theatre* (London, 1800), p. 11.

33. *Memoirs of the Colman Family,* ed. Peake, I, 191.

34. Joseph Knight, *David Garrick* (London, 1894, p. 184.
Knight says, "During the summer of 1762 accordingly, Garrick, after a long consultation with his partner Lacy, enlarged
the house until the receipts in the portion properly belonging
to the audience came to £335, which was as much as the previous
house, stage and all, could yield."

35. H. Barton Baker, *op. cit.,* I, 97.

36. The matter of stage-seating is most confusing. We know that whereas Garrick banned the practice at Drury Lane at the beginning of his management, it was not abolished finally until the enlargement of his theatre in 1762. What was done at Covent Garden is not clear either, although we know that the practice was not abandoned wholly until later in the century. Fitzgerald cites Tate Wilkinson (*A New History of the English Stage,* II, 160) as authority for an estimated 200 stage spectators on a "great benefit night." This would explain in part the maintaining of Covent Garden's capacity at about 1,335 persons until 1782.

37. While significant changes were certainly not made until this date (see note 27), certain minor alterations affecting capacity took place at Covent Garden prior to 1782. An anonymous writer calling himself "Impartial" comments upon the Drury Lane alterations of 1775 and says of its rival: "Few alterations have been made at the other house, except the converting the slips into boxes, new painting it, and other necessary decorations . . . " (*Town and Country Magazine,* September, 1775, p. 488).

38. The most complete accounts I have seen are those for 11 oratorio performances at Drury Lane in 1779. Because of the nature of the attractions and their sponsorship independent of the Drury Lane management, the accounts are set down in complete detail. They include boxoffice rates and upper-gallery tickets. These are to be found in *Memorandum Book — Nightly Accounts 1776–1779 Old Theatre,* Folger Shakespeare Library. See p. 13 above, and also Appendix B.

39. An instance of the confusion surrounding benefit receipts is noted by Genest in describing the "amphitheatre" building on the stage: "Tho' this amphitheatre seems in the first instance to have been meant for box company, yet it was not unusual in the case of an overflow, to admit persons at a lower rate — Mrs. Bellamy in relating the quarrel between herself and Mrs. Hamilton, says, that Mrs. Hamilton having a full gallery disposed of the overflow in the boxes, and upon the stage, preferring their two shillings apiece to empty benches . . ." (*English Stage,* V, 1–2). Genest also records the benefit of the Widow Milward and her 4 children, March 25, 1742, and an announcement

" . . . that many persons who had taken tickets at her former benefit could not get room and that their tickets would be received on this night, Mr. Rich having generously given her the use of his theatre" (*ibid.*, IV, 8). From Rylands English Ms. No. 1111 we learn that the first benefit (March 9, 1742) grossed £230 and that the second grossed £80.

40. William Hopkins, prompter at Drury Lane, comments upon Powell's benefit of March 31, 1764, thus: "This Night one of the greatest overflows that ever was known. The Crowd was so great it prevented the Ladies from coming to their Places in the Boxes till near seven o'clock . . ." (quoted in *Drury Lane Calendar 1747–1776,* ed. Dougald MacMillan, Oxford, 1938, p. 106). The gross that evening amounted to £268 11s. 0d.

41. Folger Shakespeare Library. Standard boxoffice rates prevail in these accounts: 5s., 3s., 2s., 1s. Scattered receipts for Covent Garden are available from its opening night, December 7, 1732, to the date of these four performances. But none of the benefit ticket totals gives the distribution previous to these four.

42. Standard entries in this Book take no account of tickets for the upper gallery. These shillings appear in "money" receipts.

43. British Museum, Egerton Ms. No. 2268.

44. The 12-night initial run of the Hoadly comedy is significant in terms of a £200 gross capacity.

February	£	*s.*	*d.*
12	205	9	6
13	170	7	6
14	197	0	0
16	199	1	0
17	188	5	0
18	174	10	0
19	189	8	0
20	191	13	0
21	199	1	0
23	189	16	6
24	184	11	6
25	186	1	0

45. Folger Shakespeare Library. See Appendix B, below.

46. See note 39, above.

47. See note 36, above.

48. From *Covent Garden Cash Book 1759–60:* December 10, £203 7s.; January 5, £222 0s. 6d.; January 24, £203 16s.; February 18, £206 11s.; March 1, £212 7s.; March 6, £207 6s.; March 29, £214 11s.; May 10, £229 15s.

49. From *Drury Lane Account Books,* Folger Shakespeare Library.

50. The date of this account is June 3, 1767.

51. See receipts in *Drury Lane Calendar,* seasons 1763–64, 1772–73, 1774–75, which are typical. Dr. Campbell wished to see Garrick in Lusignan on March 7, 1775, but found Drury Lane "full by five — tho' David appears but in one act" (*Visit to England,* p. 47); he finally saw Garrick in *Rule a Wife and Have a Wife* on March 14, " . . . which I could not have done if I had stayed half an hour longer; the pitt being full at the first rush. . . " (*ibid.,* p. 51). The gross on March 7, 1775, was £243 18s. 0d. (*Drury Lane Calendar,* p. 185); but the gross on the evening Campbell saw Garrick perform was £261 11s. 0d!

52. "The Theatre No. 65," *Town and Country Magazine,* September, 1775, p. 487.

53. Percy Fitzgerald, *The Sheridans,* II, 2: "The old house was a little larger than the late Haymarket Theatre; its nightly expenses were about £70, the profits of a full house about £160."

54. *Memorandum Book — Nightly Accounts 1776–1779 Old Theatre,* Folger Shakespeare Library. See Appendix B, below, for other receipts.

55. See note 5, above.

56. Since receipts have been taken from several sources, some of which give the daily gross in figures which have been rounded off, I have been forced to proceed in like manner with all other accounts; I may add that much care has been taken to avoid exaggeration.

57. Receipts are from the following sources: 1741–42, Rylands English Ms. No. 1111; 1747–48, 1749–50, *Diary of Richard Cross;* 1758–59, 1763–64, 1772–73, 1774–75, J. P.

Kemble's notes as they appear in *Drury Lane Calendar passim*. The total number of performances in seasons for which I have used the incomplete Kemble notes appears in brackets.

58. These receipts are taken from Rylands English Ms. No. 1111 (1740–41 season); British Museum, Egerton Ms. No. 2268 (1746–47 season); *Covent Garden Cash Book 1759–60*.

59. Appendix B.

60. See *Drury Lane Calendar*, pp. xx-xxi, for an account of the theatrical season.

61. *A Treatise on the Passions, so far as they regard the Stage; with a critical Enquiry into the Theatrical Merit of Mr. G——k, Mr. Q—n, and Mr. B——y. The first considered in the Part of Lear, the two last opposed in Othello.* Printed for C. Corbet, etc. London, n.d., Sig. A_2. This piece has been attributed to Foote.

62. M. D. George, *London Life in the Eighteenth Century* (New York, 1925), p. 323 *n*.

63. *Ibid.*, pp. 24–38.

64. Mrs. Frances Brooke, *The Excursion,* 2 vols. (London, 1777), Book V. Quoted by G. P. Baker, *Some Unpublished Correspondence of David Garrick,* Boston, 1907, p. 125.

65. Claude E. Jones, *Isaac Reed Diaries 1762–1804,* University of California Publications, Vol. X, 1946.

66. *Two Dissertations on the Theatres, An Epistle from Mr. Th. C. to D. Garrick, Esq.* (London, 1756), p. 1. Another curious statement is reported by Genest as coming from the actor Henderson. Genest tells us that the actor no longer objected to the variety of roles he had to study while at Bath and quotes him as saying: ". . . almost every part I play, however unsuited to me, does me good — in London it would do me harm, for this reason; there are computed to be 30 different audiences in London, here there are but two; and those of them who see me to a disadvantage one night, see me to an advantage the next. . . ." (*English Stage,* V, p. 594).

Chapter II: The Four Estates

1. *Town and Country Magazine,* January, 1771, p. 8.

2. Drury Lane Theatre, November, 1705.

3. *Town and Country Magazine,* October, 1776, pp. 551–52; David Garrick, *Poetical Works* (London, 1785), II, 328–29.

4. *Two Dissertations on the Theatres,* p. 5. Macky's *Journey through England,* 1714, p. 190, says, ". . . the Parterre, commonly called the Pit, contains the gentlemen on benches; and on the first story of boxes sit all the ladies of quality; in the second, the Citizens wives and daughters; and in the third, the common people and footmen."

5. *London Life in the Eighteenth Century,* p. 155.

6. *Review,* June 25, 1709.

7. J. P. Malcolm, *Anecdotes of the Manners and Customs of London during the Eighteenth Century,* II, 406 ff.

8. *Wealth, Power and Resources of the British Empire,* London, 1814. Quoted in G. D. H. Cole and Raymond Postgate, *The British People 1746–1946,* New York, 1947, p. 125.

9. M. D. George, *op. cit.,* p. 210.

10. G. D. H. Cole and Raymond Postgate, *The British People 1746–1946,* p. 66.

11. M. D. George, *op. cit.,* pp. 164 ff.

12. Elizabeth W. Gilboy, *Wages in Eighteenth Century England,* Cambridge, Mass., 1934, pp. 8–9.

13. M. D. George, *op. cit.,* p. 168.

14. *Ibid.,* p. 166.

15. See John A. Kelly, *German Visitors to English Theaters in the Eighteenth Century;* also citations in this study *passim.*

16. *Op. cit.,* p. 19.

17. *Ibid.,* p. 20.

18. *Ibid.,* pp. 36–37.

19. Quoted by M. D. George *op. cit.,* p. 205, from Middleton's *Agriculture of Middlesex,* 1798, p. 13.

20. J. P. Malcolm, *op. cit.,* I, 364–65.

21. *Ibid.,* II, 198.

22. *The Connoisseur,* No. 68 (July 15, 1755).

23. *An Enquiry into the Late Increase of Robbers,* London, 1751, sec. 1.

24. Tobias Smollett, *Roderick Random.* Quoted in *Knight's Popular History of England,* 8 vols. (New York, 1880), VI, 396.

25. *Ibid.,* p. 397. From John Forster, *The Life and Times of Oliver Goldsmith.*

26. *The Connoisseur,* June 6, 1750.

27. *Improvement of the Working People,* London, 1834, pp. 19–20.

28. For this tabulation I have employed the gross average weekly earnings of American industrial workers. As of December, 1948, this figure was $55.10 ("Hours and Earnings," *Industry Report,* United States Department of Labor, Bureau of Labor Statistics, December, 1948, p. 14). As a proportion of income, each penny spent by the eighteenth-century workman was equivalent to 38¢ spent by a modern worker. For the Elizabethan rates see Alfred B. Harbage, *Shakespeare's Audience,* p. 59.

29. P. 73.

30. See data by George Saunders, *A Treatise on Theatres,* Chapter I, p. 5.

31. Assuming of course that the cheaper seats are usually filled.

32. "Gentlemen who have no employment may sleep whole days and riot whole nights. . . . Compare the life of a careful honest man . . . with your mechanick of pleasure who is to frequent the theatre . . . He must be a fine gentleman, leave his work at five at the farthest . . . that he may be drest and at the playhouse by six, where he continues till ten and then adjourns to a publick house with fellows as idle as himself." From *A Letter to the Right Hon. Sir R. Brocas, Lord Mayor of London, by a Citizen* (R. P. Hare), 1730. Quoted in M. D. George, *op. cit.,* p. 288 *n.*

33. Although activity of the "minors" was effectively curtailed by the Licensing Act, Allardyce Nicoll lists 11 theatres of this type operating sporadically from 1737 to 1750 (*A His-*

tory of Early Eighteenth Century Drama 1700–1750, pp. 272–73). After 1750 most of these disappeared and such houses were limited to a few like Sadler's Wells, which Brayley says would accommodate about 2,200 spectators (*ibid.,* p. 56).

34. *Wynstanly's Water Theatre,* for instance, varied its show with the seasons and the humor of the public, presenting sea deities, nymphs, mermaids, tritons, and other aquatic personages, "playing and spouting out water, or sometimes water mingled with fire. . . . The quantity of water used on extraordinary occasions . . . amounted to eight hundred tuns." See G. L. Craik and C. Macfarlane, *The Pictorial History of England,* 4 vols. (New York, 1848), IV, 795. Sadler's Wells combined both tavern and playhouse, and "spectators were not only amused with songs, recitations, and spectacles, but regaled with ale, wine, cakes, and tobacco. It was chiefly a resort . . . of low and vicious company" (*ibid.*).

35. For a full account of the Half-Price Riots, see Percy Fitzgerald, *A New History of the English Stage,* II, 187 ff.

36. *Ibid.,* II, 186–87.

37. Friedrich Wilhelm von Schutz. Quoted in John A. Kelly, *op. cit.,* pp. 148–49.

38. *Natural and Political Observations and Conclusions upon the State and Condition of England,* in G. E. Barnett, ed., *Two Tracts by Gregory King,* Baltimore, 1936, p. 22.

39. *Act I, scene ii.*

40. *Act I, scene i.*

41. *Op. cit.,* II, 413–14.

42. G. D. H. Cole and Raymond Postgate, *op. cit.,* p. 61.

43. *Ibid.*

44. C. P. Moritz, "Travels . . . Through Several Parts of England, in 1782 . . ." in *A General Collection of the Best and Most Interesting Voyages and Travels,* ed. John Pinkerton, 13 vols. (London, 1808), II, 506.

45. G. D. H. Cole and Raymond Postgate, *op. cit.,* p. 61.

46. *Garrick Correspondence,* ed. James Boaden, 2 vols. (London, 1832), I, 487.

47. The play was *The Grecian Daughter* (Drury Lane, 1772). See Percy Fitzgerald, *op. cit.,* II, 244.

48. G. M. Trevelyan, *English Social History* (New York, 1944), p. 360.

49. *Garrick Correspondence,* I, 63.

50. Frederick Howard, 5th Earl of Carlisle, *op. cit.,* p. 14.

51. *The Annual Register,* February 3, 1794.

52. Epilogue to *The Clandestine Marriage* (Drury Lane, 1766). David Garrick, *Poetical Works,* I, 208 ff.

53. *Knight's Popular History of England,* VI, 416.

54. *Lethe.* David Garrick, *Dramatic Works,* 3 vols. (London, 1798), I, 23–24.

55. *The Gentleman's Magazine,* March, 1767.

56. *Drury Lane Calendar,* p. 117, and *The Journal and Letters of Samuel Curwen, 1775–1784,* ed. G. A. Ward (New York, 1842), pp. 294–95.

57. J. A. Kelly, *op. cit., passim.*

58. *Drury Lane Calendar,* p. 82.

59. *Ibid.,* pp. 133–35.

60. Peter J. Grosley, *A Tour to London; or, New Observations on England and Its Inhabitants.* Quoted by J. P. Malcolm, *op. cit.,* I, 383.

61. See pp. 27–28 and note 29, above.

62. J. P. Malcolm, *op. cit.,* I, 365–66.

63. A newspaper bill for March 31, 1770, is the earliest I have found giving the starting time later than six o'clock. This day *Isabella* was given out for six-thirty. Some days later one notice reads six-fifteen; and after that the bills regularly state the time as six-thirty until the month of May, when six o'clock is again the time (*Notebook of Clippings 1770–1777,* Folger Shakespeare Library).

64. *Drury Lane Calendar,* p. xix.

65. *Diary of William Hopkins,* October 5, 1768, Folger Shakespeare Library, quoted in *Drury Lane Calendar,* p. 134. The question of time was always an important one with Garrick's audiences. The following entries in the *Diary of Richard Cross* at Folger Library are revealing:

November 16, 1754. "We staid 'till ten Minutes after six when ye Audience made a great noise to begin, & when the Curtain went up, pelted the Actors & wou'd not suffer 'em to go on 'till Mr. Garrick told 'em, we began by the green-room Clock, & that we had not much exceeded the time — one above call'd out it was half an hour after six but we proceeded without farther Interruption."

November 18, 1754. "This Day a Paragraph appear'd in the papers that we always began by ye Green-room Clock wch was kept by Mr. Grignion's regulator of equal time, & was now slower than ye Sun 16 Minutes."

66. *Op. cit.*, p. 206 ff.

67. Mrs. George, quoting Francis Place and the *Reminiscences* of Henry Angelo, gives the following holidays for workmen: Easter, Whitsuntide, and Christmas were the three regularly recognized holidays; the hanging-days at Tyburn (eight times a year). See *ibid.*, p. 208.

68. *Anecdotes of the Manners and Customs of London during the Eighteenth Century,* II, 409–10.

69. *Ibid.*, pp. 410–11.

70. Folger Shakespeare Library, Washington, D. C.

71. *The Daily Advertiser,* March 30, 1743.

72. By 1776 Covent Garden was beginning as late as 6:15 to 6:30 p.m. Newspapers advertised the performance November 10 (?), 1776, "To begin at a Quarter after Six." This time was continued into 1777, when it reverted to 6:30 p.m. on April 30, 1777. See *Notebook of Clippings 1770–1777,* Folger Shakespeare Library; names of newspapers from which clippings are taken are not given.

73. Theophilus Cibber, *op. cit.*, p. 74.

74. This bill was presented at Drury Lane on June 26 and 29, 1761, in a summer season managed by Murphy and Foote. *Drury Lane Calendar,* p. 84.

75. Preface to *The Dramatic Timepiece,* 1767.

76. Harry William Pedicord, "Mr. and Mrs. Garrick: Some Unpublished Correspondence," *PMLA,* LX (September, 1945), 775–83. See also *Garrick Correspondence,* "Hoadly," *passim.*

77. Frederick T. Wood, "The Attack on the Stage in the Eighteenth Century," *Notes and Queries,* CLXXIII (September 25, 1937), 218–22. A good example of this material will be found in *The Stage the High Road to Hell* (London, 1767).

78. *Ibid.*

79. Theophilus Cibber, *op. cit.,* pp. 72–73.

80. As in the case of Foote's *The Minor.* See *A Letter from Mr. Foote to the Reverend Author of "Remarks, Critical and Christian," on The Minor,* in *Memoirs of Samuel Foote, Esq.,* ed. William Cooke, 3 vols. (London, 1805), III, 160–201.

81. Quoted in J. P. Malcolm, *op. cit.,* II, 111.

82. *A Solemn Protest against the Revival of Scenic Exhibitions and Interludes at the Royalty Theatre, etc.,* 2d ed. (London, 1803), p. 8. Quoted in M. D. George, *op. cit.,* p. 288 and *n.*

83. *Ibid.*

84. *The Farmer's Return from London* (Drury Lane, 1762), in *Poetical Works,* I, 186–88.

85. *Diary of Richard Cross,* Folger Shakespeare Library.

86. *Poetical Works of David Garrick,* I, 116.

87. *Drury Lane Calendar,* p. 190.

88. Allardyce Nicoll, *The English Theatre* (New York, 1936), p. 131.

Chapter III: In the Name of Freedom

1. *A History of Late Eighteenth Century Drama*, p. 5.
2. *Ibid.*
3. Friedrich Wilhelm von Schutz. Quoted by J. A. Kelly, *German Visitors to English Theatres in the Eighteenth Century*, pp. 150–51.
4. *The Morning Chronicle*, March 6, 1775.
5. *Visit to England*, pp. 43–45.
6. P. 42, above.
7. See M. D. George, *London Life in the Eighteenth Century*, pp. 288–89 and *n.*
8. *A Hundred Years of Quarter Sessions, the Government of Middlesex from 1660–1760* (Cambridge, 1932), p. 33.
9. J. P. Malcolm, *Anecdotes of the Manners and Customs of London during the Eighteenth Century*, I, 232.
10. No. 340.
11. See Chapter II, p. 42.
12. *New Brooms, An Occasional Prelude*, by George Colman (Drury Lane, September 21, 1776). A newspaper account, March 20, 1770, states: "Monday night a Lady, in the pit of Covent Garden Theatre, had her pocket cut off, in which were three guineas" (from a clipping in Folger Shakespeare Library, name of paper unknown). In 1771 J. H. L. Meyer, a German visitor, was another victim of pickpockets, losing two pocket-handkerchiefs (J. A. Kelly, *op. cit.*, p. 57).
13. *Table Talk* (New York, 1856), p. 7.
14. J. P. Malcolm, *op. cit.*, II, 408.
15. Folger Shakespeare Library.
16. *Op. cit.*, II, 408–9.
17. E. G. Dowdell, *A Hundred Years of Quarter Sessions*, p. 25.
18. W. S. Lewis, *Three Tours through London in the Years 1748–1776–1797* (New Haven, 1941), p. 75.
19. *Thoughts Upon the Present Condition of the Stage*, pp. 14–16.

20. *The Connoisseur,* Thursday, November 21, 1754.

21. *Diary of Richard Cross,* Folger Shakespeare Library.

22. J. P. Malcolm, *op. cit.,* II, 178.

23. *The Gentleman's Magazine,* March, 1765.

24. *The Town and Country Magazine,* January, 1769.

25. Cf., the riot against Macklin at the Haymarket in 1773, when bands of tailors and other laborers were recruited at a shilling a night and supper in addition to their playhouse admission. For a full account see Percy Fitzgerald, *Life of David Garrick,* II, 266 ff.

26. *Memoirs of the Life of David Garrick, Esq.,* 3d ed., 2 vols. (London, 1781), I, 81 ff.

27. January 22, 1750.

28. See biographies of Garrick and stage histories for full accounts.

29. *Op. cit.,* I, 187 ff.

30. *Op. cit.,* II, 194.

31. See Chapter II, p. 29.

32. *Drury Lane Calendar,* p. xiv.

33. *Ibid.*

34. Thomas Davies, *op. cit.,* II, 2.

35. *Ibid.,* pp. 88–90.

36. *The Covent Garden Journal,* ed. G. E. Jensen, 2 vols. (New Haven, 1915), I, 297–98.

37. "The Theatre, LXXI," in *Town and Country Magazine,* February, 1776.

38. "The Theatre, XV," *Ibid.,* March, 1770.

39. J. P. Malcolm, *op. cit.,* pp. 171–72.

40. Frederick Howard, 5th Earl of Carlisle, *op. cit.,* pp. 37–38.

41. *Op. cit.,* Tuesday, February 25, 1752, pp. 236–37.

42. Bonnell Thornton and George Colman, *op. cit.,* No. 43, November 21, 1754.

43. David Garrick, *Harlequin's Invasian,* Act II, sc. ii, in *Three Plays by David Garrick,* ed. E. P. Stein (London, 1926), p. 32.

44. *Op cit.,* pp. 297–98.

45. *Address to the Town,* in *Poetical Works,* I, 192–93.

46. *Op. cit.,* No. 43, Thursday, November 21, 1754.

47. *Drury Lane Calendar,* p. xviii.

48. *Diary of Richard Cross,* February 22, 1748.

49. Thursday, November 21, No. 43.

50. *Diary,* December 2, 1749.

51. *Ibid.,* March 14, 1748.

52. *The Connoisseur,* No. 43.

53. *Garrick and His Circle,* p. 108.

54. *Poetical Works,* I, 11.

55. *Op. cit.*

56. *Ibid.,* p. 33. Von Wimpffen, Grimm, and Gunderode were among the dissenters, according to Kelly.

57. *Ibid.,* p. 50.

58. *Ibid.,* p. 55.

59. *Ibid.*

CHAPTER IV: A BUNGLING REFORMATION

1. R. B. Sheridan, *The Critic,* I, i.
2. *Drury Lane Calendar, passim.*
3. Bickerstaffe writes to Garrick, July 27, 1767: "... I have put into your brother's hand with this letter the alteration of 'The Nonjuror,' and I flatter myself it is not ill done, because I have adhered as strictly as possible to your ideas of what it should be; and with the assistance of Moliere, I think I have made it a clean, laughable, and (what in my opinion is no small excellence in one) not too long a comedy" (*Garrick Correspondence,* I, 266–67).
4. See a "Chronology of Garrick's Dramatic Writing," Appendix A, below.
5. "Garrick's Long Lost Alteration of *Hamlet,*" *PMLA,* XLIX, September, 1934, 890–921; "Garrick's Handling of *Antony and Cleopatra,*" *RES,* XIII, January, 1937, 20–38; "*A Midsummer Night's Dream* in the Hands of Garrick and Colman," *PMLA,* LIV, June, 1939, 467–82; "Garrick and an Unknown Operatic Version of Love's Labors Lost," *RES,* XV, July, 1939, 323–28; "Garrick's Handling of *Macbeth,*" *SP,* XXXVIII, October, 1941, 609–28; "Garrick's Production of *King Lear:* A Study in The Temper of the Eighteenth-Century Mind," *SP,* XLV, January 1948, 89–103; "The God of His Idolatry: Garrick's Theory of Acting and Dramatic Composition with Especial Reference to Shakespeare," in *Joseph Quincy Adams Memorial Studies* (Folger Shakespeare Library, 1948), 115–28.
6. "Garrick's Handling of *Macbeth,*" p. 611.
7. "Garrick's Production of *King Lear,*" p. 91.
8. "The God of His Idolatry," p. 118.
9. Franz Kramer, *Das verhaltnis von David Garrick's "Every Man in His Humour" zu dem gleichnamigen lustspiel Ben Jonson's* (Halle, 1903); Heinrich Maass, *Ben Jonson's lustspiel "Every Man in His Humour" und die gleichnamige bearbeitung*

durch David Garrick (Rostock, 1903) ; R. G. Noyes, *Ben Jonson on the English Stage, 1660–1776* (Cambridge, 1935), pp. 257–65.

10. R. G. Noyes, *Ben Jonson on the English Stage, 1660–1776,* p. 258.

11. John Genest, *Some Account of the English Stage . . . 1660–1830,* V, 500.

12. *Op. cit.,* IV, 404.

13. Donald J. Rulfs, "Beaumont and Fletcher on the Stage, 1776–1833," *PMLA,* LXIII, No. 4, Pt. 1 (December 1948), 1262.

14. The text of the alteration is *The Chances . . . with Alterations* (London, 1773). References to act and scene of the original are to *The Works of Francis Beaumont and John Fletcher,* eds. Arnold Glover and A. R. Waller, 10 vols. (Cambridge, 1905–1912) ; to the first alteration, *The Chances* (London, 1682).

15. Act III, scene ii.

16. As manager, Garrick must have had such fears hanging over him more or less constantly. Hopkins the prompter notes in his Diary (October 1, 1763) concerning a performance of *Love for Love,* that "Mr. Yates in the speech where he says 'The more she cries, the less she'll p——' happened to speak the Words a little too plain, and was justly hissed by the Audience." *Drury Lane Calendar,* p. 97.

17. See note 13, above.

18. For a discussion of the authorship and its attribution to Garrick see Donald J. Rulfs, *op. cit.,* p. 1257.

19. *Dramatic Miscellanies,* 3 vols. (London, 1785), II, 410–11. Dr. Campbell, on the other hand, thought that "Leon . . . was not I think a character wherein he could display himself" (*Visit to England,* p. 52).

20. For an account of subsequent alterations of Fletcher's comedy see Donald J. Rulfs, *op. cit.,* pp. 1257–62.

21. *Drury Lane Calendar,* March 13 and 27, 1750; April 29, 1751.

22. The text for the alteration is found in *The Dramatic Works of David Garrick,* 3 vols. (London, 1798), II, 113–161.

References to act and scene of the original are to *The Works of Thomas Southerne,* 2 vols., (London, 1721), II, 97–175.

23. John Brownsmith, *The Dramatic Timepiece,* p. 12.

24. John Genest, *English Stage,* IV, 511–12.

25. Allardyce Nicoll, *A History of Early Eighteenth Century Drama 1700–1750,* p. 339.

26. John Genest, *op. cit.,* IV, 512–13. He says, "Garrick prides himself on not having borrowed any thing from Johnson, as if there were some peculiar merit in that — he would have acted more wisely, if he had adopted the best parts of the Wife's Relief, and by so doing he would have made his own alteration much better than it is at present."

27. *Ibid.*

28. The text for the alteration is found in *The Dramatic Works of David Garrick,* II, 50–112. References to act and scenes of the original are to *The Dramatic Works and Poems of James Shirley,* 6 vols. (London, 1833), III, 187–277.

29. *Garrick Correspondence,* I, 82.

30. See note 7, above.

31. *Drury Lane Calendar,* p. 251.

32. *Ibid.,* p. 228.

33. *Ibid.*

34. *Op. cit.,* V, 69.

35. *Drury Lane Calendar,* p. 227.

36. The text for the alteration is found in *The London Stage,* 4 vols. (London, 1825), Vol. I. References to act and scene of the original are to *The Complete Works of William Wycherley,* ed. Montague Summers, 4 vols. (London, 1924).

37. As Genest points out (*op. cit.,* V, 116), this incident is borrowed by Garrick from another Wycherley comedy, *The Gentleman Dancing Master.*

38. *Ibid.*

39. This song was borrowed from John Lee's alteration. See Genest, *op. cit.,* V, 116.

40. *Memoirs of Samuel Foote, Esq.,* III, 96.

41. *The Critic,* I, i.

CHAPTER V: BON TON

1. Theophilus Cibber, *Two Dissertations on the Theatres,* p. 5.
2. Prologue to *The Universal Gallant.*
3. January 21, 1758. *Garrick Correspondence,* I, 82.
4. *Memoirs,* 3d ed. (1781), I, 27.
5. September 1, 1766. *Garrick Correspondence,* I, 238–39.
6. September 8, 1766. *Ibid.,* I, 239.
7. From a copy of the *Winston Ms. Relative to Covent Garden Theatre,* Records of a court action (or several) involving Covent Garden, Folger Shakespeare Library, Washington, D. C.
8. *Poetical Works,* I, 173–74.
9. *Dramatic Works,* II, 24.
10. Sunday, April 5, 1767. *Garrick Correspondence,* I, 252. The manager's private judgment was vindicated however. Reed's tragedy expired after three performances.
11. Friday, May 22, 1772. *Ibid.,* I, 467.
12. Sunday, May 24, 1772. *Ibid.,* I, 469–70.
13. November, 1765. D. M. Little, *Pineapples of Finest Flavour* (Cambridge, Mass., 1930), p. 47.
14. Preface to *The Good-natured Man* (Covent Garden, January 29, 1768), London, 1768.
15. *The Roman and English Comedy Consider'd and Compar'd; with Remarks on The Suspicious Husband* (London, 1747), pp. 38–39.
16. *Dramatic Works,* III, 94.
17. *Ibid.,* p. 248.
18. G. P. Baker, *Some Unpublished Correspondence of David Garrick,* p. 45.
19. D. M. Little, *Pineapples of Finest Flavour,* pp. 60–61.
20. Lines in Autograph Ms. Notebook, Lot #265, Sotheby Sale Catalogue, June 19, 1928.
21. *Dramatic Works,* III, 92.
22. *Garrick Correspondence,* I, 542.

23. *Ibid.,* p. 524. Foote's "intended puppet-show" never was produced, but according to Davies, "The great success of the Stratford Jubilee . . . inspired this envious man with the design of producing a mock procession in imitation of it . . . In this mock procession a fellow was to be dressed . . . as like Mr. Garrick as possible. It was intended that some ragamuffin . . . should address Roscius in the well-known lines of the poet-laureate,

> *A nation's taste depends on you,*
> *Perhaps a nation's virtue too.*

The representer of Mr. Garrick was to make no answer, but to cry 'Cock a doodle do!' " (*Memoirs of the Life of David Garrick, Esq.,* II, 249–50).

24. *Dramatic Works,* III, 250.

25. From notes in *Autograph Ms. Notebook,* Lot #265, Sotheby Sale Catalogue, June 19, 1928.

26. Thomas Davies, *op. cit.,* I, 210–11.

27. *Ibid.*

28. *Ibid.*

29. Autograph Poem signed with initials, Lot #256, Sotheby Sale Catalogue, June 19, 1928.

30. *Poetical Works,* I, 123.

31. *A General View of the Stage* (London, 1759), p. 9.

32. *Town and Country Magazine,* August, 1776, p. 430.

33. *Memoirs,* I, 150.

34. Drury Lane, March 3, 1770.

35. *The Museum; or, The Literary and Historical Register,* No. 25, Saturday, February 28, 1747.

36. *Stage Policy Detected; or, Some Select Pieces of Theatrical Secret History Laid Open,* p. 17. Quoted by R. G. Noyes, *Ben Jonson on the English Stage, 1660-1776,* p. 127.

37. *Critical Reflections on the old Dramatic Writers addressed to David Garrick,* a preface to Mason's edition of the works of Massinger, 1779. Quoted by John Genest, *op. cit.,* VI, 123.

38. See J. P. Malcolm, *op. cit.,* II, 247–53.

39. *Op. cit.*

40. *Ibid.,* p. 97. Evidence of Karl Gottlob Kuttner, 1783.

41. *Ibid.*, p. 122. Evidence of G. F. A. Wendeborn, 1787.

42. Prologue at the opening of Drury Lane Theatre, September 20, 1747.

43. *Loc. cit.*

44. *Op cit.*, p. xxvii.

45. After 25 seasons of playing Hamlet "according to Shakespeare" Garrick substituted his own altered version for the last 4 seasons.

46. *Op. cit.*, p. 35.

47. *Ibid., n.*

48. *Op. cit.*, p. 8.

49. *A History of Early Eighteenth Century Drama 1700–1750*, p. 183.

50. *Op. cit.*, I, 108–9.

51. Allardyce Nicoll, *A History of Early Eighteenth Century Drama 1700–1750*, p. 315.

52. *Op. cit.*, I, 100.

53. *Journal and Letters 1775–1784*, ed. by G. A. Ward (New York, 1842), pp. 299–300. See also the essay by Edward Moore on the taste for pantomimes in *The World*, No. 43, Thursday, October 25, 1753.

54. *Journal and Letters 1775–1784*, p. 300.

55. See Elizabeth P. Stein, *op. cit.*, p. 125, for an account of Walpole's impressions as related to the later alteration of *Cymon.*

56. *Garrick Correspondence*, I, 249.

52. Judging from contemporary accounts we may assume that even the famous "Chinese Festival" designed by M. Noverre for Garrick, had it not been the occasion of a surge of nationalism, would have been among the successful spectacular productions. See Chapter III, above, p. 54.

58. W. S. Lewis, *op. cit.*, p. 71.

Chapter VI: Epilogue

1. Arthur Murphy, Covent Garden Theatre, September 23, 1776.

Appendix A. Chronology of Garrick's Writing for the Theatre

1739–1740 *Lethe* (Drury Lane, April 15, 1740)

1741–1742 *The Lying Valet* (Goodman's Fields, November 30, 1741)

1746–1747 *Miss in her Teens* (Covent Garden, January 17, 1747)

1748–1749 *Romeo and Juliet* * (Drury Lane, November 29, 1748)

1751–1752 *Every Man in his Humour* * (Drury Lane, November 29, 1751)

           Macbeth * (Drury Lane, January 28, 1752)

1753–1754 *Catherine and Petruchio* * (Drury Lane, March 18, 1754)

1754–1755 *The Chances* * (Drury Lane, November 7, 1754)

           The Fairies * (Drury Lane, February 3, 1755)

1755–1756 *The Winter's Tale* * (Drury Lane, January 21, 1756)

           The Tempest * (Drury Lane, February 11, 1756)

           Rule a Wife and Have a Wife * (Drury Lane, March 25, 1756)

1756–1757 *King Lear* * (Drury Lane, October 28, 1756)

           Lilliput (Drury Lane, December 3, 1756)

           The Male Coquette (Drury Lane, March 24, 1757)

1757–1758 *Isabella* * (Drury Lane, December 2, 1757)

           The Gamesters * (Drury Lane, December 22, 1757)

1758–1759 *Antony and Cleopatra* * (With Edward Capell, Drury Lane, January 3, 1759)

           The Guardian (Drury Lane, February 3, 1759)

1759–1760 *Harlequin's Invasion* (Drury Lane, December 31, 1759)

* Alteration or adaptation.

1760–1761   *The Enchanter* (Drury Lane, December 13, 1760)
1761–1762   *Cymbeline* * (Drury Lane, November 28, 1761)
            The Farmer's Return from London (Drury Lane, March 20, 1762)
1763–1764   *A Mid-Summer Night's Dream* * (Drury Lane, November 23, 1763)
1765–1766   *The Clandestine Marriage* (With George Colman, Drury Lane, February 20, 1766)
1766–1767   *The Country Girl* * (Drury Lane, October 25, 1766)
            Neck or Nothing (Drury Lane, November 18, 1766)
            Cymon (Drury Lane, January 2, 1767)
            Linco's Travels (Drury Lane, April 6, 1767)
1767–1768   *A Peep Behind the Curtain* (Drury Lane, October 23, 1767)
1769–1770   *The Jubilee* (Drury Lane, October 14, 1769)
1770–1771   *King Arthur* * (Drury Lane, December 13, 1770)
1772–1773   *The Irish Widow* (Drury Lane, October 23, 1772)
            Hamlet * (Drury Lane, December 18, 1772)
1773–1774   *Albumazar* * (Drury Lane, October 19, 1773)
            A Christmas Tale (Drury Lane, December 27, 1773)
1774–1775   *The Meeting of the Company* (Drury Lane, September 17, 1774)
            Bon Ton (Drury Lane, March 18, 1775)
1775–1776   *The Theatrical Candidates* (Drury Lane, September 23, 1775)
            May Day (Drury Lane, October 23, 1775)

* Alteration or adaptation.

ATTENDANCE CHARTS

I. Receipts on Workdays[a]

Days[b]	1740-1741	1741-1742	1746-1747	1747-1748	1749-1750	1758-1759	1759-1760	1763-1764	1772-1773	1774-1775
Ordinary Day										
D. L.		096		147	134	151		169	188	179
C. G.	115		134				145			
Opening Day										
D. L.		110		162	146	159		176	197	208
C. G.	153		172				167			
Monday										
D. L.		110		165	138	154		181	188	198
C. G.	118		135				164			
Tuesday										
D. L.		104		140	119	155		171	186	183
C. G.	110		130				144			
Wednesday										
D. L.		091		160	116	156		136	211	209
C. G.	100		123				130			
Thursday										
D. L.		097		136	141	164		202	176	209
C. G.	129		144				159			
Friday										
D. L.		091		135	127	144		128	200	179
C. G.	103		126				136			
Saturday										
D. L.		089		162	158	165		177	174	193
C. G.	128		136				140			

[a] Since many of the receipts are given in round numbers, all have been so reduced. Averages are given in pounds.

[b] In this and the two following charts, D. L. = Drury Lane; C. G. = Covent Garden.

II. Receipts on Holidays [a]

Holidays	1740–1741	1741–1742	1746–1747	1747–1748	1749–1750	1758–1759	1759–1760	1763–1764	1772–1773	1774–1775
New Year's Day										
D. L.		080		...b	140	130		215	143	221
C. G.	...b		...b				183			
Easter Monday										
D. L.		040		130	050	104		148	...c	...c
C. G.	230		141				225			
Easter Tuesday										
D. L.		150		111	150	...c		061	...c	...c
C. G.	130		069				218			
Easter Wednesday										
D. L.		180		160	160	...c		167	...c	...c
C. G.	100		137				158			
Whit-Monday										
D. L.		171		...b	...b	...c		...b	...c	...b
C. G.	100		...b				260			
Whit-Tuesday										
D. L.		...b		...b	...b	...c		...b	...c	...b
C. G.	110		...b				050			
Whit-Wednesday										
D. L.		...b		...b	...b	...c		...b	305	...b
C. G.	...b		...b				037			
Lord Mayor's Day										
D. L.		075		090	120	161		116	230	104
C. G.	130		129				165			
Anniversary of K. William										
D. L.		136		140	130	159		136	178	149
C. G.	075		119				150			
1st Week-day after Christmas										
D. L.		072		160	100	125		270	163	158
C. G.	120		105				177			
2d Week-day after Christmas										
D. L.		080		150	100	124		196	158	128
C. G.	100		077				148			
3rd Week-day after Christmas										
D. L.		070		100	070	133		179	173	226
C. G.	...b		110				132			

a Since many of the receipts are given in round numbers, all have been
 so reduced. Averages are given in pounds.

b No performance.

c Performance, but record of receipts lacking.

III. Receipts for the Theatrical Season [a]

Month	1740–1741	1741–1742	1746–1747	1747–1748	1749–1750	1758–1759	1759–1760	1763–1764	1772–1773	1774–1775
September										
D. L.		090		141	105	155		193	188	202
C. G.	084		115				063			
October										
D. L.		085		144	127	191		141	185	161
C. G.	112		104				109			
November										
D. L.		096		127	121	149		151	171	208
C. G.	126		134				132			
December										
D. L.		077		146	104	150		168	194	181
C. G.	091		116				139			
January										
D. L.		073		155	127	170		186	191	213
C. G.	116		158				143			
February										
D. L.		082		160	142	175		162	194	212
C. G.	125		166				151			
March										
D. L.		126		196	192	173		198	156	221
C. G.	159		114				208			
April										
D. L.		134		142	150	131		185	...[b]	146
C. G.	135		151				152			
May										
D. L.		108		146	164	120		095	...[b]	201
C. G.	103		105				157			

[a] Average monthly box office receipts given in pounds. Since many of these receipts are given in round numbers, all have been so reduced.

[b] No record of receipts.

SELECTED BOX OFFICE RECEIPTS

Covent Garden Theatre, 1759–1760 [a]

Nov. 30 — To Dioclesian & Judg. of Paris

	Box	Pitt	Gall.	Value
Tickets	140	74	30	51.10
Money				206.19.6
			Total	£258.17.6

Dec. 12 — To Zara & Lethe for Mr. Jackson

	Box	Pitt	Gall.	Value
Tickets	83	432	284	113.19.
Money				49.16.6
			Total	£163.15.6

Dec. 18 — Love for Love & Devil to Pay

	Box	Pitt	Gall.	Value
Tickets	137	313	418	123
Money				55.10.6
			Total	£178.10.6

Dec. 21 — To Earl of Essex wth Englishman in P.
For the gen. Lying-in Hospital in Duke
St. Grosvenor Square

	Box	Pitt	Gall.	Value
Tickets	519	53	46	142.6
Money				56
			Total	£198.6

March 17 — To Tender Husband & Honest Yorkshireman

	Box	Pitt	Gall.	Value
Tickets	230	481	314	161.1
Money				85.10.6
			Total	£246.11.6

March 18 — To Hamlet & Hob in the Well

	Box	Pitt	Gall.	Value
Tickets	399	492	135	187.1
Money				82.5.6
			Total	£269.6.6

Mar. 22 — To Consc. Lovers & Englishman Return'd
for Mr. Sparks

	Box	Pitt	Gall.	Value
Tickets	380	563	243	203.15
Money				69
			Total	£272.15

[a] *Covent Garden Cash Book 1759–60*, Folger Shakespeare Library.

March 27 — To Comus & Lethe (for Miss Brent)

	Box	Pitt	Gall.		Value
Tickets	330	95	56		92 . 7
Money					175 . 13
				Total	£268 . — —

April 8 To Romeo & Juliet wth Lethe

	Box	Pitt	Gall.		Value
Tickets	238	416	213		143 . 4
Money					75 . 5
				Total	£218 . 9

April 9 To Henry ^the 4th 1st Part w Flora (for Mr. Clark)

	Box	Pitt	Gall.		Value
Tickets	127	401	146		106 . 10 —
Money					51 . 12 . 6
				Total	£158 . 2 . 6

April 10 To Beggar's Opera & Petruchio (for Mr. Lowe)

	Box	Pitt	Gall.		Value
Tickets	259	546	163		162 . 19
Money					103 . 1
				Total	£266 .

April 11 Jovial Crew & Rape

	Box	Pitt	Gall.		Value
Tickets	133	78	55		50 . 9

April 12 Royal Merchant w. Duke & no Duke
The under-ment^d had Tickets

Messrs	Box	Pitt	Gall	Value	½ Value
Dyer Mrs.	8	35	29	10 . 3	5 . 1 . 6
Helm Miss	3	30	20	7 . 5	3 . 12 . 6
Vivier Mrs.	15	42	71	17 . 3	8 . 11 . 6
Lippie Mrs.	6	38	34	10 . 12	5 . 6
Redman "	—	40	44	9 . 16	4 . 1 . (?)
Chapman "	52	150	79	43 . 8	21 . 15
Jarvis	3	77	55	18 . 8	9 . 4
Cohayne	2	19	7	4 . 1	2 . — . 6
Dumay	17	31	36	12 . 10	6 . 5
Grenier Mrs.	—	18	16	4 . 6	2 . 3
Gratis-Davis					
Miss	23	27	13	11 . 2	5 . 11
Paddock ——	1	24	26	6 . 9	3 . 4 . 6
	17	42	3	10 . 17	5 . 8 . 6
	147	573	433	166 . —	83 . — . —
			Money		24 . 14 . 6
					107 . 14 . 6

April 14 — To Comus & Scapin (for Mr. Ryan)

	Box	Pitt	Gall.	Value
Tickets	249	190	101	100 . 17 . —
Money				66 . 7 . 6
			Total	£167 . 4 . 6

April 16   To Jovial Crew & ªDay of Taste, or London Raree
Show (for Mrs. Vincent)

	Box	Pitt	Gall.	Value
Tickets	127	208	153	83 . 5 . —
Money				76 . 4 . 6
			Total	£159 . 9 . 6

April 17   To Macbeth & Lethe (for Mr. Poitier, Jun.)

	Box	Pitt	Gall.	Value
Tickets	79	92	58	39 . 7
Money				47 ——
			Total	£86 . 7

April 18   To Coriolanus & Lethe (for Mrs. Barrington)
Mrs. Lampe

	Box	Pitt	Gall.	Value
Barrington	66	188	69	48 . 9 . —
Lampe	34	107	128	40 . 10 . —
Money				24 . 6 . 6
			Total	£113 . 5 . 5

April 19   To Earl of Essex & Miller (for Mrs. Saunders & Mrs. Lee)

	Box	Pitt	Gall.	Value
Saunders	7	68	66	18 . 11 . —
Lee	97	124	71	49 . 19 . —
Money				34 . 14 . 6
			Total	£103 . 4 . 6

April 22   To Othello & Miller (for Miss Hillyard)

	Box	Pitt	Gall.	Value
Tickets	101	278	129	79 . 17 . —
Money				24 . 4 . 6
			Total	£104 . 1 . 6

April 24   To Sir Courtly Nice (for Mr. Dunstall)

	Box	Pitt	Gall.	Value
Tickets	172	681	138	158 . 19 . —
Money				34 . 14 . —
			Total	£193 . 13 . —

April 25 To Jovial Crew & Country House (for Mattocks, Green, Pitt)

	Box	Pitt	Gall.	Value		
Mattocks	25	176	100	14.13 —	(*sic*)	[42:13]
Green	28	90	83	28.16 —		
Pitt	14	149	216	47.9 —	(*sic*)	[47:15]
Money				53.10.6		

Total £191.8.6 (*sic*) [172.14.6]

April 28 To Wit without Money & Statue ——

	Box	Pitt	Gall.	Value		
Miles	15	178	62	36.13.—		
Baker	86	124	67	46.16——		
Young	18	75	80	23.15—		
Furgeson ..	9	57	39	14.14—		
	128	434	248—			
Money				20.19—		

162.17— (*sic*) [142.17]

April 29 To Old Batchelor & Statue (for Mr. Collins & Miss Dawson)

	Box	Pitt	Gall.	Value
Collins	36	298	155	69.4.—
Dawson	122	194	144	74.—.—
	158	492	299	143.4.—
Money				84.9.6
				£227.13.6

April 30 — To Romeo & Hob (for Mr. Manet)

	Box	Pitt	Gall.	Value
Tickets	93	225	141	71.2.—
Money				72.14.—
				£143.16.—

May 1ˢᵗ To Provᵈ Husband & Statue

	Box	Pitt	Gall.	Value
Mr. Costello	102	288	246	93.6.—
Mr. Hull	72	162	47	47.—.—
	174	450	293	140.6.—
Money				39.19.—
				£180.5.—

May 2 To Funeral & Petruchio

	Box	Pitt	Gall.	Value
Tickets	260	830	247	205.4.—
Money				37.11.6
				£242.15.6

May 3ᵈ To Country Lasses & Statue
Tickets for undermᵈ ——

	Box	Pitt	Gall	Value	½ Value
Gibbs		4	22	2.16.—	1. 8.—
Courtney	30	141	39	32.11	16. 5.6
Rawlins	17	44	44	15. 5	7.12.6
A Person in distress	37	92	57	28.15	14. 7.6
Miss White	17	29	37	12. 6	6. 3.—
Goold	3	15	31	6. 2	3. 1.—
Gratis-Hitchcock	12	30	10	8.10	4. 5.—
Gratis-Gwyn	2	28	47	9. 8	4.14.—
	118	383	287	115.13	57.16.6

Money 31. 8.6

Receipt £89. 5.0

May 5 To Henry yᵉ 5ᵗʰ wᵗʰ Duke & No Duke

	Box	Pitt	Gall.	Value
Martin	55	306	204	80. 1.—
Anderson	21	280	92	56.12.—
Rᵈ Smith	30	208	192	57.15.—
				£194. 8.—

Money 32. 7.6

226.15.6

May 6 To Stratagem & Statue

	Box	Pitt	Gall.	Value
Sarjant	50	178	65	45.14.—
Roberts	100	293	135	82. 9.—
	150	471	200	128. 3.—

Money 46. 7.6

Total £174.10.6

May 7 To Merchant of Venice & Flora

	Box	Pitt	Gall.	Value
Bennet	13	408	311	95.11.—
Legge	71	305	136	77. 2.—
	84	713	447	172.13.—

Money .... 32.11.—

£205. 4.—

May 8   To Way of the World & Lethe

	Box	Pitt	Gall.	Value
Mr. Creswick	45	89	31	27 : 14 :
Depe	157	164	155	79 . 7 . —
Sledge	18	54	70	19 . 12 . —
Jonsoleen	58	179	125	53 . 17 . —
	278	486	381	180 . 10 . —
Money				32 . 2 . —
				212 . 12 . —

May 9 — To Consc. Lovers wth Duke & No Duke

	Box	Pitt	Gall.	Value
Tickets	107	478	208	119 . 5 . —
Money				26 . 2 . 6
				£145 . 7 . 6
Money				26 . 2 . 6
				£171 . 10 . —

May 12   To Fop's Fortune & Lying Valet

	Box	Pitt	Gall.	Value
Mr. Wignel	58	401	248	99 . 9 . —
Mr. Davis	90	199	166	68 . 19 . —
	148	600	414	168 . 8 . —
Money				28 . 2 . 6
			Total	£196 . 10 . 6

May 14   To Royal Merchant & Siege of Quebec

	Box	Pitt	Gall.	Value
Holton	9	109	92	27 . 16 . —
Buck	17	56	97	22 . 7 . —
Perry	10	119	191	39 . 9 . —
Weller	13	87	131	29 . 8 . —
				119 .
Money				41
			Total	£160

May 15 — To Sir Courtly Nice & Flora

	Box	Pitt	Gall	Value	½ Value
Evans	299	144	136	109 . 19 . —	
Letsam	45	46	50	23 . 3	11 . 11 . 6
Potter	28	58	79	23 . 12	11 . 16 .
Hede	12	94	84	25 . 10	12 . 15 .
	384	342	349	182 . 4	36 . 2 . 6
Money					18 . 5 . 6
Mr. Evan's deficiency					25 . 17 . 3
Rec'd by Mr. Rich					£80 . 5 . 3

May 16   To Henry the 4th & Devil to Pay

	Box	Pitt	Gall.	Value
Condell	132	212	98	74.12.—
Vaughan	151	147	113	71. 2.—
Green	206	119	45	73.13.—
	489	278	256	219.11.—
	Money			18.18.—
			Total	238. 9.—

May 19   To Bold Stroke & Contrivances

Messrs —— Tickets

	Box	Pitt	Gall.	Value	½ Value
Wilford	—	39	45	10: 7 :	5. 3.6
Ross	4	153	60	29.19	14.19.6
Mylebroke	—	40	128	18.16	9. 8
Dymuch	—	7	41	5. 3	2.11.6
Trotts	165	40	11	48. 7	20. 3.4
Bosford	—	12	38	5.12	2.16
Slater	—	56	81	16.10	8. 5
Clarke	4	33	52	11. 3	5.11.6
Toten	—	32	48	9.12	4.16
Smith	1	25	29	6.18	3. 9
S. Griffith	—	11	11	2.18	1. 9
Coles	9	45	80	17.—	8.10
Darby	—	150	161	38.12	19. 6
Clingo	4	37	39	10. 9	5. 4.6
	187	681	824	231. 6	111.12.10
		Money —			29. 8
					£141.—.10

An Oratorio Season at Drury Lane Theatre in 1779 ^a

Receipts 1st Night

Judas Macc: .... 19 Feb. 1779

		£	s	d
124	— Boxes 10^s/ each	65 "	2 "	0
152	Pitt 5^s/ each	38 "	0 "	0
427	1st Gall:^y 3/6	74 "	14 "	6
199	2nd Gall .... 2^s	19 "	18 "	0
		£197 "	14 "	6

^a *Memorandum Book — Nightly Accounts 1776–1779 Old Theatre,* Folger Shakespeare Library.

2ᵈ Night .... Esther 24ᵗʰ Feb ....

62	... Box	32 " 11 " 0
113	... Pitt	28 " 5 " 0
250	... 1ˢᵗ Gall:	43 " 15 " 0
137	... 2ᵈ Gall	13 " 14 " 0

£118 " 5 " 0

Am: 1ˢᵗ Nᵗ .... 4 " 6 " 0

£122 " 11 " 0

3ᵈ Night 26ᵗʰ Feb .... 1779 ....

Acis & Galatea .... £ S d

98 Boxes	51 " 9 " 0
156 Pitt	39 " 0 " 0
355 1ˢᵗ Gall:	62 " 2 " 6
168 2ᵈ Gall:	16 " 16 " 0
Am: 2ᵈ Night	4 " 5 " 6

£173 " 13 " 0

4th Night ....

Acis & Galatea ....

£ S d

70 Boxes	36 " 15 " 0
98 Pitt	24 " 10 " 0
369 1ˢᵗ Gall	64 " 11 " 6
139 —2ⁿᵈ Gall	13 " 18 " 0

£139 " 14 " 6

Am. 3ᵈ Nᵗ .... 5 " 10 " 6

£145 " 4 " 0

5ᵗʰ N ....

Boxes 69	36 " 4 " 6
Pitt 105	26 " 5 " 0
1ˢᵗ Gall: 299	52 " 6 " 6
2ⁿᵈ Gall 129	12 " 18 " 0

127 " 14 " 0

Am 4ᵗʰ Nᵗ .... 2 " 3 " 6

£129 " 17 " 6

6ᵗʰ Nᵗ .... £ S d

Boxes 122	64 " 1 " 0
Pitt 149	37 " 5 " 0
1ˢᵗ Gall: 394	68 " 19 " 0
2ⁿᵈ Gall 125	12 " 10 " 0

£182 " 15 " 0

5th Nᵗ Am .... 1 " 3 " 0

£183 " 18 " 0

7th Night ....   £   S   d
    Boxes 85 ....   44 " 12 " 6
    Pitt : 137 ....   34 " 5 " 0
   1st Gall : 384 ....   67 " 4 " 0
   2nd Gall : 141 ....   14 " 2 " 0
                ——————
               £160 " 3 " 6
      Am 6th Nt ....   15 " 0
               £160 " 18 " 6

8th Night ....   £   S   d
    Boxes 60 ....   31 " 10 " 0
    Pitt —106 ....   26 " 10 " 0
   1st Gall —343 ....   60 " 0 " 6
   2d Gall :—114 ....   11 " 8 " 0
               £129 " 8 " 6
      Am — 7th Nt ....   1 " 4 " 0
               £130 " 12 " 6

9th Night ....   £   S   d
    Boxes 52 ....   27 " 6 " 0
    Pitt   68 ....   17 " 0 " 0
   1st Gall : 306 ....   53 " 11 " 0
   2d Gall : 116 ....   11 " 12 " 0
               109 " 9 " 0
     2 from Pit to Boxes....................   11 " 0
               110 " 0 " 0
      Am : 8th Nt ....   2 " 14 " 6
               £112 " 14 " 6

10th Night ....   £   S   d
    Boxes 170 ....   89 " 5 " 0
    Pitt —286 ....   71 " 10 " 0
   1st Gall— 526 ....   92 " 1 " 0
   2d Gall— 259 ....   25 " 18 " 0
               £278 " 14 " 0
      Am 9th Nt ....   7 " 6
               £279 " 1 " 6

11th Night ....

			£	S	d
Boxes	....	111	58 "	5 "	6
Pitt	....	187	46 "	15 "	0
1st Gall.	....	453	79 "	5 "	6
2^d Gall	....	202	20 "	4 "	0
			204 "	10 "	0
Am 10th N^t			1 "	19 "	0
			206 "	9 "	0
Am 11th N^t			1 "	13 "	0
			208 "	2 "	0

Mr. Stanley, Acc^t.................

1st N^t	....	107 "	14 "	6
2^d	....	122 "	11 "	0
3^d	....	173 "	13 "	0
4	....	145 "	5 "	0
5	....	129 "	17 "	6
6	....	183 "	18 "	0
7	....	160 "	18 "	6
8	....	130 "	12 "	6
9	....	112 "	14 "	6
10	....	279 "	1 "	6
11	....	208 "	2 "	0
	Recp—1844 "	8 "	0	
	Exp—1672 "	0 "	5	
	£172 "	7 "	7	
	Moiety 86 "	3 "	9½	

APPENDIX C. A STATISTICAL SURVEY OF EIGHTEENTH CENTURY THEATRE REPERTOIRE

I. The Repertoire at Drury Lane Theatre. Compiled from *Drury Lane Calendar 1747–1776,* edited by Dougald Mac-Millan, Oxford, 1938.

II. The Repertoire at Covent Garden Theatre. A partial listing compiled from John Genest, *Some Account of the English Stage . . . 1660–1830,* 10 vols., Bath, 1832.

Productions are listed according to type and date of original performances, the total number of seasons in the repertoire, the greatest number of performances in a single season and the date of that "best season," and the total number of performances in the period 1747–1776.

Types of productions given in the survey agree in general with those given by Allardyce Nicoll in *A History of Restoration Drama, 1660–1700,* Cambridge, 1923; *A History of Early Eighteenth Century Drama, 1700–1750,* Cambridge, 1925; *A History of Late Eighteenth Century Drama, 1750–1800,* Cambridge, 1927.

Key to Types of Production

T.	Tragedy	M.	Masque
H.T.	Historical Tragedy	B.O.	Ballad Opera
C.	Comedy	C.O.	Comic Opera
T.C.	Tragi-Comedy	Burl.	Burletta
F.	Farce	Ent.	Entertainment, spectacle
O.F.	Operatic Farce	P.	Pantomime
O.	Opera	Dr.P.	Dramatic Poem
Ora.	Oratorio	Past.	Pastoral
D.O.	Dramatic Opera	Prel.	Prelude
H.	History	Int.	Interlude

I. Repertoire at Drury Lane Theatre, 1747–1776

Authorship	Short Title
Woodward, Henry	*Queen Mab*
Woodward, Henry	*The Genii*
Garrick, David	*Harlequin's Invasion*
Woodward, Henry	*Fortunatus*
Ravenscroft, Edward	*The Anatomist*
Garrick, David	*Lethe*
Garrick, David	*The Jubilee*
Coffey, Charles	*The Devil to Pay*
Shakespeare-Garrick	*Romeo and Juliet*
Bickerstaffe, Isaac	*The Padlock*
Townley, James	*High Life below Stairs*
Mendez, Moses	*The Chaplet*
Hoadly, Benjamin	*The Suspicious Husband*
Garrick, David	*Miss in her Teens*
Gay, John	*The Beggar's Opera*
Shakespeare (-Garrick)	*Hamlet*
Unknown	*The Elopement*
Garrick, David	*The Lying Valet*
Shakespeare	*Much Ado about Nothing*
Love, James	*The Witches*
Farquhar, George	*The Stratagem*
Shakespeare-Cibber, C.	*Richard III*
Shakespeare-Garrick	*Cymbeline*
Steele, Sir Richard	*The Conscious Lovers*
Vanbrugh, Sir John	*The Provok'd Wife*
Woodward, Henry	*Harlequin Ranger*
Fielding, Henry	*Intriguing Chambermaid*
Garrick, David and George Colman	*Clandestine Marriage*
Colman, George	*Polly Honeycombe*
Shakespeare-Tate-Garrick	*King Lear*
Cibber, C. and Vanbrugh	*The Provok'd Husband*
Jonson, Ben (-Garrick)	*Every Man in His Humour*
Congreve, William	*The Mourning Bride*
Shakespeare, *et al.*	*The Tempest*

Type	Date	Seasons	Best Season	Date of Best Season	Total Performances	Garrick Acting
P.	1750	16	45	1750–51	259	
P.	1752	12	49	1752–53	207	
P.	1759	11	25	1759–60	171	
P.	1753	14	35	1753–54	158	
F.	1697	19	20	1748–49	157	
F.	1740	23	21	1750–51	154	
Ent.	1769	3	91	1769–70	153	
B.O.	1731	28	14	1748–49	143	
T.	1594–95	25	20	1748–49	142	64
C.O.	1768	8	54	1768–69	142	
F.	1759	17	33	1759–60	140	
M.Ent.	1749	18	30	1749–50	129	
C.	1747	29	13	1747–48	126	109
F.	1747	26	18	1747–48	125	
B.O.	1727	27	11	1760–61	119	
T.	1601–02	29	6	1747–48 [a]	116	56
P.	1767	9	35	1767–68	110	
C.	1741	23	14	1747–48	106	
C.	1598–99	27	16	1748–49	105	104
P.	1762	6	43	1762–63	103	
C.	1706–07	26	7	1750–51	100	80
H.T.	1592–93	27	8	1751–52	100	35
T.	1609–10	15	16	1761–62	98	16
C.	1722	28	7	1751–52	96	
C.	1697	29	9	1747–48	95	93
P.	1751	9	26	1751–52	94	
F.	1733–34	18	19	1748–49	92	
C.	1766	11	19	1765–66	87	
F.	1760	12	30	1760–61	86	
T.	1605–06	26	8	1764–65	83	56
C.	1727–28	26	8	1763–64	82	
C.	1598	22	16	1751–52	82	81
T.	1697	24	13	1750–51	79	24
C.	1611–12	21	18	1757–58	79	

[a] Seasons being equal, the first season is indicated.

Authorship	Short Title
Centlivre, Susannah	*The Wonder*
Colman, George	*The Deuce Is in Him*
Shakespeare-Davenant-Garrick	*Macbeth*
Otway, Thomas	*The Orphan*
Colman, George	*The Jealous Wife*
Rowe, Nicholas	*The Fair Penitent*
Jonson, Ben	*The Alchymist*
Tate, Nahum	*Duke and No Duke*
Foote, Samuel	*Englishman in Paris*
Rowe, Nicholas	*Jane Shore*
Murphy, Arthur	*Way to Keep Him*
Garrick, David	*Peep behind the Curtain*
Otway, Thomas	*Venice Preserv'd*
Hill, Aaron	*Zara*
Garrick, David	*Cymon*
Cumberland, Richard	*The West Indian*
Colman, George	*Musical Lady*
Dodsley, Robert	*King & Miller of Mansfield*
Bickerstaffe, Isaac	*Daphne and Amintor*
Shakespeare	*As You Like It*
Hill, Aaron	*Merope*
Cibber, Colley	*Careless Husband*
Fielding, Henry	*Virgin Unmask'd*
Reed, Joseph	*The Register Office*
Congreve, William	*Way of the World*
Lillo, George	*The London Merchant*
Shakespeare	*Henry VIII*
Whitehead, William	*Trip to Scotland*
Garrick, David	*The Irish Widow*
Centlivre, Susannah	*The Busie Body*
Shakespeare	*Othello*
Shakespeare	*Merchant of Venice*
Foote, Samuel	*The Author*
Fielding, Henry	*The Lottery*
Woodward, Henry	*Mercury Harlequin*
Love, James	*Rites of Hecate*

Type	Date	Seasons	Best Season	Date of Best Season	Total Performances	Garrick Acting
C.	1714	18	18	1756–57	78	68
F.	1763	12	24	1763–64	78	
T.	1605–06	28	5	1748–49	77	21
T.	1680	23	9	1758–59	77	37
C.	1761	15	20	1760–61	75	36
T.	1703	23	7	1760–61	74	48
C.	1610	24	8	1755–56	74	70
F.	1684	12	17	1749–50	72	
C.	1753	10	21	1753–54	72	
T.	1713–14	24	9	1747–48	65	46
C.	1760	16	14	1759–60	65	
Burl.	1767	9	25	1767–68	65	
T.	1682	24	8	1763–64	64	24
T.	1735	23	5	1758–59	64	56
D.O.	1767	7	28	1766–67	64	
C.	1771	6	28	1770–71	63	
F.	1762	11	16	1762–63	62	
D.Tale	1736–37	23	8	1748–49	61	
C.O.	1765	7	31	1765–66	61	
C.	1600–01	22	5	1752–53	59	
T.	1749	15	11	1748–49	59	26
C.	1704	20	11	1756–57	58	
B.O.	1734–35	14	10	1748–49	58	
F.	1761	11	11	1766–67	57	
C.	1700	18	10	1750–51	56	
T.	1731	24	7	1749–50	54	
H.	1613	11	9	1761–62	54	
F.	1770	7	18	1769–70	54	
C.	1772	4	20	1772–73	54	
C.	1709	17	14	1758–59	53	
T.	1604–05	20	6	1747–48	52	7
C.	1596–97	18	8	1768–69	52	
C.	1757	8	20	1756–57	52	
B.O.	1731–32	13	8	1751–52	51	
P.	1756	3	36	1756–57	51	
P.	1763	2	47	1763–64	51	

Authorship	*Short Title*
Fletcher, John	*Rule a Wife and Have a Wife*
Buckingham (*et al.*)	*The Rehearsal*
Mendez, Moses	*Double Disappointment*
Love, James	*The Hermit*
Garrick, David (-Shakespeare)	*Catharine and Petruchio*
Southerne, Thomas (various alt.)	*Oroonoko*
Shakespeare	*Twelfth Night*
Shadwell, Charles (various alt.)	*Fair Quaker of Deal*
Congreve, William	*Love for Love*
Murphy, Arthur	*The Old Maid*
Foote, Samuel	*The Lyar*
Unknown	*Pigmy Revels*
Garrick, David	*The Guardian*
Colman, George (from Shakespeare)	*A Fairy Tale*
Rowe, Nicholas	*Tamerlane*
Farquhar, George	*Recruiting Officer*
Wycherley, Wm. (-Bickerstaffe)	*Plain-Dealer*
Murphy, Arthur	*The Apprentice*
Dibdin, Charles	*The Deserter*
Fielding, Henry	*The Mock Doctor*
Murphy, Arthur	*All in the Wrong*
Foote, Samuel	*Mayor of Garratt*
Thomson, James	*Tancred and Sigismunda*
Philips, Ambrose	*Distress'd Mother*
Garrick, David	*Institution of the Garter*
Dryden, John (-Hawkesworth)	*Amphitryon*
Burgoyne, John	*Maid of the Oaks*
Woodward, Henry	*Proteus*
Whitehead, William	*School for Lovers*
Fletcher (-Buckingham-Garrick)	*The Chances*
Garrick, David	*The Male Coquette*
Lee, Nathaniel	*The Rival Queens*
Bate (Bate-Dudley), Henry	*Rival Candidates*
Centlivre, Susannah	*Bold Stroke for a Wife*
Moore, Edward	*The Foundling*

Type	Date	Seasons	Best Season	Date of Best Season	Total Performances	Garrick Acting
C.	1624	17	6	1758–59	50	42
Burl.	1671	17	8	1752–53	49	43
F.	1745–46	8	21	1752–53	49	
P.	1766	4	29	1765–66	49	
F.	1756	15	14	1755–56	48	
T.	1696	14	10	1751–52	48	
C.	1600–01	14	14	1771–72	47	
C.	1709–10	9	14	1755–56	47	
C.	1695	17	6	1753–54	46	
C.	1761	11	17	1761–62	44	
C.	1762	9	10	1767–68	44	
P.	1772	2	36	1772–73	44	
F.	1759	13	17	1758–59	43	
Int.	1763	4	19	1763–64	43	
T.	1701	28	3	1767–68	43	
C.	1706	18	6	1750–51	42	
C.	1676	9	17	1765–66	40	
F.	1756	8	16	1755–56	40	
Int.	1773	3	15	1774–75	40	
B.O.	1732	13	7	1759–60	39	
F.	1761	11	11	1761–62	39	
C.	1763	7	10	1771–72	37	
T.	1744–45	18	6	1755–56	36	
T.	1711–12	11	8	1764–65	35	
M.	1771	2	33	1771–72	35	
C.	1756	9	11	1756–57	33	
C.O.	1774	2	25	1774–75	33	
P.	1755	1	33	1754–55	33	
C.	1762	10	13	1761–62	32	14
C.	1615	8	13	1754–55	32	31
F.	1757	8	15	1757–58	32	
T.	1677	10	9	1764–65	31	
C.O.	1775	2	17	1774–75	31	
C.	1717	12	4	1748–49	29	
C.	1747	8	15	1747–48	28	20

Authorship	*Short Title*
Bickerstaffe, Isaac (-Cibber, C.)	*The Hypocrite*
Garrick, David (-Wycherley)	*The Country Girl*
Murphy, Arthur	*The Grecian Daughter*
Moore, Edward	*The Gamester*
Macklin, Charles	*Love-a-la-Mode*
Kelly, Hugh	*School for Wives*
Mendez, Moses	*Shepherd's Lottery*
Fielding, Henry	*The Miser*
Southerne, Thomas (-Garrick)	*Fatal Marriage*
Cumberland, Richard	*Fashionable Lover*
Kelly, Hugh	*False Delicacy*
Garrick, David	*Bon Ton*
Vanbrugh, Sir John	*The Confederacy*
Steele, Sir Richard	*The Funeral*
Brown, John	*Barbarossa*
Shakespeare (-Garrick)	*The Winter's Tale*
Unknown	*Harlequin's Jacket*
Dryden, John (-Garrick)	*King Arthur*
Young, Edward	*The Revenge*
Shirley, James (-Garrick)	*The Gamester(s)*
Addison, Joseph	*The Drummer*
Murphy, Arthur	*Orphan of China*
Garrick, David	*Linco's Travels*
Hawkesworth, John	*Edgar and Emeline*
Whitehead, William	*The Roman Father*
Garrick, David	*The Enchanter*
Sheridan, Mrs. Frances	*The Discovery*
Cibber, Colley	*The Double Gallant*
Shakespeare	*Measure for Measure*
Griffith, Mrs. Elizabeth	*School for Rakes*
Lloyd, Robert	*Capricious Lovers*
Vanbrugh, Sir John	*The Relapse*
Milton, John (-Dalton, John)	*Comus*
Shakespeare	*Henry IV, Part II*
Jephson, Robert	*Braganza*
Brooke, Henry	*Earl of Essex*

Type	Date	Seasons	Best Season	Date of Best Season	Total Performances	Garrick Acting
C.	1768	7	15	1768–69	28	
C.	1766	6	14	1766–67	28	
T.	1772	5	12	1771–72	28	
T.	1753	7	12	1752–53	27	12
F.	1759	3	23	1759–60	27	
C.	1773	3	21	1773–74	27	
M.	1751	3	20	1751–52	27	
C.	1732–33	17	3	1748–49	26	
T.	1694	8	14	1757–58	26	21
C.	1772	4	18	1771–72	26	
C.	1768	4	18	1767–68	26	
F.	1775	2	18	1775–76	26	
C.	1705	12	7	1759–60	25	
C.	1701	11	6	1759–60	25	
T.	1754	5	16	1754–55	25	
C.	1610–11	5	13	1755–56	25	23
P.	1775	2	22	1774–75	25	
D.O.	1770	2	21	1770–71	25	
T.	1721	7	9	1751–52	24	
C.	1757	4	13	1772–73	24	7
C.	1715–16	9	10	1754–55	23	
T.	1759	7	9	1758–59	23	11
Int.	1767	7	8	1771–72	23	
Ent.	1761	6	10	1760–61	23	
T.	1750	5	12	1749–50	23	20
Int.	1760	3	17	1760–61	23	
C.	1763	2	17	1762–63	23	23
C.	1707	9	6	1759–60	22	
C.	1604–05	7	6	1756–57	22	
C.	1769	5	13	1768–69	22	
C.O.	1764	3	17	1764–65	22	
C.	1697	10	5	1749–50	21	
M.	1634	8	5	1749–50	21	
H.	1597–98	7	7	1762–63	21	15
T.	1775	2	15	1774–75	21	
T.	1750	9	9	1760–61	20	

Authorship	*Short Title*
Farquhar, George	*The Inconstant*
Cibber, Colley	*Love's Last Shift*
Francklin, Thomas	*Earl of Warwick*
Shakespeare	*King John*
Cumberland, Richard	*Note of Hand*
Beaumont and Fletcher (-Colman)	*Philaster*
Dibdin, Charles	*The Wedding Ring*
Garrick, David	*A Christmas Tale*
Vanbrugh, Sir John	*The Mistake*
Cibber, C. (-John Hippisley)	*Flora; or, Hob in the Well*
Cibber, Colley	*Damon and Phillida*
Cibber, Susannah M.	*The Oracle*
Colman, George	*English Merchant*
Whitehead, William	*Creusa*
Murphy, Arthur	*Zenobia*
Garrick, David	*Neck or Nothing*
Shakespeare	*Merry Wives of Windsor*
Home, John	*Douglas*
Bickerstaffe, Isaac	*Thomas and Sally*
Love, James (from Brome)	*Ladies' Frolick*
Garrick, David	*Farmer's Return from London*
Cowley, Mrs. Hannah	*The Runaway*
Garrick, David	*Theatrical Candidates*
Howard, Sir Robert	*The Committee*
Bickerstaffe, Isaac	*Maid of the Mill*
Fielding, Henry	*Tom Thumb the Great*
Murphy, Arthur	*The Upholsterer*
Smollett, Tobias	*The Reprisal*
Burney, Charles	*The Cunning Man*
Francklin, Thomas	*Matilda*
Garrick, David	*May Day*
Bickerstaffe, Isaac	*Lionel and Clarissa*
Kenrick, William	*The Widow'd Wife*
Garrick, David	*Lilliput*
Cibber, Colley	*Love Makes a Man*

Type	Date	Seasons	Best Season	Date of Best Season	Total Performances	Garrick Acting
C.	1701–02	9	6	1753–54	20	6
C.	1696	7	5	1750–51	20	6
T.	1766	6	12	1766–67	20	
H.T.	1596–97	5	8	1753–54	20	8
F.	1774	3	13	1773–74	20	
T.	1608	3	17	1763–64	20	
C.O.	1773	3	13	1772–73	20	
Ent.	1773	2	18	1773–74	20	
C.	1705	10	4	1754–55	19	13
B.O.	1729	7	6	1766–67	19	
B.O.	1729	6	6	1747–48	19	
M.	1752	6	7	1755–56	19	
C.	1767	2	15	1766–67	19	
T.	1754	5	9	1753–54	18	18
T	1768	5	7	1767–68	18	
F.	1766	2	11	1766–67	18	
C.	1601–02	13	3	1754–55	17	
T.	1756	7	6	1768–69	17	
Int.	1760	7	4	1762–63	17	
C.O.	1770	4	10	1770–71	17	
Int.	1762	2	14	1761–62	17	17
C.	1776	1	17	1775–76	17	
Int.	1775	1	17	1775–76	17	
C.	1622	10	3	1771–72	16	
C.O.	1765	6	4	1768–69	16	
Burl.	1730	5	5	1755–56	16	
F.	1758	4	12	1757–58	16	
C.	1757	4	11	1756–57	16	
Int.	1766	2	14	1766–67	16	
T.	1775	2	11	1774–75	16	
O.F.	1775	1	16	1775–76	16	
C.O.	1768	4	9	1769–70	15	
C.	1767	2	14	1767–68	15	
Int.	1756	1	15	1756–57	15	
C.	1700	9	3	1752–53	14	

Authorship	*Short Title*
King, Thomas	*Wit's Last Stake*
Clive, Mrs. Catherine	*Rehearsal: Bayes in Petti-coats*
Bickerstaffe, Isaac	*Love in a Village*
Smith, Edmund	*Phaedra and Hippolatus*
Miller, J., Hoadly, J. (-Garrick)	*Mahomet the Imposter*
Jones, Henry	*Earl of Essex*
Bickerstaffe, Isaac	*Absent Man*
Andrews, Miles Peter	*The Election*
Home, John	*Agis*
Cumberland, Richard	*The Choleric Man*
Mallet, David	*Elvira*
Shakespeare	*Henry IV, Part I*
Mallet, David	*Britannia*
Cibber, Colley	*She Wou'd and She Wou'd Not*
Hughes, John	*Siege of Damascus*
Tomkis, Thomas (-Garrick)	*Albumazar*
Foote, Samuel	*Diversions of the Morning*
Carey, Henry	*Dragon of Wantley*
Dryden, John	*All for Love*
Congreve, William	*The Double-Dealer*
Dryden, John	*The Spanish Fryar*
Congreve, William	*The Old Bachelor*
Cibber, Colley	*The Refusal*
Celesia, Mrs. D. (Mallet)	*Almida*
Garrick, D. (from Shakespeare)	*The Fairies*
Dow, Alexander	*Zingis*
Home, John	*Alonzo*
Murphy, Arthur	*The Desert Island*
Garrick, David	*Meeting of the Company*
Shakespeare (-Cumberland)	*Timon of Athens*
Dodsley, Robert	*Triumph of Peace*
Unknown	*Vertumnus and Pomona*
Crisp, Henry	*Virginia*
Murphy, Arthur	*The Citizen*

Type	Date	Seasons	Best Season	Date of Best Season	Total Performances	Garrick Acting
F.	1768	6	7	1768–69	14	
Burl.	1750	6	4	1749–50	14	
C.O.	1762	6	3	1768–69	14	
T.	1707	4	8	1751–52	14	
T.	1744	3	12	1765–66	14	
T.	1753	4	6	1755–56	13	
F.	1768	3	8	1767–68	13	
Int.	1774	2	12	1774–75	13	
T.	1758	2	11	1757–58	13	13
C.	1774	1	13	1774–75	13	
T.	1762	1	13	1762–63	13	
H.	1597–98	7	3	1769–70	12	
M.	1755	4	6	1754–55	12	
C.	1702	4	4	1747–48	12	
T.	1719–20	3	5	1758–59	12	
C.	1615	2	7	1747–48	12	
Ent.	1747	1	12	1758–59	12	
Burl.	1737	1	12	1747–48	12	
T.	1677	7	3	1772–73	11	
C.	1694	7	3	1756–57	11	
T.C.	1679–80	6	4	1762–63	11	
C.	1693	3	9	1753–54	11	
C.	1720	3	5	1747–48	11	
T.	1771	2	10	1770–71	11	
D.O.	1755	2	9	1754–55	11	
T.	1768	1	11	1768–69	11	
T.	1773	1	11	1772–73	11	
Dr. P.	1760	1	11	1759–60	11	
Prel.	1774	1	11	1774–75	11	
T.	1607–08	1	11	1771–72	11	
M.	1748–49	1	11	1748–49	11	
Ent.	1748	1	11	1748–49	11	
T.	1754	1	11	1775–76	11	11
F.	1761	6	3	1773–74	10	

Authorship	*Short Title*
Glover, Richard	*Boadicia*
Dibdin, Charles	*The Cobler*
Home, John	*The Fatal Discovery*
Rolt, Richard	*The Royal Shepherd*
Bickerstaffe, Isaac	*The Sultan*
Bickerstaffe, Isaac	*'Tis Well 'Tis No Worse*
Cibber, Colley	*The School Boy*
Bullock, Christopher	*Woman is a Riddle*
Massinger, Philip	*New Way to Pay Old Debts*
Hartson, Hall	*Countess of Salisbury*
Shakespeare	*All's Well that Ends Well*
Jonson, Ben (-George Colman)	*The Silent Woman*
Lloyd, Robert	*Arcadia*
Brown, John	*Athelstan*
Shakespeare	*Coriolanus*
Shirley, William	*Edward the Black Prince*
Moore, Edward	*Gil Blas*
Johnson, Samuel	*Mahomet and Irene*
Dow, Alexander	*Sethona*
Home, John	*Siege of Aquileia*
Cibber, Colley	*Lady's Last Stake*
Rolt, Richard	*Almena*
Garrick, David	*Ode (Shakespeare Memorial)*
Fielding, Henry (-Unknown)	*Don Quixote in England*
Young, Edward	*The Brothers*
Wycherley, William (-John Lee)	*The Country Wife*
Carey, Henry	*The Contrivances*
Macklin, Charles (from Regnard)	*A Will and No Will*
Coffey, Charles	*Phebe*
Foote, Samuel	*Taste*
Ryder, Thomas (from Vanbrugh)	*Like Master Like Man*
Vanbrugh, Sir John	*Aesop*
Rowe, Nicholas	*Ambitious Step-mother*
King, Thomas	*Love at First Sight*
Lennox, Charlotte (from Chapman, Marston, Jonson)	*Old City Manners*

Type	Date	Seasons	Best Season	Date of Best Season	Total Performances	Garrick Acting
T.	1753	1	10	1753–54	10	10
B.O.	1774	1	10	1774–74	10	
T.	1769	1	10	1768–69	10	
O.	1764	1	10	1763–64	10	
O.F.	1775	1	10	1775–76	10	
C.	1770	1	10	1770–71	10	
F.	1702	5	5	1748–49	9	
C.	1716	4	5	1759–60	9	
C.	1626	4	4	1748–49	9	
T.	1765	4	4	1767–68	9	
C.	1603–04	3	4	1757–58	9	
C.	1609	2	5	1752–53	9	
Past.	1761	1	9	1761–62	9	
T.	1756	1	9	1755–56	9	9
T.	1607–08	1	9	1754–55	9	
T.	1749–50	1	9	1749–50	9	9
C.	1751	1	9	1750–51	9	9
T.	1748–49	1	9	1748–49	9	9
T.	1774	1	9	1773–74	9	
T.	1760	1	9	1759–60	9	9
C.	1707	6	2	1755–56	8	
O.	1764	2	6	1764–65	8	
Ent.	1769	1	8	1769–70	8	8
F.	1752	1	8	1751–52	8	
T.	1753	1	8	1752–53	8	8
F.	1765	2	6	1764–65	8	
F.	1715	5	3	1760–61	7	
F.	1746	2	6	1747–48	7	
B.O.	1729	2	6	1762–63	7	
C.	1752	2	5	1751–52	7	
C.	1766	2	4	1767–68	7	
C.	1697	1	7	1758–59	7	
T.	1700	1	7	1758–59	7	
B.O.	1763	1	7	1763–64	7	
C.	1775	1	7	1775–76	7	

Authorship	*Short Title*
Colman, George	*The Spleen*
Harris, James	*The Spring*
Woodward, Henry	*Tit for Tat*
Dibdin, Charles	*The Waterman*
Lee, Nathaniel	*Theodosius*
Unknown (from Mrs. Centlivre)	*The Ghost*
Rowe, Nicholas	*Lady Jane Gray*
Foote, Samuel	*The Knights*
Addison, Joseph	*Cato*
Unknown (from Otway)	*Scapin*
Shakespeare (-Capell-Garrick)	*Antony and Cleopatra*
Noverre, M. Jean Georges	*The Chinese Festival*
Francis, Philip	*Eugenia*
Hull, Thomas	*Pharnaces*
Griffith, Mrs. Elizabeth	*Platonic Wife*
Shakespeare (-Benjamin Victor)	*Two Gentlemen of Verona*
Steele, Sir Richard	*Tender Husband*
McNamara-Morgan (from Shakespeare)	*Sheep-Shearing*
Dell, Henry (from Dryden-Cibber)	*Frenchified Lady Never in Paris*
Crowne, John	*Sir Courtly Nice*
Dodsley, Robert	*The Toy Shop*
Shakespeare	*Henry V*
Lee, John (from Vanbrugh)	*Man of Quality*
Dryden, John	*Don Sebastian*
Ravenscroft, Edward	*London Cuckolds*
Cumberland, Richard	*The Brothers*
Gay, John	*The What d'ye Call It*
Woodward, H. (from Mrs. Centlivre)	*Marplot in Lisbon*
Cibber, Colley	*The Non-Juror*
Dryden, John (adapted)	*The Secular Masque*
Mendez, Moses	*Robin Hood*
Fletcher, John (-Vanbrugh)	*The Pilgrim*
Downing, George	*Humours of the Turf*

Type	Date	Seasons	Best Season	Date of Best Season	Total Performances	Garrick Acting
F.	1776	1	7	1775–76	7	
Past.	1762	1	7	1762–63	7	
Int.	1748	1	7	1748–49	7	
B.O.	1774	1	7	1775–76	7	
T.	1680	4	2	1770–71	6	
C.	1767	3	4	1770–71	6	
T.	1715	3	3	1762–63	6	
F.	1749	2	5	1753–54	6	
T.	1713	2	4	1756–57	6	
F.	1753	2	3	1752–53	6	
T.	1606–07	1	6	1758–59	6	6
Ent.	1755	1	6	1755–56	6	
T.	1752	1	6	1751–52	6	6
O.	1765	1	6	1764–65	6	
C.	1765	1	6	1764–65	6	
C.	1594–95	1	6	1762–63	6	
C.	1705	5	1	1750–51	5	
Past.	1754	4	2	1773–74	5	
F.	1756	4	2	1757–58	5	
C.	1685	3	2	1751–52	5	
Dr. Sat.	1734–35	2	4	1756–57	5	
H.	1598–99	2	4	1747–48	5	
F.	1773	2	4	1775–76	5	
T.C.	1689	1	5	1752–53	5	
C.	1682	3	2	1749–50	4	
C.	1769	3	2	1774–75	4	
T.C.P.F.	1714–15	2	3	1747–48	4	
F.	1755	2	3	1754–55	4	
C.	1717	2	2	1752–53	4	
M.	c. 1670	1	4	1750–51	4	
M.	1750	1	4	1750-51	4	
C.	1621	1	4	1750–51	4	
C.	1772	1	4	1771–72	4	

Authorship	*Short Title*
Delap, John	*Hecuba*
Mallet, David	*Eurydice*
Bate (Bate-Dudley), Henry	*Blackamoor Wash'd White*
Arne, Thomas	*Artaxerxes*
Glover, Richard	*Medea*
Shadwell, Thomas	*Squire of Alsatia*
Farquhar, George	*Twin Rivals*
Unknown (from Fletcher)	*Tamer Tam'd*
Wycherley, William	*The Country Wife*
Unknown	*London 'Prentice*
Waldron, Francis G.	*Maid of Kent*
Murphy, Arthur	*The Choice*
Reed, Joseph	*Dido*
Arne, Thomas	*Don Saverio*
Sheridan, Mrs. Frances	*The Dupe*
Francklin, Thomas	*Electra*
Behn, Mrs. Aphra (-Unknown)	*Emperor of the Moon*
Unknown (from Sedley)	*The Grumbler*
Ford, John	*Lover's Melancholy*
Unknown (Guerini?)	*Magician of the Mountain*
Carey, Henry	*Chrononhotonthologos*
Unknown	*Mock Orators*
Hiffernan, Paul (from H. Jones)	*Heroine of the Cave*
Gentleman, Francis (from Jonson)	*The Tobacconist*
Kelly, Hugh	*A Word to the Wise*
Cumberland, Richard	*Amelia*
Cibber, Colley (from Dryden)	*Comical Lovers*
Fielding, Henry	*The Debauchees*
Theobald, Lewis	*Double Falsehood*
Unknown	*Harlequin Mountebank*
Unknown (from Fletcher, Massinger)	*Little French Lawyer*
Hiffernan, Paul	*New Hippocrates*
Gentleman, Francis	*The Pantheonites*
Unknown (from Moliere)	*No Wit Like a Woman's*
Addison, Joseph (-Unknown)	*Rosamond*

Type	Date	Seasons	Best Season	Date of Best Season	Total Performances	Garrick Acting
T.	1761	1	4	1761–62	4	
T.	1730–31	1	4	1758–59	4	4
C.O.	1776	1	4	1775–76	4	
O.	1762	1	4	1768–69	4	
T.	1767	3	1	1766–67	3	
C.	1688	3	1	1748–49	3	
C.	1702	2	2	1758–59	3	
F.	1757	2	2	1756–57	3	
C.	1672	3	1	1748–49	3	
C.O.	1754	2	2	1753–54	3	
C.	1773	2	2	1773–74	3	
C.	1765	2	2	1764–65	3	
T.	1767	1	3	1766–67	3	
C.O.	1750	1	3	1749–50	3	
C.	1763	1	3	1763–64	3	
T.	1774	1	3	1774–75	3	
F.	1687	1	3	1748–49	3	
F.	1754	1	3	1753–54	3	
T.	1628	1	3	1747–48	3	
P.	1762	1	3	1762–63	3	
Burl.	1733–34	2	1	1755–56	2	
F.	1756	2	1	1755–56	2	
T.	1774	2	1	1773–74	2	
F.	1760	2	1	1771–72	2	
C.	1770	1	2	1769–70	2	
C.O.	1768	1	2	1771–72	2	
C.	1706–07	1	2	1751–52	2	
C.	1732	1	2	1747–48	2	
Play	1727	1	2	1769–70	2	
P.	1756	1	2	1755–56	2	
F.	1749	1	2	1749–50	2	
F.	1761	1	2	1760–61	2	
Ent.	1773	1	2	1773–74	2	
F.	1769	1	2	1768–69	2	
O.	1706–07	1	2	1764–65	2	

Authorship	*Short Title*
Hill, John	*The Rout*
Bromfield, William (from Mayne)	*The Schemers*
Baker, Thomas	*Tunbridge Walks*
Townley, James	*The Tutor*
Sheridan, Thomas	*Brave Irishman*
Pye, Mrs. J. Henrietta	*Capricious Lady*
Bickerstaffe, Isaac	*The Captive*
Unknown	*Club of Fortune-Hunters*
Andrews, Miles Peter	*The Conjuror*
Unknown (from Moore)	*The Counterfeits*
Brown, John (from Handel)	*The Cure of Saul*
Hoole, John	*Cyrus*
O'Brien, William	*The Duel*
Banks, John	*Unhappy Favorite*
Chapman, Marston, Jonson	*Eastward Hoe*
Havard, William	*The Elopement*
Murphy, Arthur	*Englishman from Paris*
Foote, Samuel	*Englishman Returned from Paris*
Bickerstaffe, Isaac	*Ephesian Matron*
Clive, Mrs. Catherine	*Every Woman in Her Humour*
Clive, Mrs. Catherine	*Faithful Irishwoman*
Vanbrugh, Sir John	*The False Friend*
Kenrick, William	*Falstaff's Wedding*
Otway, Thomas	*Freindship in Fashion*
Unknown	*Galigantus*
Centlivre, Mrs. Susannah	*The Gamester*
Unknown (from Moliere)	*George Dandin*
Unknown (Levies?)	*Harlequin Enchanted*
Moseen, Thomas	*The Heiress*
Cross, Richard	*Hen-Peck'd Captain*
Pordage, Samuel	*Herod and Miriamne*
Granville, Geo., Ld. Lansdowne	*Heroic Love*
Bickerstaffe, Isaac	*He Wou'd if He Cou'd*
Thompson, Edward	*The Hobby Horse*

Type	Date	Seasons	Best Season	Date of Best Season	Total Performances	Garrick Acting
F.	1758	1	2	1758–59	2	
C.	1755	1	2	1754–55	2	
C.	1702–03	1	2	1763–64	2	
F.	1765	1	2	1764–65	2	
F.	1736–37	1	1	1769–70	1	
F.	1771	1	1	1770–71	1	
C.O.	1769	1	1	1770–71	1	
F.	1748	1	1	1747–48	1	
F.	1774	1	1	1773–74	1	
F.	1764	1	1	1763–64	1	
Ora.	1763	1	1	1762–63	1	
T.	1768	1	1	1775–76	1	
F.	1772	1	1	1772–73	1	
T.	1681	1	1	1751–52	1	
C.	1605	1	1	1751–52	1	
F.	1763	1	1	1762–63	1	
F.	1756	1	1	1755–56	1	
F.	1756	1	1	1756–57	1	
Int.	1769	1	1	1770–71	1	
F.	1760	1	1	1759–60	1	
F.	1765	1	1	1764–65	1	
C.	1701–02	1	1	1766–67	1	
C.	1766	1	1	1765–66	1	
C.	1678	1	1	1749–50	1	
Burl.	1759	1	1	1759–60	1	
C.	1704–05	1	1	1756–57	1	
F.	1747	1	1	1747–48	1	
P.	1753	1	1	1752–53	1	
F.	1759	1	1	1758–59	1	
F.	1749	1	1	1748–49	1	
T.	1673	1	1	1769–70	1	
T.	1698	1	1	1765–66	1	
Burl.	1771	1	1	1770–71	1	
F.	1766	1	1	1765–66	1	

Authorship	Short Title
Shadwell, Charles (-Unknown)	*Irish Hospitality*
Clive, Mrs. Catherine	*Island of Slaves*
Congreve, William	*Judgment of Paris*
Woodward, Henry	*A Lick at the Town*
Vaughan, Thomas	*Love's Metamorphoses*
Hill, John	*The Maiden Whim*
Unknown (from James Miller)	*Man of Taste*
Fenton, Elijah	*Miriamne*
Unknown (from Boaden's Modish Couple)	*Marriage-a-la-Mode*
Unknown (from Murphy's What We Must All Come To)	*Marriage-a-la-Mode; or, The Conjugal Douceurs*
Shakespeare (-Garrick)	*Midsummer Night's Dream*
Hiffernan, Paul	*National Prejudice*
Carey, George Saville	*The Noble Pedlar*
Unknown	*No Matter What*
Bickerstaffe, Isaac	*Recruiting Sargeant*
Arne, Thomas	*The Rose*
Beaumont & Fletcher	*The Scornful Lady*
Clive, Mrs. Catherine	*Sketch of a Fine Lady's Return from a Rout*
Unknown (from Beaumont and Fletcher)	*The Spanish Curate*
Hull, Thomas	*The Spanish Lady*
Farquhar, George	*The Stage Coach*
Baddeley, Robert	*The Swindlers*
Hoole, John	*Timanthes*
Martyn, Benjamin	*Timoleon*
Unknown	*The Tutor*
Heard, William	*Valentine's Day*
Unknown (from Charles Johnson)	*The Villagers*
Pope, Jane (from Mrs. Sheridan)	*The Young Couple*
Lillo, George (& John Hoadly)	*Arden of Feversham*

Type	Date	Seasons	Best Season	Date of Best Season	Total Performances	Garrick Acting
F.	1763	1	1	1765–66	1	
F.	1761	1	1	1760–61	1	
M.	1700–01	1	1	1747–48	1	
Prel.	1751	1	1	1750–51	1	
F.	1776	1	1	1775–76	1	
F.	1756	1	1	1755–56	1	
F.	1752	1	1	1751–52	1	
T.	1722–23	1	1	1764–65	1	
F.	1760	1	1	1759–60	1	
F.	1767	1	1	1766–67	1	
C.	1763	1	1	1763–64	1	
C.	1768	1	1	1768–69	1	
Burl.	1771	1	1	1770–71	1	
F.	1758	1	1	1757–58	1	
Int.	1770	1	1	1770–71	1	
C.O.	1772	1	1	1772–73	1	
C.	c. 1615	1	1	1747–48	1	
F.	1763	1	1	1762–63	1	
F.	1622	1	1	1749–50	1	
Int.	1765	1	1	1775–76	1	
F.C.	1703–04	1	1	1763–64	1	
F.	1774	1	1	1773–74	1	
T.	1770	1	1	1774–75	1	
T.	1729–30	1	1	1771–72	1	
Burl.	1759	1	1	1759–60	1	
O.F.	1776	1	1	1775–76	1	
F.	1756	1	1	1755–56	1	
F.	1767	1	1	1766–67	1	
T.	1759	1	1	1759(summer)	1	

II. Repertoire at Covent Garden Theatre, 1747 – 1776

Authorship	Short Title
Unknown	*The Coronation*
Shakespeare	*Romeo and Juliet*
Sheridan, Richard B.	*The Duenna*
Gay, John	*Beggar's Opera*
Unknown	*Perseus and Andromede*
Shakespeare	*Richard III*
Unknown	*Mother Shipton*
Bickerstaffe, Isaac	*Love in a Village*
Shakespeare	*Hamlet*
Cibber, Colley and Sir John Vanbrugh	*Provok'd Husband*
Shakespeare	*Merchant of Venice*
Jones, Henry	*Earl of Essex*
Shakespeare	*Othello*
Rowe, Nicholas	*Jane Shore*
Philips, Ambrose	*Distress'd Mother*
Lee, Nathaniel	*The Rival Queens*
Bickerstaffe, Isaac	*Maid of the Mill*
Farquhar, George	*The Stratagem*
Shakespeare	*King Lear*
Shakespeare	*Macbeth*
Unknown	*Orpheus and Eurydice*
Unknown	*Harlequin Sorcerer*
Unknown	*The Sylphs*
Rowe, Nicholas	*Tamerlane*
Rowe, Nicholas	*Fair Penitent*
Otway, Thomas	*Venice Preserv'd*
Centlivre, Mrs. Susannah	*Busie Body*
Shakespeare	*Henry IV, Part I*
Milton, John	*Comus*
Macklin, Charles	*Love-a-la-Mode*
Shakespeare	*Henry V*
Brome, Richard	*Jovial Crew*
Steele, Sir Richard	*Conscious Lovers*

Type	Date	Seasons	Best Season	Date of Best Season	Total Performances
Ent.	1761	6	68	1761–62	180
T.	1594–95	27	23	1750–51	88
C.O.	1775	1	75	1775–76	75
B.O.	1727	23	38	1759–60	70
P.	1749	2	63	1749–50	64
H.T.	1592–93	26	14	1761–62	62
Ent.	? ?	2	57	1770–71	58
C.O.	1762	11	40	1762–63	55
T.	1601–02	28	5	1754–55	52
C.	1727–28	26	6	1754–55	51
C.	1596–97	23	6	1771–72	44
T.	1753	17	17	1752–53	43
T.	1604–05	23	5	1750–51	41
T.	1713–14	22	5	1750–51	40
T.	1711–12	12	9	1748–49	39
T.	1677	19	5	1758–59	38
C.O.	1765	10	29	1764–65	38
C.	1706–07	25	4	1748–49	37
T.	1605–06	16	6	1755–56	36
T.	1605–06	21	5	1773–74	35
O.	1718	4	31	1754–55	34
P.	1741	3	31	1751–52	34
P.	1774	1	34	1773–74	34
T.	1701	24	3	1750–51	33
T.	1703	16	5	1750–51	33
T.	1682	16	8	1752–53	33
C.	1709	22	5	1762–63	32
H.	1597–98	21	4	1750–51	32
M.	1634	15	11	1759–60	32
F.	1759	15	5	1771–72	32
H.	1598–99	19	6	1766–67	31
C.	1641	9	19	1759–60	30
C.	1722	21	3	1749–50	29

Authorship	*Short Title*
Mason, William	*Elfrida*
Jonson, Ben	*Every Man in His Humour*
Shakespeare	*King John*
Fielding, Henry	*The Miser*
Cibber, Colley	*The Refusal*
Shakespeare	*Cymbeline*
Hoole, John	*Cyrus*
Cumberland, Richard	*The Brothers*
Otway, Thomas	*The Orphan*
Farquhar, George	*Recruiting Officer*
Shakespeare	*Merry Wives of Windsor*
Hoadly, Benjamin	*Suspicious Husband*
Lee, Nathaniel	*Theodosius*
Fletcher, John	*Rule a Wife and Have a Wife*
Dodsley, Robert	*Cleone*
Shakespeare	*Henry VIII*
Colman, George	*The Fairy Prince*
Cibber, Colley	*She Wou'd and She Wou'd Not*
Johnson, Charles	*Country Lasses*
Centlivre, Mrs. Susannah	*The Wonder*
Hill, Aaron	*Zara*
Hull, Thomas	*Henry II*
Cibber, Colley	*Love Makes a Man*
Congreve, William	*Love for Love*
Congreve, William	*Way of the World*
Vanbrugh, Sir John	*The Confederacy*
Dryden, John	*All for Love*
O'Hara, Kane	*Midas*
Congreve, William	*The Mourning Bride*
Southerne, Thomas	*Oroonoko*
Murphy, Arthur	*The Citizen*
Farquhar, George	*Constant Couple*
Rowe, Nicholas	*Lady Jane Gray*
Hoole, John	*Timanthes*

Type	Date	Seasons	Best Season	Date of Best Season	Total Performances
D.P.	1752	3	27	1772–73	29
C.	1598	11	15	1762–63	28
H.	1596–97	10	5	1750–51	28
C.	1732–33	21	3	1755–56	27
C.	1720–21	12	6	1750–51	27
T.C.	1609–10	9	7	1773–74	27
T.	1768	5	21	1768–69	27
C.	1769	3	22	1769–70	27
T.	1680	18	3	1752–53	26
C.	1706	22	2	1754–55	25
C.	1601–02	18	4	1761–62	24
C.	1746–47	17	2	1747–48	23
T.	1680	16	4	1752–53	23
C.	1624	14	7	1772–73	23
T.	1750	6	16	1758–59	23
H.	1613	6	16	1772–73	23
M.	1771	1	23	1771–72	23
C.	1702	19	3	1757–58	22
C.	1714–15	16	5	1751–52	22
C.	1714	14	7	1760–61	22
T.	1735	11	7	1751–52	22
T.	1773	4	17	1773–74	22
C.	1700	18	3	1762–63	21
C.	1695	17	2	1755–56	20
C.	1700	14	4	1764–65	20
C.	1705	14	3	1767–68	19
T.	1677	13	5	1750–51	19
Burl.	1762	6	9	1763–64	19
T.	1697	13	4	1754–55	19
T.	1696	15	2	1748–49	18
F.	1761	12	3	1762–63	18
C.	1699	9	3	1749–50	18
T.	1715	8	10	1749–50	18
T.	1700	5	13	1769–70	18

Authorship	*Short Title*
Farquhar, George	*The Inconstant*
Hughes, John	*Siege of Damascus*
Goldsmith, Oliver	*She Stoops to Conquer*
Centlivre, Mrs. Susannah	*Bold Stroke for a Wife*
Norris, Henry	*Royal Merchant*
Home, John	*Douglas*
Behn, Mrs. Aphra	*The Rover*
Betterton, Thomas	*The Prophetess*
Sheridan, Richard B.	*The Rivals*
Howard, Sir Robert	*The Committee*
Addison, Joseph	*Cato*
Congreve, William	*Double-Dealer*
Farquhar, George	*Twin Rivals*
Colman, George	*Man and Wife*
Griffith, Mrs. Elizabeth	*Double Mistake*
Murphy, Arthur	*Three Weeks After Marriage*
Dryden, John	*Spanish Fryar*
Steele, Sir Richard	*The Funeral*
Shakespeare	*As You Like It*
Garrick, David (from Shakespeare)	*Catharine and Petruchio*
Fletcher, John	*Wit Without Money*
Shakespeare	*Henry IV, Part II*
Jonson, Ben	*Volpone*
Reed, Joseph	*Tom Jones*
Shakespeare	*Julius Caesar*
Cibber, Colley	*Love's Last Shift*
Garrick, David	*Miss in Her Teens*
Murphy, Arthur	*The Upholsterer*
Lillo, George	*London Merchant*
Shakespeare	*All's Well That Ends Well*
Arne, Thomas	*Artaxerxes*
Colman, George	*Man of Business*
Congreve, William	*Old Batchelor*
Foote, Samuel	*The Knights*
Buckingham, Duke of (*et al.*)	*The Rehearsal*

Type	Date	Seasons	Best Season	Date of Best Season	Total Performances
C.	1701–02	15	2	1753–54	17
T.	1719–20	12	4	1751–52	17
C.	1773	4	12	1772–73	17
C.	1717	16	1	1757–58	16
C.	1706	9	7	1767–68	16
T.	1756	7	9	1756–57	16
C.	1677	6	10	1756–57	16
D.O.	1690	3	13	1757–58	16
C.	1775	2	14	1774–75	16
C.	1622	13	2	1747–48	15
T.	1713	11	3	1775–76	15
C.	1694	10	3	1754–55	15
C.	1702	10	3	1756–57	15
F.	1769	3	12	1769–70	15
C.	1766	1	15	1765–66	15
F.	1776	1	15	1775–76	15
T.C.	1679–80	13	2	1758–59	14
C.	1701	13	2	1753–54	14
C.	1600–01	11	3	1774–75	14
F.	1756	10	3	1756–57	14
C.	c. 1614	9	6	1756–57	14
H.	1597–98	7	5	1766–67	14
C.	1606	7	7	1771–72	14
C.O.	1769	2	13	1768–69	14
H.T.	1600–01	10	4	1750–51	13
C.	1696	10	2	1747–48	13
F.	1746–47	10	2	1749–50	13
F.	1758	10	3	1763–64	13
T.	1731	9	2	1767–68	13
C.	1603–04	6	6	1762–63	13
O.	1762	4	9	1761–62	13
C.	1774	1	13	1773–74	13
C.	1693	10	3	1754–55	12
C.	1749	9	2	1754–55	12
Burl.	1671	5	5	1754–55	12

Authorship	*Short Title*
Thomson, James	*Tancred and Sigismunda*
Goldsmith, Oliver	*Good-Natur'd Man*
Colman, George	*Jealous Wife*
Otway, Thomas	*Cheats of Scapin*
Vanbrugh, Sir John	*The Relapse*
Garrick, David	*Lethe*
Shakespeare	*Measure for Measure*
Fletcher, John	*Humourous Lieutenant*
Dell, Henry	*Frenchified Lady*
Brown, John	*Barbarossa*
Thomson, James	*Coriolanus*
Cradock, Joseph	*Zobeide*
Ravenscroft, Edward	*London Cuckolds*
Rowe, Nicholas	*Royal Convert*
Foote, Samuel	*The Minor*
Murphy, Arthur	*No One's Enemy*
Kelly, Hugh	*Romance of an Hour*
Hull, Thomas	*The Perplexities*
Toms, Edward	*Accomplished Maid*
Murphy, Arthur	*Alzuma*
Kelly, Hugh	*Clementine*
Hoole, John	*Cleonice*
Sheridan, Thomas	*Coriolanus*
Macklin, Charles	*Married Libertine*
Cumberland, Richard	*Summer's Tale*
Cibber, Colley	*Double Gallant*
Young, Edward	*The Revenge*
Foote, Samuel	*Englishman Returned*
Shadwell, Thomas	*Squire of Alsatia*
Cibber, Colley	*Careless Husband*
Addison, Joseph	*The Drummer*
Cibber, Colley	*The Non-Juror*
Murphy, Arthur	*The Old Maid*
Murphy, Arthur	*The Apprentice*
Carey, Henry	*The Contrivances*
Morgan, McNamara	*Sheep-Shearing*

Type	Date	Seasons	Best Season	Date of Best Season	Total Performances
T.	1744–45	5	6	1758–59	12
C.	1768	3	10	1767–68	12
C.	1761	11	1	1761–62	11
F.	1677	10	2	1754–55	11
C.	1697	9	2	1747–48	11
F.	1740	8	3	1756–57	11
C.	1604–05	6	3	1769–70	11
C.	c. 1619	4	8	1756–57	11
F.	1756	3	8	1756–57	11
T.	1754	2	10	1770–71	11
T.	1749	2	10	1748–49	11
T.	1771	1	11	1771–72	11
C.	1682	10	1	1747–48	10
T.	1707	4	7	1762–63	10
C.	1760	2	7	1760–61	10
C.	1764	2	6	1774–75	10
C.	1774	2	9	1774–75	10
C.	1767	1	10	1766–67	10
C.O.	1766	1	9	1766–67	9
T.	1773	1	9	1772–73	9
T.	1771	1	9	1770–71	9
T.	1775	1	9	1774–75	9
T.	1754	1	9	1774–75	9
C.	1761	1	9	1760–61	9
C.O.	1765	1	9	1765–66	9
C.	1707	8	2	1757–58	9
T.	1721	7	2	1752–53	9
F.	1756	5	4	1755–56	9
C.	1688	3	7	1763–64	9
C.	1704	6	2	1758–59	8
C.	1715–16	6	2	1751–52	8
C.	1717	6	3	1754–55	8
C.	1761	5	3	1765–66	8
F.	1756	7	2	1762–63	8
F.	1715	7	2	1758–59	8
Past.	1754	4	2	1753–54	8

Authorship	*Short Title*
Pordage, Samuel	*Herod and Mariamne*
Tate, Nahum	*Duke and No Duke*
Garrick, David and George Colman	*Clandestine Marriage*
Foote, Samuel	*Englishman in Paris*
Fielding, Henry	*Mock Doctor*
Carey, Henry	*Honest Yorkshireman*
Cumberland, Richard	*The West Indian*
Beaumont and Fletcher	*Philaster*
Sheridan, Richard B.	*Saint Patrick's Day*
Murphy, Arthur	*Way to Keep Him*
Wycherley, William	*The Country Wife*
Foote, Samuel	*The Author*
Foote, Samuel	*The Commissary*
Shakespeare	*Coriolanus*
O'Brien, William	*Cross Purposes*
Smith, Edmund	*Phaedra and Hippolitus*
Whitehead, William	*Roman Father*
Crowne, John	*Sir Courtly Nice*
Foote, Samuel	*Taste*
Thomson, James (-Thomas Hull)	*Edward and Eleonora*
Cibber, Colley	*School Boy*
Moncrieff, John	*Appius*
Arne, Thomas	*Guardian Outwitted*
Murphy, Arthur	*School for Guardians*
Banks, John	*Albion Queens*
Coffey, Charles	*Devil to Pay*
Colman, George	*English Merchant*
Carey, Henry	*Dragon of Wantley*
Garrick, David	*The Guardian*
Fielding, Henry	*Intriguing Chambermaid*
Miller, James, and J. Hoadly	*Mahomet the Imposter*
Gay, John	*What D'ye Call It*
Banks, John	*Virtue Betrayed*
Foote, Samuel	*The Lyar*
Unknown	*Merry Counterfeit*
Unknown (from Fielding)	*Country Madcap*

Type	Date	Seasons	Best Season	Date of Best Season	Total Performances
T.	1673	2	7	1757–58	8
F.	1684	7	1	1755–56	7
C.	1766	6	2	1767–68	7
C.	1753	6	2	1755–56	7
B.O.	1732	5	2	1747–48	7
B.O.	1735	4	2	1755–56	7
C.	1771	3	3	1774–75	7
T.C.	c. 1608	2	6	1774–75	7
F.	1775	2	6	1774–75	7
C.	1760	6	1	1767–68	6
C.	1672	5	2	1767–68	6
C.	1757	4	3	1770–71	6
C.	1765	4	2	1771–72	6
T.	1607–08	4	3	1758–59	6
F.	1772	4	2	1772–73	6
T.	1707	4	2	1754–55	6
T.	1750	4	3	1768–69	6
C.	1685	4	2	1759–60	6
C.	1752	4	3	1755–56	6
T.	1775	2	4	1774–75	6
F.	1702	2	4	1754–55	6
T.	1755	1	6	1754–55	6
C.O.	1764	1	6	1764–65	6
C.	1767	1	6	1766–67	6
T.	1684	5	1	1749–50	5
B.O.	1731	5	1	1747–48	5
C.	1767	5	1	1767–68	5
Burl.	1737	4	2	1761–62	5
F.	1759	4	2	1775–76	5
F.	1733–34	4	2	1762–63	5
T.	1744	4	2	1767–68	5
T.C.P.F.	1714–15	4	2	1751–52	5
T.	1682	3	2	1749–50	5
C.	1762	2	4	1761–62	5
F.	1762	2	4	1761–62	5
O.F.	1770	4	1	1770–71	4

Authorship	*Short Title*
Shadwell, Charles (*et al.*)	*Fair Quaker of Deal*
Garrick, David	*The Lying Valet*
Colman, George	*The Musical Lady*
Fletcher, John	*The Pilgrim*
Bickerstaffe, Isaac	*Thomas and Sally*
Shakespeare	*Winter's Tale*
Hill, Aaron	*Almira*
Dryden, John	*Don Sebastian*
Francklin, Thomas	*Earl of Warwick*
Cibber, Mrs. Susannah M.	*The Oracle*
Murphy, Arthur	*Grecian Daughter*
Bickerstaffe, Isaac	*Love in the City*
Woodward, Henry (from Davenant)	*The Man's the Master*
Colman, George	*Deuce is in Him*
Southerne, Thomas	*Fatal Marriage*
Fielding, Henry	*The Lottery*
Glover, Richard	*Medea*
Loveridge, Richard	*Pyramis and Thisbe*
Hull, Thomas	*Spanish Lady*
Vanbrugh, Sir John	*Aesop*
Vanbrugh, Sir John	*Country House*
Carey, Henry	*Dragoness*
Pix, Mrs. (Mary Griffith)	*False Friend*
Colman, George	*Oxonian in Town*
Colman, George	*Polly Honeycombe*
Dibdin, Charles	*Shepherd's Artifice*
Farquhar, George	*Stagecoach*
Foote, Samuel	*Foote's "Tea"*
Johnson, Charles	*Wife's Relief*
Cumberland, Richard	*Amelia*
Hartson, Hall	*Countess of Salisbury*
Dryden, John	*Oedipus*
Rich, John	*Spirit of Contradiction*
Baker, Thomas	*Tunbridge Walks*
Betterton, Thomas	*Amorous Widow*

Type	Date	Seasons	Best Season	Date of Best Season	Total Performances
C.	1709–10	4	1	1747–48	4
C.	1741	4	1	1753–54	4
F.	1762	4	1	1764–65	4
C.	c. 1621	4	1	1747–48	4
Int.	1760	4	1	1760–61	4
C.	1610–11	4	1	1770–71	4
T.	1736	3	2	1757–58	4
T.C.	1689	3	2	1757–58	4
T.	1766	3	2	1769–70	4
M.	1732	3	2	1751–52	4
T.	1772	2	3	1775–76	4
B.O.	1767	1	4	1766–67	4
C.	1775	1	4	1775–76	4
F.	1763	3	1	1770–71	3
T.	1694	3	1	1754–55	3
B.O.	1731–32	3	1	1748–49	3
T.	1767	3	1	1767–68	3
M.	1716	3	1	1747–48	3
Int.	1765	3	1	1764–65	3
C.	1697	2	2	1747–48	3
F.	1698	2	2	1759–60	3
Burl.	1738	2	2	1754–55	3
C.	1699	2	2	1751–52	3
F.	1767	2	2	1767–68	3
F.	1760	2	2	1762–63	3
Past.	1764	2	2	1764–65	3
F.C.	1703–04	2	2	1749–50	3
Ent.	1747	2	2	1747–48	3
C.	1711	2	2	1760–61	3
C.O.	1768	1	3	1767–68	3
T.	1765	1	3	1768–69	3
T.	1678	1	3	1754–55	3
C.	1760	1	3	1759–60	3
C.	1702–03	1	3	1747–48	3
C.	1670	2	1	1751–52	2

Authorship	Short Title
Dryden, John	*Amphitryon*
Mendez, Moses	*Double Disappointment*
Hawkesworth, John	*Edgar and Emeline*
O'Hare, Kane	*Golden Pippen*
Woodward, Henry	*Harlequin's Jubilee*
Etheridge, Sir George	*Man of Mode*
Lee, John (from Vanbrugh)	*Man of Quality*
Shakespeare	*Much Ado about Nothing*
Coffey, Charles	*Phebe*
Addison, Joseph	*Rosamond*
Banks, John	*Unhappy Favorite*
Fielding, Henry	*Virgin Unmask'd*
Hughes, John	*Apollo and Daphne*
Worsdale, James	*Cure for a Scold*
Unknown (from Fielding)	*Don Quixote in England*
Theobald, Lewis	*Double Falsehood*
Wilder, James (?)	*Gentleman Gardner*
Garrick, David	*Irish Widow*
Southerne, Thomas (-Garrick)	*Isabella*
Unknown	*Love Match*
Bickerstaffe, Isaac	*The Padlock*
Shakespeare	*Twelfth Night*
O'Hara, Kane	*Two Misers*
Griffith, Mrs. Elizabeth	*Wife in the Right*
Hull, Thomas	*Absent Man*
Colman, George (from Gay)	*Achilles in Petticoats*
Hull, Thomas	*All in the Right*
Murphy, Arthur	*All in the Wrong*
Tenducci, Ferdinande	*Amintas*
Unknown	*The Anniversary*
Unknown	*Athanias*
Fielding, Henry	*Author's Farce*
Sheridan, Thomas	*Irishman in London*
Young, Edward	*Busiris*
Mendez, Moses	*The Chaplet*
Murphy, Arthur	*The Choice*

Type	Date	Seasons	Best Season	Date of Best Season	Total Per- formances
C.	1690	2	1	1772–73	2
F.	1745–46	2	1	1753–54	2
Ent.	1761	2	1	1767–68	2
Burl.	1773	2	1	1772–73	2
P.	1770	2	1	1769–70	2
C.	1676	2	1	1748–49	2
F.	1773	2	1	1772–73	2
C.	1598–99	2	1	1774–75	2
B.O.	1729	2	1	1747–48	2
O.	1706	2	1	1753–54	2
T.	1681	2	1	1749–50	2
B.O.	1734–35	2	1	1754–55	2
M.	1715–16	1	2	1748–49	2
B.O.	1734–35	1	2	1749–50	2
C.	1734	1	2	1758–59	2
Play	1727	1	2	1766–67	2
B.O.	1749	1	2	1748–49	2
C.	1772	1	2	1775–76	2
T.	1757	1	1	1769–70	2
F.	1762	1	1	1761–62	2
C.O.	1768	1	1	1770–71	2
C.	1600–01	1	1	1771–72	2
O.F.	1775	1	1	1774–75	2
C.	1772	1	1	1771–72	2
F.	1764	1	1	1763–64	1
C.O.	1773	1	1	1773–74	1
F.	1766	1	1	1765–66	1
C.	1761	1	1	1775–76	1
O.	1769	1	1	1769–70	1
F.	1758	1	1	1757–58	1
T.	? ?	1	1	1759–60	1
Burl.	1730	1	1	1747–48	1
F.	1736	1	1	1754–55	1
T.	1718–19	1	1	1755–56	1
Ent.	1749	1	1	1761–62	1
C.	1765	1	1	1771–72	1

Authorship	*Short Title*
Carey, Henry	*Chrononhotonthologos*
Bullock, Christopher	*Cobler of Preston*
Shakespeare	*Comedy of Errors*
Unknown	*Comical Resentment*
Francis, Philip	*Constantine*
Unknown	*Counterfeit Heiress*
Brown, John (from Handel)	*Cure of Saul*
Cibber, Colley	*Damon and Phillida*
Unknown	*Drones Demolished*
Kenrick, William	*The Duellist*
Jackson, John	*Eldred*
Behn, Mrs. Aphra	*Emperor of the Moon*
Unknown	*English Tars in America*
Townley, James	*False Concord*
Home, John	*Fatal Discovery*
Hippisley, J. (from Colley Cibber)	*Flora; or, Hob in the Well*
Moore, Edward	*The Foundling*
Chapman, George	*Gentleman Usher*
Goldsmith, Oliver	*The Grumbler*
Woodward, Henry	*Harlequin Dr. Faustus*
Bate (Bate-Dudley), Henry	*Henry and Emma*
Unknown	*Hour before Marriage*
Bickerstaffe, I. (from Colley Cibber)	*The Hypocrite*
Reed, Joseph	*The Imposters*
Macklin, Charles	*Irish Fine Lady*
Dodsley, Robert	*King and Miller of Mansfield*
Hiffernan, Paul	*Lady's Choice*
Cibber, Colley	*Lady's Last Stake*
Langford, Abraham	*Lover His Own Rival*
Jackson, William	*Lycidas*
Garrick, David	*Male Coquette*
Kelly, Hugh	*Man of Reason*
Woodward, Henry (from Susannah Centlivre)	*Marplot in Lisbon*

Type	Date	Season	Best Seasons	Date of Best Season	Total Per-formances
Burl.	1733–34	1	1	1771–72	1
F.	1715–16	1	1	1758–59	1
C.	1592–93	1	1	1761–62	1
O.F.	1759	1	1	1758–59	1
T.	1754	1	1	1753–54	1
F.	1762	1	1	1761–62	1
Ora.	1763	1	1	1770–71	1
B.O.	1729	1	1	1747–48	1
Int.	1742–43	1	1	1747–48	1
C.	1773	1	1	1773–74	1
T.	1773	1	1	1775–76	1
F.	1687	1	1	1748–49	1
Droll	? ?	1	1	1760–61	1
F.	1764	1	1	1763–64	1
T.	1769	1	1	1775–76	1
B.O.	1729	1	1	1769–70	1
C.	1747	1	1	1772–73	1
T.C.	1606	1	1	1763–64	1
F.	1773	1	1	1772–73	1
P.	1766	1	1	1766–67	1
Int.	1774	1	1	1773–74	1
F.	1772	1	1	1771–72	1
C.	1768	1	1	1773–74	1
F.	1776	1	1	1775–76	1
F.	1767	1	1	1767–68	1
Tale	1736–37	1	1	1769–70	1
F.	1759	1	1	1758–59	1
C.	1707	1	1	1747–48	1
B.O.	1735–36	1	1	1754–55	1
Int.	1767	1	1	1767–68	1
F.	1757	1	1	1764–65	1
C.	1776	1	1	1775–76	1
F.	1755	1	1	1761–62	1

Authorship	Short Title
Chetwood, William	The Medley
Unknown	The Modern Wife
Unknown	Muses' Looking Glass
Theobald, Lewis	Orestes
Unknown	Peep into the Green Room
Morgan, McNamara	Philoclea
Unknown	Plume and Rose
Colman, George	The Portrait
Addington, Sir William	Prince of Agra
Theobald, Lewis	Rape of Proserpine
Unknown	Rival Queens; Alexander Little
Unknown	Scheming Lieutenant
Granville, Geo., Ld. Lansdowne	The She-Gallants
Etheridge, Sir George	She Wou'd if She Cou'd
Unknown	Siege of Quebec
Jonson, Ben	Silent Woman
Lennox, Charlotte	The Sister
Unknown (from Otway)	Soldier's Fortune
Unknown	The South Briton
Unknown	The Sultan
Thomson, Edward	The Syrens
Arthur, John	Tanner of York
Steele, Sir Richard	Tender Husband
Fielding, Henry	Tom Thumb
Whitehead, William	Trip to Scotland
Brooks, Henry	Triumph of Hibernia
Rowe, Nicholas	Ulysses
Cibber, Colley	Venus and Adonis
Hill, Aaron	Walking Statue
Forrest, Theodosius	The Weathercock
Murphy, Arthur	What We Must All Come To
Bullock, Christopher	Woman's a Riddle
Cibber, Colley	Ximena

Type	Date	Seasons	Best Season	Date of Best Season	Total Performances
B.O.	1729	1	1	1753–54	1
C.	1771	1	1	1770–71	1
F.	? ?	1	1	1748–49	1
D.O.	1731	1	1	1768–69	1
Int.	? ?	1	1	1775–76	1
T.	1754	1	1	1753–54	1
?	? ?	1	1	1755–56	1
Burl.	1770	1	1	1770–71	1
T.	1774	1	1	1773–74	1
B.O.	1726	1	1	1760–61	1
F.	1764	1	1	1764–65	1
F.	? ?	1	1	1774–75	1
C.	1696	1	1	1758–59	1
C.	1668	1	1	1750–51	1
P.	1760	1	1	1759–60	1
C.	1609	1	1	1747–48	1
C.	1769	1	1	1768–69	1
F.	1748	1	1	1747–48	1
C.	1774	1	1	1773–74	1
M.	1759	1	1	1758–59	1
M.	1776	1	1	1775–76	1
B.O.	1738	1	1	1755–56	1
C.	1705	1	1	1759–60	1
Burl.	1730	1	1	1750–51	1
F.	1770	1	1	1772–73	1
M.	1745	1	1	1751–52	1
T.	1705	1	1	1755–56	1
M.	1714–15	1	1	1747–48	1
F.	1709–10	1	1	1768–69	1
O.F.	1775	1	1	1775–76	1
C.	1764	1	1	1763–64	1
C.	1716	1	1	1747–48	1
T.	1712	1	1	1771–72	1

LIST OF WORKS CITED

Adam, Robert and James. The Works in Architecture of Robert and James Adam. Country Life Press, 1931.

Angelo, Henry. The Reminiscences of Henry Angelo. 2 vols. London, 1828.

Annual Register, The. London, 1794.

Baker, George Pierce. Some Unpublished Correspondence of David Garrick. Boston, 1907.

Baker, H. Barton. History of the London Stage, 1576–1888. New York, 1904.

Beaumont, Francis, and John Fletcher. Arnold Glover and A. R. Waller, eds., The Works of Francis Beaumont and John Fletcher. 10 vols. Cambridge, 1905–12.

Bell, Hamilton. "Three Plans by Sir Christopher Wren," *The Architectural Record,* XXXIII (1913), 359–63.

Brayley, Edward W. Historical and Descriptive Accounts of the Theatres of London. London, 1826.

British Museum. Egerton Ms. No. 2268.

Brooke, Mrs. Frances. The Excursion. 2 vols. London, 1777.

Brownsmith, John. The Dramatic Timepiece. London, 1767.

Campbell, Thomas. Dr. Campbell's Diary of a Visit to England in 1775. Ed. James L. Clifford. Cambridge, 1947.

Carlisle, Frederick Howard, Fifth Earl of. Thoughts Upon the Present Condition of the Stage, and upon the Construction of a New Theatre. New ed. London, 1800.

Cibber, Colley. An Apology for the Life of Mr. Colley Cibber. Ed. R. W. Lowe. 2 vols. London, 1888.

Cibber, Theophilus. Two Dissertations on the Theatres, an Epistle from Mr. Th. C. to D. Garrick, Esq. London, 1756.

Cole, G. D. H., and Raymond Postgate. The British People 1746–1946. New York, 1947.

Colman, George. "Critical Reflections on the old Dramatic Writers addressed to David Garrick." A preface to William Mason's edition of *The Works of Philip Massinger.* London, 1779.

——Memoirs of the Colman Family. Ed. R. B. Peake. 2 vols. London, 1841.

——New Brooms, an Occasional Prelude. London, 1776.

Colquhoun, Patrick. Wealth, Power and Resources of the British Empire. London, 1814.

Covent Garden Theatre. Covent Garden Account Book (1740–1741). Folger Shakespeare Library, Washington, D. C.

——Covent Garden Cash Book 1759–60. Folger Shakespeare Library, Washington, D. C.

Cross, Richard. Diary of Richard Cross. Folger Shakespeare Library, Washington, D. C.

Curwen, Samuel. Journals and Letters of Samuel Curwen, 1775–1784. Ed. G. A. Ward. New York, 1842.

Daily Advertiser, The. London, 1743.

Davies, Thomas. Memoirs of the Life of David Garrick, Esq. 3d ed. 2 vols. London, 1781.

——Dramatic Miscellanies. 3 vols. London, 1785.

Defoe, Daniel. *The Review*. June 25, 1709.

Doran, John. Their Majesties' Servants: Annals of the English Stage, from Thomas Betterton to Edmund Kean. 2 vols. London, 1860.

Dowdell, E. G. A Hundred Years of Quarter Sessions, the Government of Middlesex from 1660–1760. Cambridge, 1932.

Drury Lane Theatre. Drury Lane Account Books. Folger Shakespeare Library, Washington, D. C.

——Memorandum Book — Nightly Accounts 1776-1779 Old Theatre. Folger Shakespeare Library, Washington, D. C.

——Drury Lane Calendar 1747–1776. Ed. Dougald MacMillan. Oxford, 1938.

Fielding, Henry. An Enquiry into the Late Increase of Robbers. London, 1751.

——*The Covent Garden Journal*. Ed. G. E. Jansen. 2 vols. New Haven, 1915.

Fitzgerald, Percy. A New History of the English Stage. 2 vols. London, 1882.

——Life of David Garrick. 2 vols. London, 1868.

——The Sheridans. 2 vols. London, 1886.

Foote, Samuel. Memoirs of Samuel Foote, Esq. Ed. William Cooke. 3 vols. London, 1805.

——The Roman and English Comedy Consider'd and Compar'd, with remarks on the Suspicious Husband. London, 1747.

[——] A Treatise on the Passions, so far as they regard the Stage; with a critical Enquiry into the Theatrical Merit of Mr. G——k, Mr. Q——n, and Mr. B——y; The first considered in the Part of Lear, the two last opposed in Othello. London, n.d.

Forster, John. The Life and Times of Oliver Goldsmith. London, 1877.

Garrick, David. The Dramatic Works of David Garrick. 3 vols. London, 1798.

——The Poetical Works of David Garrick. 2 vols. London, 1785.

——The Private Correspondence of David Garrick. Ed. James Boaden. 2 vols. London, 1832.

——The Chances . . . with Alterations. London, 1773.

Genest, John. Some Account of the English Stage . . . 1660–1830. 10 vols. Bath, 1832.

Gentleman's Magazine, The. March, 1765; January, 1767.

George, M. Dorothy. London Life in the Eighteenth Century. New York, 1925.

Gilboy, Elizabeth W. Wages in Eighteenth Century England. Cambridge, 1934.

Goldsmith, Oliver. Preface to The Good-natured Man. London, 1768.

Grosley, Peter J. A Tour to London; Or, New Observations on England and Its Inhabitants. Trans. Thomas Nugent. 2 vols. London, 1765.

Harbage, Alfred B. Shakespeare's Audience. New York, 1941.

Hopkins, William. Diary of William Hopkins. Folger Shakespeare Library, Washington, D. C.

Kelly, John A. German Visitors to English Theaters in the Eighteenth Century. Princeton, 1936.

King, Gregory. "Natural and Political Observations and Conclusions upon the State and Condition of England," in George

E. Barnett, ed., *Two Tracts by Gregory King*. Baltimore, 1936.

Knight, Charles. Knight's Popular History of England. 8 vols. New York, 1880.

Knight, Joseph. David Garrick. London, 1894.

Kramer, Franz. Das verhaltnis von David Garrick's Every Man in His Humour zu dem gleichnamigen lustspiel Ben Jonson's. Halle, 1903.

Lewis, W. S. Three Tours through London in the Years 1748–1776–1797. New Haven, 1941.

Little, D. M. Pineapples of Finest Flavour, or a Selection of Sundry Unpublished Letters of the English Roscius, David Garrick. Cambridge, Mass., 1930.

The London Stage, 4 vols. London, [182?].

Maass, Heinrich. Ben Jonson's lustspiel Every Man in His Humour und die gleichnamige bearbeitung durch David Garrick. Rostock, 1903.

Macky, John. Journey through England. London, 1714.

Malcolm, James P. Anecdotes of the Manners and Customs of London during the Eighteenth Century, 2d ed. 2 vols. London, 1810.

Moritz, C. P. "Travels . . . through Several Parts of England, in 1782," in *A General Collection of the Best and Most Interesting Voyages and Travels,* ed. John Pinkerton. 13 vols. London, 1808.

Morning Chronicle, The. London, 1775.

Museum, The; or The Literary and Historical Register. No. 25, Saturday, February 28, 1747.

Nicoll, Allardyce. The English Theatre. New York, 1936.

——A History of Restoration Drama 1660–1700. Cambridge, 1923.

——A History of Early Eighteenth Century Drama 1700–1750. Cambridge, 1925.

——A History of Late Eighteenth Century Drama 1750–1800. Cambridge, 1927.

Notebook of Clippings 1770–1777. Folger Shakespeare Library, Washington, D. C.

Noyes, R. G. Ben Jonson on the English Stage, 1660–1776. Cambridge, Mass., 1935.

Odell, G. C. D. Shakespeare from Betterton to Irving. 2 vols. New York, 1920.

Parsons, Mrs. Clement. Garrick and His Circle. 2d ed. London, 1906.

Pedicord, Harry William. "Mr. and Mrs. Garrick: Some Unpublished Correspondence," *PMLA*, LX (September, 1945), 775–83.

Perry, Lawrence. Syndicated column, North American Newspaper Alliance. New York, February 5, 1949.

Pictorial History of England. Ed. G. L. Craik and C. Macfarlane. 4 vols. New York, 1848.

Place, Francis. Improvement of the Working People. London, 1834.

Reed, Isaac. Isaac Reed Diaries 1762–1804. Ed. Claude Jones. University of California Publications, Vol. X, 1946.

Rogers, Samuel. Table Talk. New York, 1856.

Rulfs, Donald J. "Beaumont and Fletcher on the Stage, 1776–1833," *PMLA* LXIII, No. 4, Pt. 1 (December, 1948), 1245–64.

Rylands English Ms. No. 1111. John Rylands Library, University of Manchester, England.

Saunders, George. A Treatise on Theatres. London, 1790.

Sheridan, Richard Brinsley. The Critic. London, 1781.

Shirley, James. The Dramatic Works and Poems of James Shirley. 6 vols. London, 1833.

Smollett, Tobias. Roderick Random. Oxford, 1925–26 (Shakespeare Head).

Solemn Protest against the Revival of Scenic Exhibitions and Interludes at the Royalty Theatre, A. 2d ed. London, 1803.

Sotheby and Company, London. Sale Catalogue, June 19, 1928.

Stage the High Road to Hell, The. London, 1767.

Stein, Elizabeth P. David Garrick, Dramatist. New York, 1938.

——Three Plays by David Garrick. London, 1926.

Stone, G. W., Jr. "Garrick's Long Lost Alteration of *Hamlet*." *PMLA*, Vol. XLIX, September, 1934.

——"Garrick's Handling of *Antony and Cleopatra,*" *RES,* Vol. XIII, January, 1937.

——"*A Midsummer Night's Dream* in the Hands of Garrick and Colman," *PMLA,* Vol. LIV, June, 1939.

——"Garrick and an Unknown Operatic Version of *Love's Labors Lost,*" *RES,* Vol. XV, July 1939.

——"Garrick's Handling of *Macbeth,*" *SP,* XXXVIII, October, 1941.

——"Garrick's Production of *King Lear:* a Study in the Temper of the Eighteenth-Century Mind," *SP,* Vol. XIV, January 1948.

——"The God of His Idolatry: Garrick's Theory of Acting and Dramatic Composition with Especial Reference to Shakespeare," in *Joseph Quincy Adams Memorial Studies,* Folger Shakespeare Library, 1948.

Southerne, Thomas. The Works of Thomas Southerne. 2 vols. London, 1721.

Thaler, Alwin. From Shakespeare to Sheridan: a Book about the Theatre of Yesterday and Today. Cambridge, Mass., 1922.

Theatrical Monitor, No. 18. April 16, 1768.

Thornton, Bonnell. *The Connoisseur,* No. 18 (June 9, 1754); No. 43 (November 21, 1754); No. 68 (July 15, 1755). London, 1754, 1755.

Town and Country Magazine, The. London, 1769, 1770, 1771, 1775, 1776.

Townley, James. High Life below Stairs. London, 1759.

Trevelyan, G. M. English Social History. New York, 1944.

Universal Spectator, The, No. 340. London, 1735.

Villiers, George, Duke of Buckingham. The Chances. London, 1682.

Wilkes, Thomas. A General View of the Stage. London, 1759.

Wood, Frederick T. "The Attack on the Stage in the Eighteenth Century," *Notes and Queries,* CLXXIII (September 25, 1937), 218–22.

World, The, No. 43. Thursday, October 25, 1753.

Wycherley, William. The Complete Works of William Wycherley. Ed. Montague Summers. 4 vols. London, 1924.

INDEX